Course | Workbook/Laboratory Manual to accompany Nachalo, Second Edition, Book 1
Sophia Lubensky

http://create.mheducation.com

Copyright 2018 by McGraw-Hill Education. All rights reserved. Printed in the United States of America. Except as permitted under the United States Copyright Act of 1976, no part of this publication may be reproduced or distributed in any form or by any means, or stored in a database or retrieval system, without prior written permission of the publisher.

This McGraw-Hill Create text may include materials submitted to McGraw-Hill for publication by the instructor of this course. The instructor is solely responsible for the editorial content of such materials. Instructors retain copyright of these additional materials.

ISBN-10: 1260781860   ISBN-13: 9781260781861

Contents

i. Preface 1
1. Chapter 7
2. Chapter 51
3. Chapter 87
4. Chapter 123
5. Chapter 163
6. Chapter 207
7. Chapter 249

Credits

i. Preface: *Chapter from Workbook/Laboratory Manual to accompany Nachalo, Second Edition, Book 1 by Lubensky, Ervin, McLellan, Jarvis, 2002* 1
1. Chapter: *Chapter 1 from Workbook/Laboratory Manual to accompany Nachalo, Second Edition, Book 1 by Lubensky, Ervin, McLellan, Jarvis, 2002* 7
2. Chapter: *Chapter 2 from Workbook/Laboratory Manual to accompany Nachalo, Second Edition, Book 1 by Lubensky, Ervin, McLellan, Jarvis, 2002* 51
3. Chapter: *Chapter 3 from Workbook/Laboratory Manual to accompany Nachalo, Second Edition, Book 1 by Lubensky, Ervin, McLellan, Jarvis, 2002* 87
4. Chapter: *Chapter 4 from Workbook/Laboratory Manual to accompany Nachalo, Second Edition, Book 1 by Lubensky, Ervin, McLellan, Jarvis, 2002* 123
5. Chapter: *Chapter 5 from Workbook/Laboratory Manual to accompany Nachalo, Second Edition, Book 1 by Lubensky, Ervin, McLellan, Jarvis, 2002* 163
6. Chapter: *Chapter 6 from Workbook/Laboratory Manual to accompany Nachalo, Second Edition, Book 1 by Lubensky, Ervin, McLellan, Jarvis, 2002* 207
7. Chapter: *Chapter 7 from Workbook/Laboratory Manual to accompany Nachalo, Second Edition, Book 1 by Lubensky, Ervin, McLellan, Jarvis, 2002* 249

Workbook/Laboratory Manual to accompany Nachalo, Second Edition, Book 1

Preface

TO THE INSTRUCTOR

ORGANIZATION OF THE WORKBOOK/LABORATORY MANUAL

The purpose of this Workbook/Laboratory Manual is to give students additional opportunities to practice Russian outside of class. Lesson 1 focuses mainly on the Russian alphabet and on teaching students how to write in Russian script. The setup is similar to that of subsequent lessons except there are no **Понимание текста** or **Диалоги** sections. Lessons 2 through 7 of the Workbook/Laboratory Manual are organized as follows:

Часть первая/вторая/третья/четвёртая
    Работа дома (*Homework*)
        Письмо (*Written Exercises*)
            Понимание текста
            Grammar Points
            Перевод (*Translation*)
            Повторение — мать учения (*Practice makes perfect*)
            Ситуации (*Situations*)
            Ваша очередь! (*It's your turn!*)
            Сочинение (*Composition*)
            Fun with grammar! Case review (at end of Part 4 only)
    Работа в лаборатории (*Laboratory Exercises*)
        Диалоги (*Dialogues*)
            Диалог 1
            Диалог 2
        Аудирование (*Listening Comprehension*)
            Three or more listening exercises
        Говорение (*Speaking Drills*)
            Three or more speaking exercises

Like the main text, the Workbook/Laboratory Manual is divided into Parts (**Части**), thus allowing students to work concurrently on assignments in corresponding sections. The Audio Program, which is also available on either audio cassettes or audio CDs for students to purchase, must be used with the Laboratory Exercises.

About the Workbook Exercises

The Workbook exercises section of each **Часть** (except in Lesson 1) opens with the **Понимание текста,** an exercise that checks students' comprehension of the reading that appears in the corresponding **Часть** in the main text. These exercises occur in a variety of formats including true/false, sentence completion, and matching.

    The discrete grammar points are practiced in the same order as they occur in the main text. At least one exercise is provided for each point. Although many of the exercises have been contextualized, most of the formats are traditional: question/answer, fill-in-the-blank, and so forth.

    At the end of each **Часть** is a series of exercises that reviews vocabulary and grammar in a holistic manner. The first exercise is a short **Перевод** (*Translation*). Following the **Перевод** is the **Повторение — мать учения** (*Practice makes perfect*) exercise, which is a cloze passage based on the reading in the corresponding **Часть**. The missing words are listed in dictionary form alongside the exercise, and students must place them in the appropriate blank in the correct declined or conjugated form. Next is the **Ситуации** (*Situations*) exercise, for which students must provide a Russian question or statement appropriate for the situation given. Then there is **Ваша очередь!** (*It's your turn!*), which asks a series of personalized questions to which students must respond. The last of the written exercises is **Сочинение** (*Composition*), which allows students to creatively combine vocabulary and grammar from the current

Preface vii

Часть with that from previous lessons. It also helps prepare students for the composition portion of the corresponding lesson test. At the end of the fourth **Часть** only is **Fun with grammar! Case review**, a crossword puzzle that reviews and consolidates case material covered through that lesson.

About the Audio Program

Each Audio Program (available on either CD or cassette) contains all of the Laboratory exercises as they appear in the Workbook/Laboratory Manual. A written version of the Laboratory exercises, including the dialogues and the cues for the listening comprehension exercises and speaking drills, can be found in the Audioscript that appears in the Instructor's Manual.

The Laboratory exercises (in Lessons 2 through 7) begin with the **Диалоги**. These functional dialogues, which appear in the corresponding **Части** of the main text, have been recorded to provide students with additional listening and speaking practice. The **Диалоги** are practiced in three phases: (1) pauses for students to repeat each line of the dialogue, (2) pauses in which students speak the lines of the second speaker, and (3) pauses in which students speak the lines of the first speaker. Following each **Диалог** is at least one printed comprehension question.

After the dialogues are several listening comprehension exercises (**Аудирование**) in various formats. Some exercises focus on a particular problem in pronunciation; others ask students to perform a specific task or answer questions based on information that they hear. The answers for these exercises are provided in the Answer Key, which is part of the Instructor's Manual.

The Laboratory exercises conclude with several speaking drills (**Говорение**). Here students are required to respond verbally to an aural and written cue. After a pause, the correct answer is given as part of the recorded material. Because students are given immediate feedback on the recording, the answers are not included as part of the Answer Key.

NEW TO THIS EDITION

This edition of the **НАЧАЛО** Workbook/Laboratory Manual has been revised, incorporating new art as well as new exercises, to provide students with more exposure to spoken and written Russian in addition to enhancing students' studies outside of class. Below is a list of new exercises in the order in which they appear in each **Часть**:

- **Повторение — мать учения** (*Practice makes perfect*) These activities consist of cloze passages based on the corresponding readings in the main text. The missing words are listed in dictionary form alongside each exercise, and students must place them in the appropriate blank using the correct declined or conjugated form.
- **Ситуации** (*Situations*) Here students are asked to provide a Russian question or statement appropriate for the given situation.
- **Ваша очередь!** (*It's your turn!*) These exercises present a series of personalized questions to which students must respond.
- **Сочинение** (*Composition*) Brief writing assignments such as these allow students to creatively combine vocabulary and grammar from the current **Часть** with that from previous lessons. They also help students prepare for the composition portion of the corresponding lesson test.
- **Fun with grammar! Case review** These activities appear only at the end of the fourth **Часть** of each lesson. The exercises contain crossword puzzles that review and consolidate case material covered through that lesson.
- **Говорение** (*Speaking drills*) New to the Laboratory Manual, the speaking drills require students to respond verbally to an aural and written cue. After a pause, the correct answer is given as part of the recorded material.

SUGGESTIONS FOR ASSIGNING THE WORKBOOK AND LABORATORY MATERIAL

We highly recommend that you assign the Workbook and Laboratory Manual activities for a given grammar topic as you cover the corresponding topics of the text in class. Once students have become familiar with the new vocabulary and structures presented in the reading portion of a **Часть**, we recommend that they listen to the recordings of functional dialogues (which take about five minutes). These dialogues present only vocabulary and structures already encountered in the reading or in earlier lessons. You can assign the **Аудирование** and **Говорение** exercises as the final activities for that **Часть**, though some students may find they can do them easily before that time.

If students do this outside preparation faithfully, it should not be necessary to spend class time doing "listen and repeat" work except, perhaps, for an occasional checkup to determine their progress. Class time can then be used for guided practice and communicative, interactive activities, in which instructor monitoring and on-the-spot feedback are irreplaceable.

An Answer Key to the exercises that focus on grammatical forms in this Workbook/Laboratory Manual can be found in the Instructor's Manual. You may wish to provide students with a copy of the Answer Key to facilitate independent study and self-checking. Another possibility is to provide students with an abridged Answer Key containing answers to only the first few items in each grammatical exercise so that they can make sure they understand the topic (and review the grammar explanations in the textbook, if necessary) before completing the remaining items.

ACKNOWLEDGMENTS

The authors of **НАЧАЛО** would like to express their heartfelt appreciation to Tatiana Smorodinskaya, whose tireless work on the first edition provided a solid foundation for this book, and to Valentina Lebedeva and Nelly Zhuravlyova, who read the manuscript of the Book 1 Workbook/Laboratory Manual for authenticity of language and provided many constructive suggestions for improving it. Further thanks are due Jennifer Bown of The Ohio State University for preparing the Answer Key. We would also like to thank Stacy Kendrick and David Sweet, who put in many hours of careful editorial work, and Rich DeVitto and David Sutton, who shepherded this Workbook/Laboratory Manual through production. Finally, we would like to express our gratitude to Thalia Dorwick and Leslie Oberhuber for their many developmental suggestions and ongoing support in this project.

TO THE STUDENT

There is probably no more important key to success in language learning than regular, daily, and systematic contact with the language. You can learn Russian with success by conscientiously preparing your homework assignments, whether they are from your instructor, the main text, or this Workbook/Laboratory Manual. For every hour you spend in class, you should plan on spending at least another hour each day outside of class.

ACCOMPLISHING YOUR DAILY WORK

It is important that you do all exercises and other class work on time, as it is assigned. Your instructor will be coordinating each day's classroom work on the assumption that you have done the assignment for that day and previous days. If you fall behind on those assignments, you will find it difficult to keep up with the class and to participate fully in class activities.

DOING THE WRITTEN EXERCISES

The exercises in this Workbook/Laboratory Manual are intended to be done outside of class. There is at least one Workbook exercise for each grammar point in the main text. Be sure to write out all your answers in full. Once you've become familiar with a grammar point, you can apply it to classroom activities, which are often of a real-life, communicative nature.

LEARNING FROM YOUR MISTAKES

Language is perhaps the most complex form of observable human behavior. In learning a new language, therefore, you'll find that mistakes are inevitable. Don't be distressed by them, but rather learn from them. When you correct your written work (or when you receive corrections from your instructor), whether it is an in-class assignment, a homework assignment, or a test, go over the corrections carefully and mark your mistakes in a distinctive color so that you can review them easily.

REVIEWING

When you have completed an exercise in this Workbook/Laboratory Manual and it has been corrected, keep it handy so that you can look at it over the next few days. Pay particular attention to reviewing your errors so that you can learn from them. Over the longer term, keep all of your corrected written work in a special file or binder. If you file all of your corrected assignments and tests, you will be able to locate them quickly whenever you need to review them.

USING THE AUDIO PROGRAM

For each lesson in the main text, there is a corresponding Audio CD or Cassette that runs approximately forty-five to fifty minutes. You should listen to this recording section by section, several times per section, over the days that you are working on a given **Часть** (*Part*). Many students find that they learn the words to popular songs effortlessly just by hearing them often on the radio; you can learn Russian the same way by listening to your Audio Program again and again. You might follow a schedule like this:

As you work through each **Часть** (*Part*) *of a lesson:* Listen to the first portion of the audio CD or cassette, where the functional dialogues (**Диалоги**) (which also appear in the main text for in-class work), are read aloud by native speakers of Russian. Each **Диалог** is first read in its entirety; it is then broken down into individual lines, with pauses for you to repeat or take a speaker's role.

Following each **Диалог** is at least one question about the grammar, vocabulary, or content of the dialogue. Don't be satisfied, however, with simply answering the question; rather, go back and listen to the dialogue again. The more often you listen to the **Диалоги,** the more comfortable you will become with their grammar, vocabulary, intonation patterns, word stress, and content. In particular, you should try to approximate the speakers' intonation and rate of speech. Don't worry about perfection; just try to come as close as you can.

As you complete each **Часть** (*Part*) *of a lesson:* After the last **Диалог** in each **Часть** there are several listening comprehension exercises (**Аудирование**) that will give you further practice in understanding Russian. As with the

Диалоги, listen to each **Аудирование** as often as you need to; do not feel that you must "get it" the first time around.

Following the listening comprehension exercises are several speaking drills (**Говорение**). Once again, perform each exercise as often as you need to. Check your responses with the given responses on the recording. If at first you are not sure how to respond, listen to the given responses, then go back and try again. Do the exercise again the next day to see if you are able to respond more quickly. Before the oral portion of your test, go back and review all the speaking exercises.

ESTABLISHING A DAILY ROUTINE

Most students find it helpful to do their class preparation (written homework, lab work, studying with a friend, and so forth) on a fixed schedule. Pick a convenient time each day to prepare your Russian work; then stick to that schedule. For example, if you will be listening to the audio CDs or cassettes in your school's language laboratory, you might make that part of your daily routine. Go to the lab and listen to the appropriate portion of the recorded program several times as needed. Then do your written homework, while still in the lab. Finish up your daily study session by reviewing the same portion of the recorded program again. The entire process will probably take no more than one hour each day. In this way, you will have heard each portion of the lab program several times. Each day you should also listen to the reading on the Listening Comprehension Audio CD or Cassette (supplied with the main text) that corresponds to the **Часть** you are currently working on.

If you faithfully follow a daily schedule of outside preparation, including doing your assigned written homework, reviewing errors on corrected papers, and reviewing the audio CDs or cassettes, you will find that in only a few days what may have at first sounded like incomprehensible gibberish will have become familiar and understandable. Then you know that you're ready to move on!

Name_____ Date_____ Class_____

ДОБРО ПОЖАЛОВАТЬ В РОССИЮ!

УРОК 1

ЧАСТЬ ПЕРВАЯ

РАБОТА ДОМА (*Homework*)

ПИСЬМО (*Written exercises*)

New Letters and Sounds: Group A

Я пишу по-русски

The letters	
Printed	Written
А а	*А а*
Б б	*Б б*
В в	*В в*
Г г	*Г г*
Д д	*Д д*
Е е	*Е е*
Ё ё	*Ё ё*
Ж ж	*Ж ж*
З з	*З з*
И и	*И и*
Й й	*Й й*

The letters	
Printed	Written
К к	*К к*
Л л	*Л л*
М м	*М м*
Н н	*Н н*
О о	*О о*
П п	*П п*
Р р	*Р р*
С с	*С с*
Т т	*Т т*
У у	*У у*
Ф ф	*Ф ф*

The letters	
Printed	Written
Х х	*Х х*
Ц ц	*Ц ц*
Ч ч	*Ч ч*
Ш ш	*Ш ш*
Щ щ	*Щ щ*
Ъ ъ	*ъ*
Ы ы	*ы*
Ь ь	*ь*
Э э	*Э э*
Ю ю	*Ю ю*
Я я	*Я я*

Урок 1, Часть первая

Russians do not, as a general rule, print. Fortunately, Russian cursive script has many features in common with English cursive script and with Russian block letters. Nevertheless, developing good Russian cursive handwriting takes practice. The following pages provide hints on how to form Russian letters in cursive script. The arrows indicate the direction in which you should move your pen or pencil when you make the capital letters.

A. Fill the lines below as you practice writing the cursive forms of Russian capital and lowercase letters. Say the names of the letters aloud in Russian each time you write them.

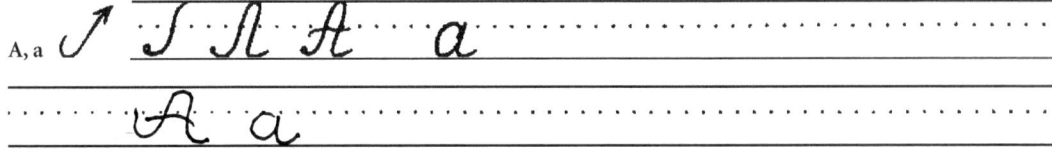

М, м begin with a small hook just above the line (even in the middle of a word). This hook is very small; it does not look like the letter *c*.

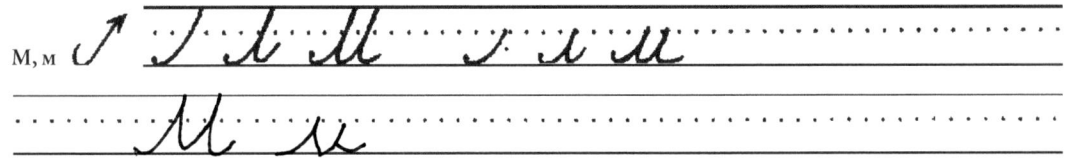

The small **к** is half the height of the capital **К**. Do not make a loop or extend the small letter above the middle, or dotted, line.

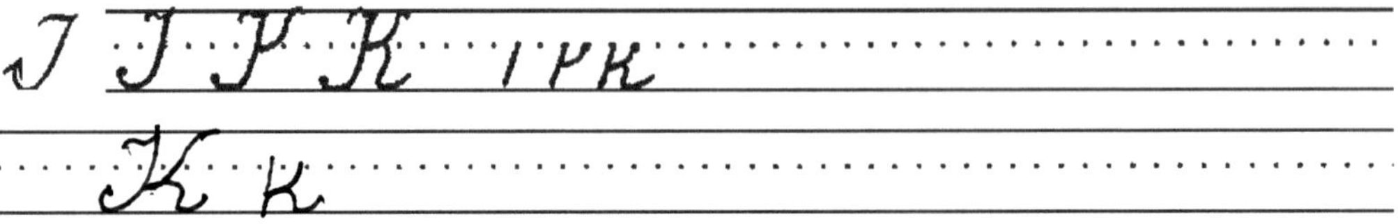

The capital **Т** requires four strokes (three vertical and one top horizontal). The small **т** is like the English script *m*. Sometimes a line is written above it.

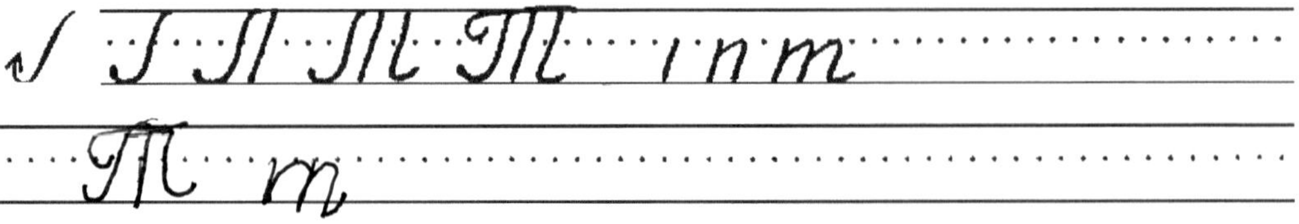

Some Russians prefer an alternate form of the cursive lower case **т**. If you choose to write with this variant, be sure that the **т** is only a half space high (the same height as an **а** or **о**) and that the stem comes straight down and does not curve to the right.

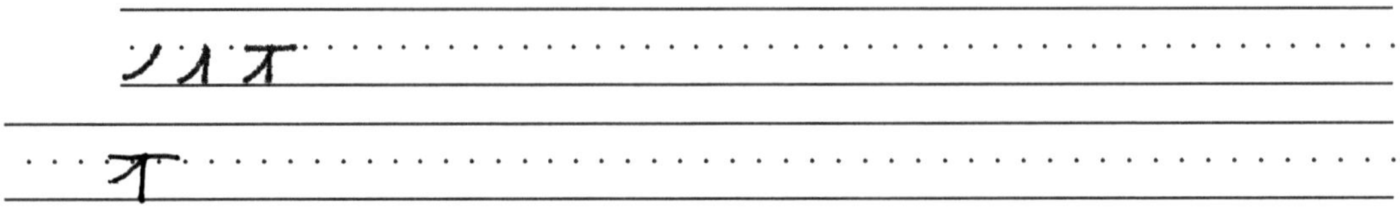

2   Урок 1, Часть первая

Name_____ Date_____ Class_____

О, о *О о*

Now practice writing the following words. Russians do not write stress marks, but your instructor may have you write them for practice.

Как, как *Как, как*

Кто, кто *Кто, кто*

Ма́ма, ма́ма *Мама, мама*

The left bar of the small **р** extends straight below the line and the part of the letter above the line does not close (contrast this to the cursive small-letter *p* in English).

Р, р *Р р*

В, в *В в*

Н, н *Н н*

Workbook/Laboratory Manual to accompany Nachalo, Second Edition, Book 1

Е, е — *Е е*

The final stroke of the capital **У** remains on the line and turns to the left and stops. It does not extend below the line, as the small **у** does.

У, у — *У У у у*

Most Russian letters connect from the baseline to the following letter. As you can see in the examples below, this connecting stroke is drawn to about half the height of the next letter. Practice writing the following words.

Тама́ра — *Тамара*

Ку́ртка, ку́ртка — *Куртка, куртка*

Вот, вот — *Вот, вот*

Б. As you practice writing cursive forms of the capital and small letters, continue to say the names of the letters aloud in Russian each time you write them.

Make the **Б** with three strokes: a vertical downstroke, a horizontal cross stroke, and a looping stroke. The small **б** looks somewhat like the English cursive *d* but terminates by trailing off to the top right.

Б, б — *Б Б Б б б*

П, п — *П П П п п*

Уро́к 1, Часть пе́рвая

Name_____ Date_____ Class_____

The top of the small **г** must be rounded. Do not make it angular or flat like the English cursive *r*.

Г, г

The next letter looks like the numeral 10 with a bar in between.

Ю, ю

The small **и** does not have the hook that **М, м** have (and that's the only difference!).

И, и

Ш, ш should not be made to look like the English cursive *W, w*. The middle stroke is the same height as the first and last strokes, and the last stroke returns all the way down to the line and bends to the right. Sometimes the small **ш** is underlined to help it stand out.

Ш, ш

Л, л begin with a small hook (like **М, м**). The hook is important to help distinguish **Л, л** from **Г, г**.

Л, л

Like **М, м** and **Л, л**, **Я, я** (both capital and small) must always be preceded by a tiny hook.

Я, я

Урок 1, Часть первая   5

The capital **З** is indented on the right side, very much like the numeral 3. Make it in one stroke.

З, з

Make **Э, э** by forming a backward *C* and then adding a cross stroke. Do not indent it on the right like the **З**.

Э, э

The two dots that distinguish **Е** from **Ё** are not usually used by Russians, but you should make a habit of using them.

Ё, ё

Now make a series of the upper- and lowercase **З, Э,** and **Е**, one after the other. Remember the distinctive features of each!

Now practice writing some words and phrases with these letters.

Привет!

Кто это?

6   Урок 1, Часть первая

Name_____ Date_____ Class_____

Не знаю. *Не знаю.*

Don't forget the hooks before **л**, **м**, and **я**!

Германия *Германия*

Япония *Япония*

Ирландия *Ирландия*

Америка *Америка*

Как тебя зовут? *Как тебя зовут?*

Меня зовут *Меня зовут*

Как дела? *Как дела?*

Хорошо́, спаси́бо. *Хорошо, спасибо.*

B. Write the following words in cursive script. Say them aloud as you write them.

Как? *Как?*

его́ *его*

её *её*

Как её зову́т? *Как её зовут?*

Как его́ зову́т? *Как его зовут?*

кто *кто*

э́то *это*

Name_____ Date_____ Class_____

ВВ. Now you will hear a series of words that sound similar to their English counterparts. Number them in the order that they are read. In the right-hand column, write what you think the English meaning is. The first one has been done for you.

Аме́рика	_____	_____
аппети́т	_____	_____
Берли́н	_____	_____
гита́ра	_____	_____
Ита́лия	____1____	___Italy___
кака́о	_____	_____
капитали́зм	_____	_____
парк	_____	_____
тала́нт	_____	_____
термо́метр	_____	_____

ГОВОРЕНИЕ (*Speaking drills*)

ГГ. Repeat the words and phrases after the speaker.

1. Приве́т!
2. Как тебя́ зову́т?
3. Как её зову́т?
4. Её зову́т Ната́ша.
5. Как его́ зову́т?
6. Его́ зову́т Анто́н.
7. Кто э́то?
8. Не зна́ю.
9. Э́то Па́вел.

ДД. Answer the speaker's questions with the cued response.

ОБРАЗЕЦ: *You hear:* Кто э́то?
You see: Кто э́то? (Анто́н)
You say: Э́то Анто́н.

1. Кто э́то? (Гали́на)
2. Как её зову́т? (Тама́ра)
3. Как тебя́ зову́т? (*Male:* Джон) (*Female:* Ро́бин)
4. Как его́ зову́т? (Ян)

ЕЕ. How would you ask each of the following?

ОБРАЗЕЦ: *You hear and see:* How would you ask "Who is that?"
You say: Кто э́то?

1. How would you ask the name of a student you have just met?
2. You see a man and you want to know his name. What would you ask your classmate?
3. You see a woman and you want to know her name. What would you ask your classmate?
4. How would you ask "Who is that?"

Name_____ Date_____ Class_____

ЧАСТЬ ВТОРАЯ

РАБОТА ДОМА (*Homework*)

ПИСЬМО (*Written exercises*)

New letters and sounds: Group B

A. Fill the lines below as you practice writing the cursive forms of Russian capital and lowercase letters. Say the names of the letters aloud in Russian each time you write them.

Д, д

Note carefully the strokes used to form **Ф, ф**.

Ф, ф

Note carefully the strokes used to make **Ж, ж**.

Ж, ж

Х, х

Й, й always have the "half-moon" over them. It is never omitted. It is what distinguishes the consonant **й** from the vowel **и**.

Й, й

The final stroke of **Ч, ч** must turn to the right. It never goes below the line.

Ч, ч

С, с

The **ь** (**мя́гкий знак** [*soft sign*]) has no sound of its own. It never starts a word, so there is no capital letter for it in cursive script.

ь

Б. Write the following words in cursive script. Pay close attention to how you join the letters. Say the words aloud and remind yourself of their meaning.

Здра́вствуйте.

Letters should connect into **ж** at the top of the left stroke.

Меня́ зову́т Наде́жда Миха́йловна.

16   Уро́к 1, Часть втора́я

Name_____ Date_____ Class_____

Óчень прия́тно. *Очень приятно.*

Что э́то? *Что это?*

Не зна́ю. *Не знаю.*

Спаси́бо. *Спасибо.*

Пожа́луйста. *Пожалуйста.*

B. The following Russian words are new to you, but they sound similar to their English counterparts. Match the words on the left with the corresponding pictures.

1. _____ авто́бус
2. _____ детекти́в
3. _____ диск
4. _____ ка́ктус
5. _____ ма́ски
6. _____ па́льма
7. _____ ра́дио
8. _____ стадио́н
9. _____ телефо́н
10. _____ флаг
11. _____ компью́тер

Уро́к 1, Часть втора́я 17

Г. **More food, flowers, and animals!** Choose the proper category for each of the words on the left. Then write the English translation in the right-hand column.

		FOOD	FLOWER	ANIMAL	ENGLISH TRANSLATION
1.	беф-стро́ганов	[ ]	[ ]	[ ]	_____
2.	тюльпа́н	[ ]	[ ]	[ ]	_____
3.	жира́ф	[ ]	[ ]	[ ]	_____
4.	крокоди́л	[ ]	[ ]	[ ]	_____
5.	жасми́н	[ ]	[ ]	[ ]	_____
6.	свинья́	[ ]	[ ]	[ ]	_____
7.	абрико́с	[ ]	[ ]	[ ]	_____
8.	дельфи́н	[ ]	[ ]	[ ]	_____

Names and nicknames

Д. It is sometimes challenging for Americans to read Russian novels because of the frequent use of nicknames as well as first names with patronymics. See how well you can match the following nicknames with the correct first names. In the first half of the blank line, write the letter that corresponds to the correct nickname. In the second half, indicate whether the name refers to a man (M) or a woman (W).

ОБРАЗЕЦ: __г__ / __М__ Пётр

1. ____ / ____ Ви́ктор
2. ____ / ____ Влади́мир
3. ____ / ____ Дми́трий
4. ____ / ____ Екатери́на
5. ____ / ____ Еле́на
6. ____ / ____ Елизаве́та
7. ____ / ____ Ива́н
8. ____ / ____ Ири́на
9. ____ / ____ Михаи́л
10. ____ / ____ Ната́лья
11. ____ / ____ Никола́й
12. ____ / ____ Светла́на
13. ____ / ____ Татья́на
14. ____ / ____ Алекса́ндр *or* Алекса́ндра

а. Ли́за
б. Ми́ша
в. Ко́ля
г. ~~Пе́тя~~
д. И́ра
е. Ната́ша
ж. Ви́тя
з. Ле́на
и. Све́та
к. Та́ня
л. Ва́ня
м. Ди́ма
н. Са́ша
о. Воло́дя
п. Ка́тя

Name_____ Date_____ Class_____

Patronymics and last names

Е. Here is a list of common Russian first names.

MEN'S NAMES		WOMEN'S NAMES	
Ива́н	Анто́н	Наде́жда	О́льга
Макси́м	Вади́м	Людми́ла	А́нна
Ви́ктор	Алекса́ндр	Мари́на	Еле́на

1. If **А́нна Ива́новна** is **А́нна,** daughter of **Ива́н,** then . . .

    О́льга Ива́новна is _____

    Наде́жда Вади́мовна is _____

    Мари́на Ви́кторовна is _____

2. If **Ива́н Ви́кторович** is **Ива́н,** son of **Ви́ктор,** then . . .

    Вади́м Алекса́ндрович is _____

    Ива́н Вади́мович is _____

    Макси́м Анто́нович is _____

3. What is the suffix for *son of*? _____
4. What is the suffix for *daughter of*? _____
5. If **Еле́на** and **Ви́ктор** are brother and sister, and **Алекса́ндр** is their father, how would you address the siblings in a formal setting?

    _____
    _____

6. If **Людми́ла** and **Макси́м** are brother and sister, and their father's name is **Макси́м Вади́мович Кругло́в,** what would be the full name (all three parts—**и́мя, о́тчество, фами́лия**) of both children?

    _____
    _____

Formal greetings and introductions

Ж. Write out in cursive Russian what you would say when . . .

1. you say hello to your professor when you first see her in the morning.

    _____

2. you say hello to your professor whose name is **Людми́ла Анто́новна Вели́чкина.**

    _____
    _____

3. you say hello to your professor whose name is **Михаи́л Ива́нович Степа́нов.**

    _____
    _____

Уро́к 1, Часть втора́я   19

Requesting, giving, and receiving

З. The following dialogue takes place at the snack bar of a theater. How would you translate it into Russian? Use cursive.

"A [*small filled*] pastry and tea, please." _____

"Here you are." _____

"Thanks." _____

"You're welcome." _____

Informal greetings: "Hi, how are things?"

И. Fill in the blanks of the dialogue with the appropriate words.

    А. Приве́т, Га́ля!

    Б. _____, Ви́тя!

    А. Как _____?

    Б. Ничего́, спаси́бо. А у _____?

    А. Хорошо́.

Now copy the complete dialogue in cursive script.

    А. _____

    Б. _____

    А. _____

    Б. _____

    А. _____

Formal greetings: "Hello. How are you?"

К. Fill in the blanks of the dialogue with the appropriate words.

    А. Здра́вствуйте, Наде́жда Миха́йловна!

    Б. _____, Ви́ктор Ива́нович!

    А. Как у _____ дела́?

    Б. Хорошо́, _____.

Now copy the complete dialogue in cursive script.

    А. _____

    Б. _____

    А. _____

    Б. _____

Л. Compare the dialogues in exercises **И** and **К**. What three clues tell you that the speakers in the dialogue of exercise **И** are using the familiar form of address with each other?

    1. _____

    2. _____

    3. _____

Name_____ Date_____ Class_____

What three clues tell you that the speakers in the dialogue of exercise **K** are using the formal form of address with each other?

1. _____
2. _____
3. _____

М. What would you most likely say or hear in each of the following situations? You may use a letter more than once.

1. _____ You say good-bye to your professor.
2. _____ You say hello to two schoolchildren.
3. _____ A neighbor woman asks how you are doing.
4. _____ You say hello to the parents of a Russian friend.
5. _____ You are talking to a Russian student in the cafeteria and ask his name.
6. _____ You are petting the neighbor's dog and playfully ask it what its name is.
7. _____ You run into a fellow student and ask her how things are going.
8. _____ You were just introduced to a professor, but you have already forgotten his name.
9. _____ You say good-bye to your roommate.

а. Пока́, Са́ша!
б. Как дела́?
в. Ди́ма, Са́ша Приве́т!
г. Извини́те, как вас зову́т?
д. Здра́вствуйте!
ж. Как у вас дела́?
з. Как тебя́ зову́т?
и. До свида́ния, О́льга Петро́вна!

Повторе́ние — мать уче́ния (*Practice makes perfect*)

Н. Determine how the Russian words below must be placed in the boxes of the grid so that their first letters spell out a question in Russian. Then write the English translation on the line next to each word. The first one has been done for you. Once you have completed the puzzle, answer the questions on the following page.

1. А́ДРЕС _____
2. А́РМИЯ _____
3. А́ТОМ _____
4. ВА́ЗА _____
5. ДО́КТОР _____
6. ЕВРО́ПА _____
7. КАКА́О _____*cocoa*_____
8. КО́СМОС _____
9. ЛА́МПА _____
10. СЕКРЕ́Т _____
11. УНИВЕРСИТЕ́Т _____

Уро́к 1, Часть втора́я   21

What are three possible responses to the question in the grid?

1. _____
2. _____
3. _____

РАБОТА В ЛАБОРАТОРИИ (*Laboratory exercises*)

АУДИРОВАНИЕ (*Listening comprehension*)

АА. A series of fourteen letters will be read to you. Number them in the order that they are read. The first one has been done for you.

Ч, ч _____   С, с _____

Ф, ф _____   Е, е _____

Э, э _____   Х, х ___1___

Ж, ж _____   Р, р _____

Д, д _____   З, з _____

Ш, ш _____   В, в _____

Л, л _____   П, п _____

ББ. You are in the Moscow airport listening for flight announcements. Each announcement consists of a destination city and a departure time. Circle the cities that you hear.

ОБРАЗЕЦ: Тель-Авив — 3.15

Париж   Да́р-эс-Сала́м

То́кио   Москва́

Ки́ев   Пеки́н

(Тель-Ави́в)   Торо́нто

Мадри́д   Копенга́ген

Бо́стон   Найро́би

Нью-Йо́рк   Бангко́к

Лиссабо́н   Бейру́т

Монреа́ль   Санкт-Петербу́рг

Вашингто́н   Берли́н

Name_____ Date_____ Class_____

ВВ. Here is a conversation between three people—a teacher, a male student, and a female student—who are getting acquainted. Listen carefully and number the lines below to correspond to the order in which they are spoken. The first one has been done for you. You will hear this dialogue twice.

_____ О́чень прия́тно, Марк. О́чень прия́тно, Ири́на.

_____ Меня́ зову́т Ири́на.

___1___ Приве́т! Меня́ зову́т Марк. А тебя́?

_____ Не зна́ю, э́то не студе́нт.

_____ О́чень прия́тно, Серге́й Миха́йлович.

_____ Здра́вствуйте. Меня́ зову́т Серге́й Миха́йлович.

_____ Меня́ зову́т Ири́на. А э́то кто?

_____ Меня́ зову́т Марк.

ГОВОРЕ́НИЕ (*Speaking drills*)

ГГ. Repeat the following words after the speaker and follow along closely with the printed words. Each word contains one or more letter «**о**». Circle each «**о**» that is unstressed (and thus sounds more like "ah" or "uh") and underline each «**о**» that is stressed (and thus sounds like "oh"). The first one has been done for you.

1. п(о)жалуйста
2. это
3. зовут
4. кто
5. кофе
6. очень
7. приятно
8. пока
9. до свидания
10. хорошо

ДД. Answer each of the speaker's questions or statements using the cued response in parentheses. Then indicate whether you are using the formal or informal form of address with each person.

ОБРАЗЕ́Ц: *You hear:* Здра́вствуйте!
         You see: Здра́вствуйте! (*Hello, Natalya Ivanovna!*)
         You say: Здра́вствуйте, Ната́лья Ива́новна!
         You check: Formal ☒

1. Как вас зову́т? (*Use your own name.*) Formal ☐ Informal ☐
2. Приве́т! (*Hi!*) Formal ☐ Informal ☐
3. Как дела́? (*Not bad.*) Formal ☐ Informal ☐
4. До свида́ния! (*Good-bye!*) Formal ☐ Informal ☐
5. Как у вас дела́? (*Very well, thanks.*) Formal ☐ Informal ☐
6. Как тебя́ зову́т? (*Use your own name.*) Formal ☐ Informal ☐

Уро́к 1, Часть втора́я

EE. Many Russian words look and sound much like their English counterparts. This similarity can help us understand what others are saying or writing. When we pronounce these words, however, we often revert to an American pronunciation that is unintelligible to native Russian speakers. Repeat the following words after the speakers and carefully mimic their pronunciation. Write the English meaning of the word in the space at the right. The first one has been done for you.

1. Вашингто́н _____ Washington _____
2. дире́ктор _____
3. исто́рия _____
4. Кана́да _____
5. контра́кт _____
6. ко́фе _____
7. Кремль _____
8. литерату́ра _____
9. Ме́ксика _____
10. миллионе́р _____
11. партнёр _____
12. президе́нт _____
13. Росси́я _____
14. саксофо́н _____
15. тури́ст _____
16. Япо́ния _____

ЖЖ. **And you?** Answer each of the following questions with the cued response and the appropriate form of "*And you?*" as required by context.

ОБРАЗЕЦ: *You hear:* Как тебя́ зову́т?
You see: (*Sasha. And you?*)
You say: Са́ша. А тебя́?

1. (*Fine, thanks. And you?*)
2. (*Yes, and you?*)
3. (*Anton Mikhailovich. And you?*)
4. (*Yes, and you?*)

Name_____ Date_____ Class_____

ЧАСТЬ ТРЕТЬЯ

РАБОТА ДОМА (*Homework*)

ПИСЬМО (*Written exercises*)

New Letters and Sounds: Group C

A. As you practice writing the cursive forms of the capital and small letters, say the names of the letters aloud in Russian each time you write them.

Щ, щ have a small tail that dips just below the line. It does not descend fully such as that on the small **у** or **р**. The tail is important, for it is what distinguishes **Щ, щ** from **Ш, ш**.

Щ, щ

Ц, ц also have the small tail that dips just below the line. The tail is what distinguishes cursive **Ц, ц** from **И, и**.

Ц, ц

No word begins with **ы**, so it has no capital letter in cursive script.

ы

The **ъ** (**твёрдый знак** [*hard sign*]) has no sound of its own. It never starts a word, so there is no capital letter for it in cursive script. Note the small horizontal stroke that distinguishes **ъ** from **ь** (**мягкий знак** [*soft sign*]).

ъ

Урок 1, Часть третья   25

Workbook/Laboratory Manual to accompany Nachalo, Second Edition, Book 1

Б. Write the following words in cursive script. Say them aloud as you write them.

борщ (*borshch*) *борщ*

цыган (*gypsy*) *цыган*

му́зыка *музыка*

объе́кт (*object, objective*) *объект*

В. Congratulations! You now know all the letters of the Russian alphabet. Here are a few review questions.

1. Which three letters *always* have a hook before them? _____

   Keeping this in mind, write out the following words:

   Росси́я _____

   февра́ль _____

   до́ма _____

   земля́ (*earth*) _____

2. When learning the Russian alphabet, students sometimes confuse certain letters, both in how they sound and in how they are written in cursive script. Write the following letters in cursive. Next to the letter pair, explain why you think English speakers might have problems with these letters.

   REASON FOR PROBLEMS

   Б, б _____ *vs.* В, в _____ _____

   П, п _____ *vs.* Р, р _____ _____

   Э, э _____ *vs.* З, з _____ _____

   И, и _____ *vs.* У, у _____ _____

   Г, г _____ *vs.* Ч, ч _____ _____

   Т, т _____ *vs.* М, м _____ _____

   К, к _____

Урок 1, Часть тре́тья

Name _____ Date _____ Class _____

Г. Rewrite the following words in the correct category below.

профе́ссор   фле́йта
джи́нсы
курс   о́пера
гита́ра   авто́бус
трамва́й
   конце́рт
студе́нт   шарф
блу́зка   автомоби́ль
университе́т
   сви́тер
мотоци́кл

COLLEGE	TRANSPORTATION	MUSIC	CLOTHING
_____	_____	_____	_____
_____	_____	_____	_____
_____	_____	_____	_____
_____	_____	_____	_____

Д. Many names of people and places that are well known to you can seem strange in Cyrillic. What is the English equivalent of the following names?

1. Эйнште́йн _____
2. Пи́цца Хат _____
3. Ле́нин _____
4. Мо́царт _____
5. Бах _____
6. Ба́скин-Ро́ббинс _____
7. Пика́ссо _____
8. Ре́мбрандт _____
9. Джо́ди Фо́стер _____
10. Ке́лвин Клайн _____
11. Ге́нрих VIII _____
12. Джон Сте́йнбек _____

Уро́к 1, Часть тре́тья

Е. Following is a list of American states and Canadian provinces. Some of the Russian spellings and stresses differ slightly from those in English. In the first column, rewrite the list in cursive script using Russian alphabetical order. Then give the English equivalent. Ask your instructor to show you how your state or province is rendered on Russian maps.

1. _____ _____ Теха́с
2. _____ _____ Ога́йо
3. _____ _____ Манито́ба
4. _____ _____ Флори́да
5. _____ _____ Иллино́йс
6. _____ _____ Арканза́с
7. _____ _____ Калифо́рния
8. _____ _____ Вашингто́н
9. _____ _____ Онта́рио
10. _____ _____ Колора́до
11. _____ _____ Нью-Йо́рк
12. _____ _____ Квебе́к

Ж. Match the countries with their respective capitals.

1. _____ Аргенти́на   а. Буэ́нос-А́йрес
2. _____ Испа́ния   б. О́сло
3. _____ Ита́лия   в. Мадри́д
4. _____ Кита́й   г. Москва́
5. _____ Норве́гия   д. Пари́ж
6. _____ Росси́я   е. Пеки́н
7. _____ Фра́нция   ж. Рим
8. _____ Япо́ния   з. То́кио

З. Are the following countries in South America, Europe, or Asia? Check the correct box.

	Ю́ЖНАЯ АМЕ́РИКА	ЕВРО́ПА	А́ЗИЯ
1. А́встрия	[ ]	[ ]	[ ]
2. Аргенти́на	[ ]	[ ]	[ ]
3. Бе́льгия	[ ]	[ ]	[ ]
4. Брази́лия	[ ]	[ ]	[ ]
5. Венесуэ́ла	[ ]	[ ]	[ ]
6. Вьетна́м	[ ]	[ ]	[ ]

Name_____ Date_____ Class_____

	ЮЖНАЯ АМЕРИКА	ЕВРОПА	АЗИЯ
7. Голландия	[ ]	[ ]	[ ]
8. Индия	[ ]	[ ]	[ ]
9. Колумбия	[ ]	[ ]	[ ]
10. Корея	[ ]	[ ]	[ ]
11. Парагвай	[ ]	[ ]	[ ]
12. Португалия	[ ]	[ ]	[ ]
13. Таиланд	[ ]	[ ]	[ ]
14. Польша	[ ]	[ ]	[ ]
15. Япония	[ ]	[ ]	[ ]

И. From the following words, put together a grocery list, a list of classes that you might take, and a list of currencies that you might need when traveling abroad.

архитектура   пепси-кола   рубль   франк
брокколи   песо   статистика   экономика
макароны   пицца   физика   грейпфрут
марка   программирование   иена

MY SHOPPING LIST   CLASSES I MIGHT TAKE   CURRENCIES I MIGHT NEED

_____   _____   _____
_____   _____   _____
_____   _____   _____
_____   _____   _____
_____   _____   _____

Asking and answering questions

К. Answer the following questions as cued.

   ОБРАЗЕЦ: — Это Нина?

   — Да, <u>это Нина.</u>

   — Вадим врач? (музыкант)

   — Нет, <u>он не врач. Он музыкант.</u>

1. — Это Виктор Михайлович?

   — Да, _____

2. — Вера аспирантка? (студентка)

   — Нет, _____

3. — Это Máша? (Наташа)

   — Нет, _____

4. — Это Аргенти́на? (Брази́лия)

   — Нет, _____

5. — Ми́ша музыка́нт?

   — Да, _____

6. — Это Любо́вь Андре́евна? (Мари́на Влади́мировна)

   — Нет, _____

7. — Это Аризо́на?

   — Да, _____

8. — Это Торо́нто? (Отта́ва)

   — Нет, _____

Discussing location: where, here, at home

Л. You are visiting an apartment that is shared by several Russian women. Their names are **Валенти́на Серге́евна Петро́ва, Людми́ла Анто́новна Касья́нова, Еле́на Петро́вна Ивано́ва,** and **Татья́на Бори́совна Майо́рова.** Each is momentarily preoccupied with dinner preparations. The doorbell rings and you must answer it. It is an agent collecting information for the census. He wants to know if certain people live there and if they are at home. How might the conversation go if he asked for the person whose name is given in parentheses?

ОБРАЗЕЦ: (Валенти́на Ива́новна Петро́ва)

— <u>Здесь живёт (lives) Валенти́на Ива́новна Петро́ва?</u>

— <u>Нет, здесь живёт Валенти́на Серге́евна Петро́ва.</u>

or
   (Людми́ла Анто́новна Касья́нова)

— <u>Здесь живёт Людми́ла Анто́новна Касья́нова?</u>

— <u>Да, здесь.</u>

— <u>Она́ до́ма?</u>

— <u>Да, до́ма.</u>

1. (Еле́на Петро́вна Ивано́ва)

   _____
   _____
   _____
   _____

2. (Татья́на Влади́мировна Майо́рова)

   _____
   _____
   _____

Name _____ Date _____ Class _____

O. Your host brother Vanya is packing for the weekend. He's in a hurry and can't seem to find any of his clothing. Tell him where the items are, using the grammatically correct form of the pronoun for *it* or *they*.

ОБРАЗЕЦ: _____Где брюки?_____
_____Они здесь._____

1. _____
2. _____
3. _____
4. _____
5. _____
6. _____

Урок 1, Часть третья   33

Повторе́ние — мать уче́ния (*Practice makes perfect*)

П. Complete the following crossword puzzle. If an English word is given as a clue, write the Russian equivalent. Otherwise write the Russian word that best completes the sentence. HINT: You may need to refer to p. 17 of the textbook for some answers. One word has been filled in for you.

ГОРИЗОНТА́ЛЬ

5 *hat*
7 *boots*
10 — Как дела́? — _____.
13 *a type of flower*
14 *a girl's name*
15 Как _____ зову́т?
18 — Где А́нна? — Она́ _____.
20 *slacks*
22 _____ Ви́ктор? Он здесь?
23 — _____ э́то? — Не зна́ю.
25 _____, Мари́я Петро́вна!
28 *overcoat*
29 _____ зову́т Та́ня. Как тебя́ зову́т?
32 О́чень _____.

ВЕРТИКА́ЛЬ

1 *jeans*
2 *tie*
3 Что _____?
4 *tank top*
6 *gloves*
8 _____ прия́тно.
9 *a guy's name*
11 *Bye!*
12 — Как у вас дела́? — _____, спаси́бо.
16 _____ вас зову́т?
17 _____, Во́ва!
18 Как _____?
19 Как его́ _____?
21 *jacket*
24 *dress*
25 — Ю́ра _____? — Нет, он до́ма.
26 Как _____ зову́т?
27 — Э́то Ле́на? — Нет, э́то _____ Ле́на. Э́то Лю́да.
28 *a guy's name*
30 *a girl's name*
31 _____ э́то? Газе́та?

34 Уро́к 1, Часть тре́тья

Name_____ Date_____ Class_____

РАБОТА В ЛАБОРАТОРИИ (*Laboratory exercises*)

АУДИРОВАНИЕ (*Listening comprehension*)

АА. Which groceries should you pick up at the store? Listen carefully as the speaker reads a list and check the items you hear. You will hear each item twice. The first one has been done for you.

_____ бана́ны   _____ макаро́ны

_____ бро́кколи   _____ пе́пси-ко́ла

_____ гре́йпфруты   _____ пи́цца

_____ конфе́ты   _____ спаге́тти

__X__ ко́фе   _____ торт

_____ лимо́н   _____ чай

_____ лимона́д

ББ. Is the speaker asking a question or making a statement? Circle what you hear.

ОБРАЗЕЦ: Ни́на студе́нтка?

(Ни́на студе́нтка?)   Ни́на студе́нтка.

1. Э́то Анто́н Па́влович?   Э́то Анто́н Па́влович.
2. Да́ша до́ма?   Да́ша до́ма.
3. Он студе́нт?   Он студе́нт.
4. Пётр музыка́нт?   Пётр музыка́нт.
5. Она́ аспира́нтка?   Она́ аспира́нтка.
6. Мари́я Дми́триевна здесь?   Мари́я Дми́триевна здесь.

ВВ. You will hear a series of questions. Place the letter of the question next to the most appropriate response.

ОБРАЗЕЦ: Ко́ля <u>до́ма?</u>

1. _____ Она́ здесь.
2. _____ Да, Ве́ра.
3. __Об.__ Нет, он здесь.
4. _____ Нет, э́то Та́ня.
5. _____ Он до́ма.
6. _____ Ири́на.

ГОВОРЕНИЕ (*Speaking drills*)

ГГ. You will hear a series of questions, each beginning with a question word. Repeat the question after the speaker and pay close attention to the intonation.

4. Как у вас дела?
5. Где Вера и Дима?
6. Как его зовут?

Now check yourself. Ask the questions after the cued introduction. Then check your intonation with the speaker's.

1. Ask what that is.
2. Ask where the sneakers are.
3. Ask the two neighbor children what their names are.
4. Ask your classmate how he is doing.
5. Ask where Slava and Vika are.
6. Ask your classmate what the new (female) student's name is.

ДД. You will hear a series of yes/no questions and similar statements. Repeat after the speaker and pay close attention to the intonation.

1. Валя дома?   Валя дома.
2. Она аспирантка?   Она аспирантка.
3. Саша студент?   Саша студент.
4. Это Гена?   Это Гена.
5. Тамара Васильевна здесь?   Тамара Васильевна здесь.

Again, check yourself. Follow the instructions and either ask a question or make a statement. Then check your intonation with the speaker's.

1. Ask if Valya is at home.
2. Ask if she is a graduate student.
3. Tell your classmate that Sasha is a student.
4. Tell your classmate that that is Gena.
5. Ask if Tamara Vasilevna is here.

ЕЕ. You will hear a series of questions asking you where certain items are. Respond by saying that it is (they are) here. Be sure to use the correct form of *it* or *they*.

ОБРАЗЕЦ: *You hear and see:* Где брюки?
          You say: Они здесь.

1. Где билет?
2. Где виза?
3. Где паспорт?
4. Где письмо?
5. Где сумка?
6. Где туфли?

Name_____ Date_____ Class_____

ГГ. Repeat the following words after the speaker. Pay close attention to each stressed or unstressed «е» and «я». Circle each «е» or «я» that receives full pronunciation. The first one has been done for you.

1. воскрес(е)нье
2. день
3. газета
4. до свидания
5. тебя
6. неделя
7. неплохо
8. октябрь
9. пятница
10. сегодня

ГОВОРЕНИЕ (*Speaking drills*)

ДД. You will hear a series of sentences with a singular noun and a possessive adjective. Repeat the same sentence changing the noun and the adjective to the plural.

ОБРАЗЕЦ: *You hear and see:* Где мой журна́л?
You say: <u>Где мои́ журна́лы?</u>

1. Это на́ша газе́та.
2. Где моя́ ру́чка?
3. Где ваш биле́т?
4. Это её чемода́н.
5. Это твоя́ блу́зка?
6. Где его́ руба́шка?

ЕЕ. You will now hear a similar series of sentences, but the noun and the possessive adjective will be in the plural. This time change the noun and the adjective to the singular.

ОБРАЗЕЦ: *You hear and see:* Это мои́ су́мки.
You say: <u>Это моя́ су́мка.</u>

1. Это на́ши кни́ги.
2. Где твои́ журна́лы?
3. Это его́ га́лстуки.
4. Это мои́ футбо́лки.
5. Где её ю́бки?
6. Это ва́ши рюкзаки́?

ЖЖ. Answer the following questions positively, using the appropriate possessive adjective.

ОБРАЗЕЦ: *You hear and see:* Это твой журна́л?
You say: <u>Да, мой.</u>

1. Это его́ ку́ртка?
2. Это твой рюкза́к?

5. Э...
6. Это её ру́чка?

урок 1, Часть четвёртая

Name_____ Date_____ Class_____

Перево́д (*Translation*)

И. Translate the following dialogues into Russian.

1. "Does Anna Pavlovna live here?"

   "No. Her address is building two, apartment three."

   _____
   _____

2. "Is that your sister?"

   "No! That's my mother!"

   _____
   _____

Повторе́ние — мать уче́ния (*Practice makes perfect*)

К. Following is a summary of the reading of Part 1. Fill in the blanks with words that maintain the context of the reading. Use each word only once.

Вот дом три, кварти́ра де́сять. Здесь _____¹ муж и _____² Кругло́вы. Их _____³ Са́ша то́же _____⁴ здесь. Он — _____⁵ Вот кварти́ра пять. Здесь живёт _____⁶ Петро́вский. А э́то Джим, _____⁷ аспира́нт. Он — _____⁸.	америка́нец внук его́ жена́ живёт живу́т пиани́ст профе́ссор

Ситуа́ции (*Situations*)

Л. How would you . . .

1. tell somebody that this is your apartment?

   _____

2. tell somebody that your parents live here?

   _____

3. tell somebody that this is your sister (brother, mother, or father), and her (his) name is . . . ? (Give the name of your own sister, brother, or parents.)

   _____

4. write out your telephone number?

   _____

5. say that this is Mark, an American?

   _____

Ваша о́чередь! (*It's your turn!*)

M. Answer these questions about yourself, using complete sentences.

1. Как тебя́ зову́т? _____

2. Ты студе́нт и́ли аспира́нт (студе́нтка и́ли аспира́нтка)?

   _____

3. Како́й твой но́мер телефо́на?

   _____

4. (*Looking at a picture of your parents' home.*) Кто здесь живёт?

   _____

РАБО́ТА В ЛАБОРАТО́РИИ (*Laboratory exercises*)

ДИАЛО́ГИ (*Dialogues*)

Диало́г 1 Здесь живёт . . . ? (Asking where someone lives)

АА. Follow along as you listen to the dialogue.

  А. Э́то кварти́ра шесть?
  Б. Да.
  А. Здесь живёт Во́ва Си́лин?
  Б. Здесь.
  А. А кто ещё живёт здесь?
  Б. Его́ роди́тели, сестра́ Ле́на и их соба́ка Бе́лка.

  - Now read and repeat aloud in the pause after each phrase.
  - Now read the lines for speaker **Б** aloud.
  - Now read the lines for speaker **А** aloud.

If speaker **А** asked about **Ле́на Си́лина** instead of **Во́ва Си́лин**, how would the last line read?

_____

Диало́г 2 Как её зову́т? (Finding out someone's identity)

ББ. Follow along as you listen to the dialogue.

  А. Как её зову́т?
  Б. А́нна Смит.
  А. Она́ америка́нка?
  Б. Нет, но её муж — америка́нец.

  - Now read and repeat aloud in the pause after each phrase.
  - Now read the lines for speaker **Б** aloud.
  - Now read the lines for speaker **А** aloud.

Rewrite the above dialogue so that it is about Viktor Sorokin and his wife, who is an American. Make any necessary changes.

  А. _____
  Б. _____
  А. _____
  Б. _____

50 Уро́к 2, Часть пе́рвая

Name _____ Date _____ Class _____

АУДИРОВАНИЕ (*Listening comprehension*)

ВВ. A typical address in Russia consists of a building (**дом,** abbreviated **д.**) number followed by an apartment (**квартира,** abbreviated **кв.**) number. Write down the addresses you hear.

    ОБРАЗЕЦ: *You hear:*   дом пять, квартира девять
                    You write: д. 5, кв. 9

1. д. _____, кв. _____
2. д. _____, кв. _____
3. д. _____, кв. _____
4. д. _____, кв. _____
5. д. _____, кв. _____
6. д. _____, кв. _____

ГГ. Listen carefully to the following statements, then match each person with the correct apartment number.

1. _____ Таня   а. кв. 7
2. _____ Дима   б. кв. 10
3. _____ Витя   в. кв. 3
4. _____ Маша   г. кв. 9
5. _____ Петя   д. кв. 2
6. _____ Нина   е. кв. 12

ДД. It is often difficult for beginning learners of Russian to differentiate between the numbers starting with the letter **д**. The numbers 2, 9, 10, and 12 will be read in Russian four times, each time in different order. Write them down in the order that you hear them.

    ОБРАЗЕЦ: *You hear:*   девять, двенадцать, десять, два
                    You write: 9   12   10   2

1. _____ _____ _____ _____
2. _____ _____ _____ _____
3. _____ _____ _____ _____
4. _____ _____ _____ _____

ГОВОРЕНИЕ (*Speaking drills*)

ЕЕ. Answer the following questions with the cued information. Make sure you place the new information at the end of the sentence.

    ОБРАЗЕЦ: *You hear and see:*   — Там живёт Дима? (нет, Володя)
                  You say: — <u>Нет, там живёт Володя.</u>

1. Кто здесь живёт? (Даша)
2. Где живёт Софья Петровна? (здесь)
3. Там живёт Юра? (нет, Саша)
4. Тамара живёт здесь? (нет, там)

ЖЖ. Practice reading the following addresses. Begin now.

ОБРАЗЕЦ: *You see:* д. 4, кв. 12
You say: дом четы́ре, кварти́ра двена́дцать

1. д. 5, кв. 3
2. д. 2, кв. 9
3. д. 10, кв. 4
4. д. 11, кв. 7
5. д. 8, кв. 6

Name_____ Date_____ Class_____

Spelling rules

Д. Before doing exercise **E**, review the spelling rules.

1. «Кни́ги» rule (ы and и): After г, к, х, ж, ч, ш, or щ, always write _____, never _____.

   ОБРАЗЕЦ: plural of *magazine*   журна́л_____

   BUT   plural of *book*   кни́г_____

2. «Хоро́шее» rule (о and е): After ж, ч, ш, щ, or ц, write _____ if the syllable is stressed;

   write _____ if the syllable is unstressed.

   ОБРАЗЕЦ: *a large dormitory*   больш_____е общежи́тие

   BUT   *a good dormitory*   хоро́ш_____е общежи́тие

3. «Роя́ли» rule (ы and и): When replacing **-ь, -й,** or **-я** (as, for example, when forming plural nouns), always

   use _____, never _____.

   ОБРАЗЕЦ: singular   биле́т   plural   биле́т_____

   BUT   singular   рубль   plural   рубл_____

   singular   музе́й   plural   музе́_____

   singular   фами́лия   plural   фами́ли_____

Adjectives: Gender and number

E. Below are combinations of adjectives and nouns. The adjectives are all given in the dictionary form (that is, the masculine singular form). Rewrite them so that they agree with the given noun. Keep in mind the three spelling rules and change the adjectives (when necessary) to agree with the nouns.

ОБРАЗЕЦ: (наш ма́ленький) _____наши ма́ленькие_____ де́ти

1. (твой большо́й) [ая ая] _____ кварти́ра
2. (её но́вый) [ая] _____ ру́чка
3. (ваш большо́й) [ое] ваше _____ окно́
4. (мой дорого́й) [ои ие] _____ вну́ки
5. (мой ма́ленький) _____ упражне́ние
6. (его́ но́вый) _____ журна́л
7. (твой хоро́ший) [ое ее] _____ письмо́
8. (ваш но́вый) _____ блу́зки
9. (наш ма́ленький) [а ая] _____ ку́хня
10. (их но́вый) _____ лифт

Уро́к 2, Часть втора́я   55

Ж. You are looking through magazines and pointing out famous people, describing them to a classmate. Using the adjectives on pages 55–56 of the textbook, write a sentence describing each of the famous people listed below. Remember, in most instances you can add the prefix **не-** to negate the meaning of the adjective or express the opposite quality.

ОБРАЗЕЦ: Лиз Тэйлор   Она́ о́чень культу́рная.

1. Билл Кли́нтон *Он очень талантливый*
2. Джо́ди Фо́стер *Она очень культурная*
3. Джу́лия Ро́бертс *Она очень культурная*
4. Том Хэнкс *Он очень талантливый*
5. Майкл Джо́рдан *Он очень талантливый*
6. Билл Гейтс *Он очень талантливый*
7. Леона́рдо Дика́прио *Он очень талантливый*

Перево́д (*Translation*)

3. Translate the following dialogues into Russian.

(*An adult is speaking to a child.*)

1. "Hello, are you (*informal*) our new neighbor?"

   "Yes, my name is Pasha. And yours (*formal*)?"

   Привет ты наш новый сосед?
   Да, мое имя паша и ваш?
   а ваc

2. "Is your apartment large?"

   "No, our apartment is small. And yours?"

   а твоя
   ваша квартира большая
   Нет наша квартира маленькая и ваши

Повторе́ние — мать уче́ния (*Practice makes perfect*)

И. Following is a shortened version of the reading of Part 2. Fill in the blanks with words that maintain the context of the reading. Do not use any of the words more than once.

ДЕ́ВОЧКА.	Вон наш эта́ж и на́ши _____.¹	дом
	Сле́ва — моя́ _____.² Вот моё	до́ма
	_____.³ А где твои́ о́кна?	здесь
МА́ЛЬЧИК.	Мой _____⁴ не здесь.	ко́мната
ДЕ́ВОЧКА.	А где твоя́ ма́ма?	о́кна
МА́ЛЬЧИК.	Ма́ма и па́па _____,⁵ А	окно́
	де́душка и ба́бушка _____.⁶ Вон они́.	хоро́ший
ДЕ́ВОЧКА.	А кто э́то?	э́то
МА́ЛЬЧИК.	_____⁷ Са́ша Кругло́в. Он	
	_____⁸ музыка́нт.	

56 Уро́к 2, Часть втора́я

Name: Shawn Simon

Ситуа́ции (*Situations*)

К. How would you...

1. ask whose letters these are? Чьи письма это?
2. ask whose pen this is? Чья это ручка?
3. tell somebody that this is your (your family's) new house?
   Это мой новый дом
4. ask your friend if this is her pen? Это твоя ручка?
5. tell somebody that your parents are talented and cultured?
   Мои родители талантлывы и культурны
6. tell somebody that your brother is not very serious?
   Мой брат не очень серьезен

Ва́ша о́чередь! (*It's your turn!*)

Л. Try to answer the following questions.

1. (*Pointing to your books.*) Чьи э́то кни́ги?
   Да это мои книги
2. (*Pointing to your family's house.*) Чей э́то дом?
   Да, наш дом
3. Твои́ роди́тели серьёзные? Несерьёзные?
   Нет, мои родители не серьезно
4. Твой профе́ссор энерги́чный? Тала́нтливый?
   Мой профессор талантливый
5. Твой дом но́вый? Ста́рый?
   Мой дом новый
6. Твой брат (твой оте́ц, твой де́душка) (*choose one*) романти́чный? Энерги́чный?
   Мой брат и отец энергичный
7. Твоя́ сестра́ (твоя́ мать, твоя́ ба́бушка) (*choose one*) тала́нтливая? Эксцентри́чная?
   Моя сестра и мать талантливая

Сочине́ние (*Composition*)

М. Write a short paragraph (five or six sentences) describing your family and its members. Ideas: Is your family small? large? Are your parents and brothers or sisters talented? energetic? serious? eccentric? Are any of them musicians? doctors? college students? grade-school students?

РАБОТА В ЛАБОРАТОРИИ (Laboratory exercises)

ДИАЛОГИ (Dialogues)

Диалог 1 Наша новая квартира (Making strong contrasts)

АА. Follow along as you listen to the dialogue.

А. Ваша новая квартира большая?
Б. Большая, но (but) плохая. А ваша?
А. Наша маленькая, но хорошая.

- Now read and repeat aloud in the pause after each phrase.
- Now read the lines for speaker **Б** aloud.
- Now read the lines for speaker **А** aloud.

Rewrite the above conversation so that each speaker is talking about her apartment building (**дом**) rather than her apartment. Make any changes necessary.

А. _____
Б. _____
А. _____

Диалог 2 Ты наш новый сосед? (Meeting a new neighbor)

ББ. Follow along as you listen to the dialogue.

A child greets an older person on a staircase.

А. Здравствуйте!
Б. Здравствуй! Ты наш новый сосед?
А. Да. (*Pointing to an apartment door.*) Вот наша квартира.
Б. А как тебя зовут?
А. Петя. А вас?
Б. Николай Иванович.

- Now read and repeat aloud in the pause after each phrase.
- Now read the lines for speaker **Б** aloud.
- Now read the lines for speaker **А** aloud.

List at least three things you heard in this dialogue that tell you one of the speakers is a child and the other an older person.

1. _____
2. _____
3. _____

Name_____ Date_____ Class_____

АУДИРОВАНИЕ (*Listening comprehension*)

ВВ. You will hear a series of sentences. For each one, put an **X** by the object that the speaker is talking about. Listen carefully to the pronouns and the adjective endings. They will indicate whether the item being referred to is masculine, feminine, neuter, or plural.

    ОБРАЗЕЦ: *You hear:*   Она́ о́чень ма́ленькая.

                    You check: __X__ ку́ртка

                                  _____ жаке́т

                                  _____ пла́тье

                                  _____ брю́ки

1. _____ ру́чка
   _____ каранда́ш
   _____ окно́
   _____ кни́ги

2. _____ ру́чка
   _____ биле́т
   _____ письмо́
   _____ журна́лы

3. _____ блу́зка
   _____ га́лстук
   _____ пла́тье
   _____ джи́нсы

4. _____ руба́шка
   _____ га́лстук
   _____ пла́тье
   _____ кроссо́вки

5. _____ ла́мпа
   _____ журна́л
   _____ письмо́
   _____ кни́ги

6. _____ столо́вая
   _____ дом
   _____ окно́
   _____ ко́мнаты

ГГ. Is the noun that you hear singular or plural? Remember: The endings of feminine singular nouns may sound similar to those of neuter plural nouns. Listen for adjective endings that will also give you a clue.

    ОБРАЗЕЦ: *You hear:*   Где твои́ ту́фли?
                 You circle: (plural)

1. singular   plural
2. singular   plural
3. singular   plural
4. singular   plural
5. singular   plural
6. singular   plural
7. singular   plural
8. singular   plural

Урок 2, Часть втора́я   59

ДД. It is always important to note whether others are using formal or informal language with you. For each sentence you hear, mark **F** for formal, **I** for informal.

ОБРАЗЕЦ: *You hear:* Это твой дедушка?
You write: ____I____

1. _____   5. _____
2. _____   6. _____
3. _____   7. _____
4. _____   8. _____

ГОВОРЕНИЕ (*Speaking drills*)

ЕЕ. For each number below, the name of an object will be given. Describe each object with the given adjective. Change the adjective ending where necessary to describe a feminine, neuter, or plural noun.

ОБРАЗЕЦ: *You hear:* (pen)
You see: (хороший)
You say: Это хорошая ручка.

1. (большой)
2. (мой)
3. (наш)
4. (новый)
5. (маленький)
6. (хороший)

ЖЖ. Answer the questions with the cued response.

ОБРАЗЕЦ: *You hear:* Чья это куртка?
You see: (my)
You say: Это моя куртка.

1. (your, *informal*)
2. (his)
3. (our)
4. (your, *formal*)
5. (her)
6. (their)
7. (my)

33. As in exercise **EE**, you will again hear the name of an item. How would you ask to whom that item belongs?

ОБРАЗЕЦ: *You hear:* (pencil)
You say: Чей это карандаш?

1. (apartment)
2. (suitcase)
3. (dog)
4. (dress)
5. (backpack)
6. (dogs)

60 Урок 2, Часть вторая

Name_____ Date_____ Class_____

5. In a later chapter you will learn that the Russian word **кла́ссика** can refer to classical music, like that of Tchaikovsky. It may also refer to classical literature, art, and so on. In this ad it is contrasted with the Russian word **моде́рн**. Since it obviously does not refer to music, literature, or art in this case, what do you think it means?

_____

Перево́д (*Translation*)

Ж. Translate the following dialogue into Russian.

SASHA. Boris Antonovich, this is my sister, Anna.
BORIS ANTONOVICH. Hello, Anna. Pleased to meet you.
ANNA. Nice to meet you, Boris Antonovich.
SASHA. (*To Boris Antonovich.*) My sister is a pianist.
(*To Anna.*) Boris Antonovich is also a musician.

_____
_____
_____
_____
_____

Повторе́ние — мать уче́ния (*Practice makes perfect*)

З. Following is a shortened version of the reading of Part 3. Fill in the blanks with words that maintain the context of the reading. You will have to change the form of some of the words. Do not use any of the words more than once.

СЕРГЕ́Й ПЕТР.	Здесь _____[1] музыка́нт?		ваш
ДЕ́ДУШКА.	Да, э́то _____[2] внук. А кто вы?		ужа́сно
СЕРГЕ́Й ПЕТР.	А мы _____[3] сосе́ди.		студе́нт
НАТА́ЛЬЯ ИВ. (*To Sasha.*)	Так, вы _____?[4]		хоро́ший
СА́ША.	Да, я _____,[5] пиани́ст.		живёт
НАТА́ЛЬЯ ИВ. (*Aside.*)	Нет, э́то _____![6]		музыка́нт
ЛЁНА. (*Later.*)	Кака́я _____[7] му́зыка!		мой

Ситуа́ции (*Situations*)

И. How would you ...

1. ask somebody if he is a graduate student?

2. say that your apartment is large?

3. ask somebody if her brothers are musicians?

4. ask if the neighbors are Germans?

5. say that our houses (buildings) are big and new?

Ва́ша о́чередь! (*It's your turn!*)

К. Answer the following questions.

1. Я музыка́нт. А ты?

2. Моя́ ко́мната больша́я. А твоя́?

3. Мои́ роди́тели америка́нцы. А твои́?

4. Мои́ сосе́ди япо́нцы. А твои́?

5. Мой компью́тер не о́чень но́вый. А твой?

Сочине́ние (*Composition*)

Л. Write a short paragraph (five to six sentences) describing a member of your family. Introduce her/him. Is she/he a musician? a student? Use some of the adjectives from Part 2 to help describe her/him. Is her/his room large or small? Is her/his computer American or Japanese? You can also compare yourself with the person by using the word **то́же**.

Name_____ Date_____ Class_____

РАБОТА В ЛАБОРАТОРИИ (*Laboratory exercises*)

ДИАЛОГИ (*Dialogues*)

Диалог 1 Очень приятно! (Making introductions; *two young people and an older gentleman*)

АА. Follow along as you listen to the dialogue.

> ВОЛОДЯ. Максим Петрович, познакомьтесь, это мой друг (*friend*) Сергей.
> МАКСИМ ПЕТРОВИЧ. Здравствуйте, Сергей, очень приятно.
> ВОЛОДЯ. Сергей, Максим Петрович — наш сосед.
> СЕРГЕЙ. Очень приятно, Максим Петрович.

- Now read and repeat aloud in the pause after each phrase.
- Now read the lines for speaker **Б** aloud.
- Now read the lines for speaker **А** aloud.

1. What is the relationship between Volodya and Sergei?

   _____

2. What is the relationship between Volodya and Maksim Petrovich?

   _____

3. What is the relationship between Sergei and Maksim Petrovich?

   _____

Диалог 2 Вы брат и сестра? (Getting acquainted; *a teenager talks to two adults*)

ББ. Follow along as you listen to the dialogue.

> ОЛЕГ. Вы наши соседи?
> МАРИЯ МИХАЙЛОВНА. Да.
> ОЛЕГ. А как вас зовут?
> МАРИЯ МИХАЙЛОВНА. Мария Михайловна и Пётр Михайлович.
> ОЛЕГ. Вы брат и сестра?
> ПЁТР МИХАЙЛОВИЧ. Нет, (*laughing*) мы муж и жена.

- Now read and repeat aloud in the pause after each phrase.
- Now read the lines for speaker **Б** aloud.
- Now read the lines for speaker **А** aloud.

1. Why does Oleg think that Maria and Pyotr might be brother and sister?

   _____

2. How would the fourth line read if Maria's and Pyotr's fathers were named Anton (**Антон**)?

   _____

АУДИРОВАНИЕ (*Listening comprehension*)

ВВ. Referring to the family tree in exercise **B** on page 62, decide if the sentences you hear are true or false. If the statements are correct, circle **В** for **ве́рно**. If the statements are incorrect, circle **Н** for **неве́рно**.

ОБРАЗЕЦ: *You hear:*   Антóн Васи́льевич и Тóля — дéдушка и внук.
           You circle: (В)

1. В   Н
2. В   Н
3. В   Н
4. В   Н
5. В   Н
6. В   Н

ГГ. Is the noun that you hear singular or plural?

ОБРАЗЕЦ: *You hear:*   Это вáши сыновья́?
           You circle: (plural)

1. singular   plural   4. singular   plural
2. singular   plural   5. singular   plural
3. singular   plural   6. singular   plural

ДД. Circle the letter of the most appropriate response to each of the statements and questions that you hear.

ОБРАЗЕЦ: *You hear:*   Где твоя́ ру́чка?
                         а. Он там.
           You circle: (б. Онá там.)
                         в. Они́ там.

1. а. Где он живёт?
   б. Где онá живёт?
   в. Где они́ живу́т?

2. а. Я тóже музыкáнт.
   б. Я тóже студéнт.
   в. Я тóже аспирáнт.

3. а. Да, вáша.
   б. Да, твоя́.
   в. Да, нáша.

4. а. Это наш профéссор, Ири́на Влади́мировна.
   б. Это наш дом.
   в. Это нáша квартúра.

5. а. Его́ тóже.
   б. Я тóже.
   в. Меня́ тóже.

Name_____ Date_____ Class_____

ГОВОРЕНИЕ (*Speaking drills*)

EE. You will hear a series of sentences in the singular. Change the subject to the plural and make any other necessary changes.

    ОБРАЗЕЦ: *You hear:* Её сын — студе́нт.
                   You say: Её сыновья́ — студе́нты.

1. Моя́ сестра́ — аспира́нтка.
2. Здесь живёт япо́нец.
3. Наш сосе́д — италья́нец.
4. Мой брат — тала́нтливый музыка́нт.
5. Где живёт его́ дочь?

ЖЖ. Respond to each of the statements that you hear with a statement about yourself, using the word **то́же**.

    ОБРАЗЕЦ: *You hear:* Его́ ба́бушка — ру́сская.
                   You say: Моя́ ба́бушка то́же ру́сская.

1. Его́ сосе́д — украи́нец.
2. Их дом но́вый и большо́й.
3. Её зову́т Же́ня.
4. Её сестра́ — о́чень серьёзная.
5. Его́ тётя — врач.
6. Их мать — пиани́стка.

33. Your classmates ask you questions as you show them pictures of your family and home. Answer each affirmatively.

    ОБРАЗЕЦ: *You hear:* Кто э́то? Твоя́ сестра́?
                   You say: Да, моя́ сестра́.

1. Чья э́то семья́? Твоя́?
2. Кто здесь живёт? Твой брат?
3. Это твоя́ кварти́ра?
4. Кто э́то? Твоя́ тётя?
5. Это твой де́душка?
6. Здесь живу́т твои́ роди́тели?

ИИ. Now, you and your brother are answering questions about pictures of your family. Answer each affirmatively. Remember that you will have to answer with the plural *our* since the questions are addressed to you and your brother.

ОБРАЗЕЦ: *You hear:* Кто это? Ваша сестра?
You say: Да, наша сестра.

1. Это ваши родители?

2. Чья это машина? Ваша?

3. Кто здесь живёт? Ваша бабушка?

4. Это ваш дом?

5. Чья это семья? Ваша?

6. Кто это? Ваш дядя?

Name_____ Date_____ Class_____

Exclamations

Г. What might you exclaim if you encountered the following items during the course of your day? Remember: If the noun is feminine, the adjectives should also be feminine; the same is true for masculine, neuter, and plural nouns and their respective adjectives.

большо́й краси́вый
ма́ленький
некраси́вый
плохо́й хоро́ший
ста́рый

ОБРАЗЕЦ: _Како́й большо́й чемода́н!_

1. _____
2. _____
3. _____
4. _____
5. _____
6. _____

Д. Using **како́й** and an adjective, how would you make an exclamation referring to an item you are asking about? Choose from the adjectives listed here. Various responses are possible.

ОБРАЗЕЦ: Э́то ва́ша соба́ка? _Кака́я больша́я!_

1. Э́то ваш кот? _____
2. Э́то ва́ши брю́ки? _____
3. Э́то ва́ша ко́мната? _____
4. Э́то ваш роя́ль? _____
5. Э́то ва́ша у́лица? _____
6. Э́то ва́ши ту́фли? _____

Уро́к 2, Часть четвёртая

Перево́д (*Translation*)

E. Translate the following dialogues into Russian.

1. "Excuse me, what is your name?"

   "Karina."

   "What a pretty name!"

   _____

   _____

   _____

2. "Who lives here?"

   "Sonya. Her brother Petya lives here, too."

   _____

   _____

Повторе́ние — мать уче́ния (*Practice makes perfect*)

Ж. Following is a shortened version of the reading of Part 4. Fill in the blanks with words that maintain the context of the reading. You will have to change the form of some of the words. Do not use any of the words more than once.

СА́ША. _____,¹ э́то ва́ша соба́ка? _____² краси́вая!	большо́й
	ваш
ЛЕ́НА. Моя́. _____³ зову́т Бе́лка. А э́то _____⁴ ко́шка? Кака́я _____!⁵	его́
	её
СА́ША. Э́то кот. _____⁶ зову́т Матве́й, Мо́тя. А я Са́ша.	извини́те
	како́й
ЛЕ́НА. Ле́на.	сосе́д
СА́ША. О́чень прия́тно. Мы, ка́жется, _____.⁷	

Name_____ Date_____ Class_____

Ситуа́ции (*Situations*)

З. How would you . . .

1. express delight at seeing your neighbor's large kitchen?
   _____

2. tell somebody that your floor (the floor your family lives on) is the fourth?
   _____

3. ask a student you just met if he is called by his full name or his nickname? (You choose a name to put in!)
   _____

4. express dismay at your terrible neighbors?
   _____

5. express delight at the beautiful (Moscow) subway?
   _____

Ва́ша о́чередь! (*It's your turn!*)

И. Answer the questions that are asked of you.

1. Твоя́ кварти́ра ста́рая? Но́вая? _____

2. Твоя́ ко́мната больша́я? Ма́ленькая? _____

3. Сосе́ди хоро́шие? _____

   You are asked the following questions while looking at photos:

4. Э́то твоя́ ко́шка? Как её зову́т? _____

5. Э́то твоя́ соба́ка? Как её зову́т? _____

Сочине́ние (*Composition*)

К. Write a short paragraph (five or six sentences) describing your family's house. Is it old or new? Who lives there? Are the rooms large or small? What are the neighbors like?

_____

_____

_____

_____

_____

Уро́к 2, Часть четвёртая

Fun with grammar! Case review

Л. Fill in the blanks of the following sentences with the appropriate case endings. Not all blanks, however, will have an ending. Then enter the words into the crossword puzzle below to help check your spelling. The letter-number combinations (e.g., **г**12) at the end of each sentence indicate the location of the word or words in the puzzle. The first letter and number are for the first word and so on. Note that **г** is for **горизонта́ль,** or horizontal; **в** is for **вертика́ль** or vertical.

1. Ри́та — мо_____ двою́родн_____ сестра́. (г16)(в8)
2. Ви́ка и Ва́ня о́чень хоро́ш_____ де́ти. (г12)
3. Ваш_____ внук ма́леньк_____? (г9) (г7)
4. Как_____ больш_____ ко́шка! (г11) (в3)
5. Вот мо_____ дорог_____ внук. (в16) (г14)
6. Э́то наш_____ но́в_____ но́мер телефо́на. (в6) (в2)
7. Мо_____ окно́ ма́леньк_____. (в10) (в7)
8. Наш_____ метро́ о́чень хоро́ш_____. (г17) (в13)
9. Мо_____ кроссо́вки но́в_____, а тво_____ стар_____. (г15) (г4) (г5) (в1)

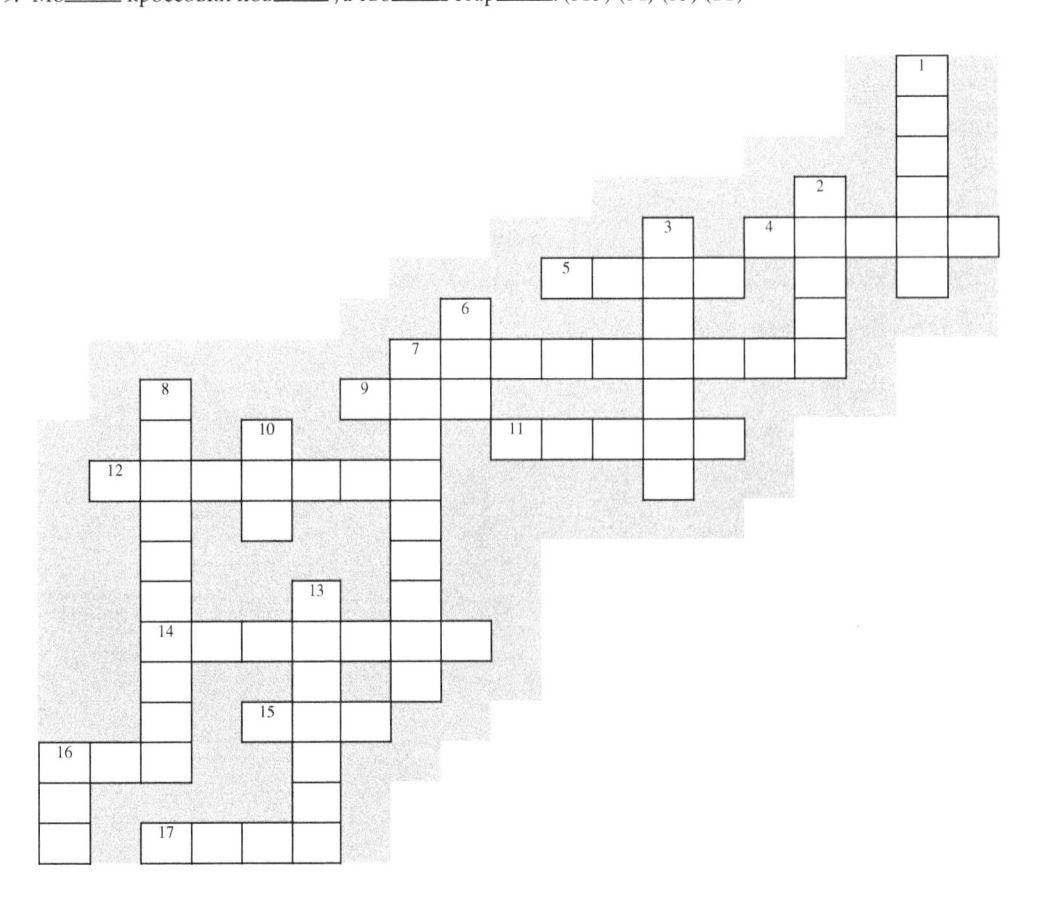

Name _____ Date _____ Class _____

РАБОТА В ЛАБОРАТОРИИ (*Laboratory exercises*)

ДИАЛОГИ (*Dialogues*)

Диалог 1 Хоро́шая профе́ссия! (Getting acquainted)

АА. Follow along as you listen to the dialogue.

    А. Извини́те, как вас зову́т?
    Б. Кристи́на.
    А. Како́е краси́вое и́мя! А я Татья́на, Та́ня. Я архите́ктор.
    Б. Хоро́шая профе́ссия, Та́ня! А я исто́рик.
    А. Кака́я интере́сная профе́ссия!

- Now read and repeat aloud in the pause after each phrase.
- Now read the lines for speaker **Б** aloud.
- Now read the lines for speaker **А** aloud.

Rewrite the dialogue so that it is between Brandon (**Брэ́ндон**), a musician, and **Михаи́л,** a journalist. (Refer to page 69 in the textbook for the correct nickname.)

    А. _____
    Б. _____
    А. _____
    Б. _____
    А. _____

Диалог 2 Кто здесь живёт? (Establishing who lives where)

ББ. Follow along as you listen to the dialogue. Begin now.

    А. Кто здесь живёт?
    Б. Здесь живу́т Кругло́вы. Их внук Са́ша то́же живёт здесь.
    А. А Джим то́же живёт здесь?
    Б. Нет, он живёт не здесь.

- Now read and repeat aloud in the pause after each phrase.
- Now read the lines for speaker **Б** aloud.
- Now read the lines for speaker **А** aloud.

1. What is Sasha's relationship to the Kruglovs? _____

2. Does Jim also live with the Kruglovs? _____

АУДИРОВАНИЕ (*Listening comprehension*)

ВВ. Indicate whether the sentence you hear is a statement, a question, or an exclamation.

ОБРАЗЕЦ: *You hear:* Это твоя рубашка?
You check: QUESTION
[X]

	STATEMENT	QUESTION	EXCLAMATION
1.	[ ]	[ ]	[ ]
2.	[ ]	[ ]	[ ]
3.	[ ]	[ ]	[ ]
4.	[ ]	[ ]	[ ]
5.	[ ]	[ ]	[ ]
6.	[ ]	[ ]	[ ]
7.	[ ]	[ ]	[ ]
8.	[ ]	[ ]	[ ]

ГГ. Which item is the speaker talking about?

ОБРАЗЕЦ: *You hear:* Сегодня — четвёртый день.

You check: _____ first day

_____ second day

_____ third day

__X__ fourth day

1. _____ first floor
   _____ second floor
   _____ third floor
   _____ fourth floor

2. _____ first house
   _____ second house
   _____ third house
   _____ fourth house

3. _____ first apartment
   _____ second apartment
   _____ third apartment
   _____ fourth apartment

4. _____ first window
   _____ second window
   _____ third window
   _____ fourth window

5. _____ first building entrance
   _____ second building entrance
   _____ third building entrance
   _____ fourth building entrance

6. _____ first lesson
   _____ second lesson
   _____ third lesson
   _____ fourth lesson

Name_____ Date_____ Class_____

ДД. You will hear a series of questions in which the speaker is asking for information. Place the letter of the question next to the appropriate situation below.

    ОБРАЗЕЦ: *You hear:*   Извините, где квартира десять?
                     You check: where apartment ten is.

The speaker wants to know:

1. _____ where Chekhov Street is.
2. _____ if that is the other person's dog.
3. __Об.__ where apartment ten is.
4. _____ where Professor Rugaleva lives.
5. _____ if this is Pushkin Street.
6. _____ what the other person's name is.
7. _____ if this is building twelve.

ГОВОРЕНИЕ (*Speaking drills*)

ЕЕ. Repeat after the speaker as a series of voiced and voiceless paired consonant sounds is read to you.

	VOICED	VOICELESS
1.	б	п
2.	д	т
3.	г	к
4.	в	ф
5.	з	с
6.	ж	ш

Now the speaker will read one of the paired sounds. Circle the sound that you hear.

The "Stroganoff" Effect

ЖЖ. Listen to and repeat each of the following words after the speaker. Indicate in writing what *sound* (not what *letter*) you hear at the end of each word.

    ОБРАЗЕЦ: сосед   [т]

1. рад   [   ]
2. Чехов   [   ]
3. геолог [   ]
4. муж   [   ]
5. хлеб   [   ]
6. Волгоград [   ]
7. этаж   [   ]

Урок 2, Часть четвёртая

The "Vodka" Effect

33. Listen to and repeat each of the following words after the speaker. Indicate in writing what *sound* (not what *letter*) combination you hear for the underlined letters.

ОБРАЗЕЦ: за́<u>втр</u>а   [фт]

1. А<u>вс</u>тра́лия   [   ]
2. Вашин<u>гт</u>о́н   [   ]
3. блу́<u>зк</u>а   [   ]
4. фу<u>тб</u>о́лка   [   ]
5. ю́<u>бк</u>а   [   ]
6. бли́<u>зк</u>о   [   ]

ИИ. Read each of the following sentences. Then check your intonation with that of the speaker.

1. Кака́я больша́я ко́мната!
2. Э́то твоя́ ко́мната?
3. Э́то моя́ ко́мната.
4. Како́й краси́вый костю́м!
5. Э́то ваш костю́м?
6. Э́то мой костю́м.

Name_____ Date_____ Class_____

МЫ И НАШИ СОСЕДИ урок 3

ЧАСТЬ ПЕРВАЯ
Интере́сная профе́ссия

РАБО́ТА ДО́МА (*Homework*)

ПИСЬМО́ (*Written exercises*)

Понима́ние те́кста

А. The following statements about the reading on page 83 of the textbook are incorrect. Rewrite them so that they are correct.

1. Ле́на игра́ет в ша́хматы.
   _____

2. Её те́ма — «музыка́нты».
   _____

3. Журнали́ст — неинтере́сная профе́ссия.
   _____

4. Ната́лья Ива́новна гуля́ет.
   _____

5. Серге́й Петро́вич пи́шет статью́.
   _____

6. Во́ва чита́ет три́ллер.
   _____

«-ешь» Verbs: Basic (чита́ть) type

Б. The «-ешь» verbs are conjugated in the same pattern as the verb **чита́ть**. Fill in the blanks with the appropriate endings for the verb **чита́ть**. Then conjugate the verbs **гуля́ть** (the stem is **гуля́-**) and **рабо́тать** (the stem is **рабо́та-**) in the spaces provided.

ЧИТА́ТЬ	ГУЛЯ́ТЬ	РАБО́ТАТЬ
я чита́ _____	я _____	я _____
ты чита́ _____	ты _____	ты _____
он (она́) чита́ _____	он (она́) _____	он (она́) _____
мы чита́ _____	мы _____	мы _____
вы чита́ _____	вы _____	вы _____
они́ чита́ _____	они́ _____	они́ _____

В. Match the incomplete sentences in the left column with the proper conclusion in the right column. Use each letter once. The first one has been done for you.

1. Что она́ ___б___
2. Что ты _____
3. Где вы _____
4. Я э́то _____
5. Где они́ _____
6. Мы о́чень хорошо́ _____
7. Же́ня хорошо́ _____
8. Ма́льчик и соба́ка _____
9. Где Ми́ша _____

а. зна́ем их.
б. чита́ет? (crossed out)
в. игра́ет в ша́хматы.
г. живёт?
д. понима́ю.
е. рабо́таете?
ж. гуля́ют.
з. де́лаешь?
и. живу́т?

Г. Refer to the following pictures. How would you tell what each of the people is doing? Use exercise **В** to remind you of some of the verbs from which you can choose.

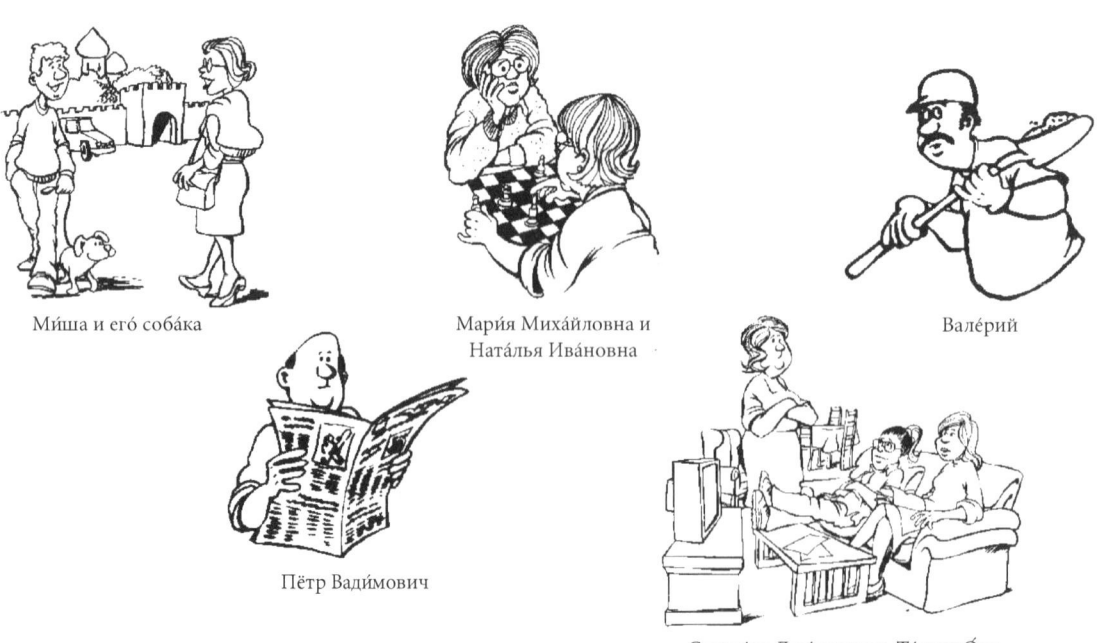

Ми́ша и его́ соба́ка

Мари́я Миха́йловна и Ната́лья Ива́новна

Вале́рий

Пётр Вади́мович

Светла́на Дми́триевна, Та́ня и О́ля

Name_____ Date_____ Class_____

Telling where someone lives: The Prepositional case

3. Use the geographical names on the left to make up sentences describing where each member of this family lives.

ОБРАЗЕЦ: (Индиа́на) Сын <u>живёт в Индиа́не.</u>

1. (Ло́ндон) Роди́тели <u>живут в Лондоне</u>
2. (Варша́ва) Ба́бушка <u>живёт в Варшаве</u>
3. (Вашингто́н) Де́душка <u>живёт в Вашингтоне</u>
4. (Ки́ев) Брат <u>живёт в Киеве</u>
5. (Калифо́рния) Сестра́ <u>живёт в Калифорнии</u>
6. (Кана́да) Де́ти <u>живут в Канаде</u>
7. (А́фрика) Тётя <u>живёт в Африке</u>
8. (Фра́нция) Дя́дя <u>живёт в Франции</u>

«-ешь» Verbs: писа́ть variation

И. Fill in the blanks with the correct endings and mark the stresses.

МАРИ́НА БОРИ́СОВНА. Что вы пи́ш**ете**?

КА́ТЯ. Я пиш__ курсову́ю рабо́ту, а что пи́ш__ет__

Вале́ра, я не зна́ю.

ЗО́Я И ВАЛЕ́РА. А мы пи́ш__ем__ письмо́.

МАРИ́НА БОРИ́СОВНА. А ты что пи́ш__ешь__ Ле́на?

ЛЕ́НА. Я пиш__ статью́.

ВАЛЕ́РА. А они́ пи́ш__ут__ кни́гу.

К. Elena has written this note to a new pen pal. Fill in the blanks with the correct form of the following verbs.

чита́ть жить писа́ть знать де́лать рабо́тать

Меня́ зову́т Еле́на, а э́то кварти́ра, где я _____живу́_____. Мои́ роди́тели, ба́бушка и де́душка то́же

___живут___¹ здесь. Моя́ мать — пиани́стка. Мой оте́ц — журнали́ст и мно́го

_____² до́ма. Он _____³ кни́ги и статьи́. Ба́бушка

и де́душка не _____.⁴ Они́ _____⁵ кни́ги и

журна́лы. Я не _____,⁶ я студе́нтка. Там _____⁷

на́ши сосе́ди. Я не _____,⁸ как их зову́т и что они́

_____.⁹

Verb stress patterns

Л. Conjugate the following three verbs and indicate which syllables take stress.

ЧИТА́ТЬ	ЖИТЬ	ПИСА́ТЬ
я _____	я _____	я _____
ты _____	ты _____	ты _____
он (она́) _____	он (она́) _____	он (она́) _____
мы _____	мы _____	мы _____
вы _____	вы _____	вы _____
они́ _____	они́ _____	они́ _____

1. Verbs similar to **чита́ть** are always stressed on the _____.
2. Verbs similar to **жить** are always stressed on the _____.
3. Verbs similar to **писа́ть** are stressed on the _____ of the _____ form.

   All other forms are stressed on the _____.

Перево́д (*Translation*)

М. Translate the following dialogue into Russian.

"Where do your parents live?"
"In Denver."
"Does your sister live there, too?"
"No, she lives in Boston."

_____

_____

_____

_____

Повторе́ние — мать уче́ния (*Practice makes perfect*)

Н. Following is a summary of the reading of Part 1. Fill in the blanks with words that maintain the context of the reading. You will have to change the form of some of the words. Do not use any of the words more than once.

Си́лины все (*all*) до́ма. Ната́лья Ива́новна _____.¹	де́лать
Ле́на _____² статью́. Это её	курсова́я рабо́та
_____.³ Те́ма _____,⁴ но	ша́хматы
о́чень _____.⁵ А что	интере́сный
_____⁶ Серге́й Петро́вич и Во́ва? Они́ игра́ют в	писа́ть
_____.⁷	чита́ть
	тру́дный

86 Уро́к 3, Часть пе́рвая

Name _____ Date _____ Class _____

Ситуа́ции (*Situations*)

О. How would you ...

1. ask someone what he is doing?

2. tell somebody that you live in Russia?

3. ask your classmate what her father is reading?

4. ask your Russian host mother where she works?

5. tell somebody that your brothers are writing an article?

Ва́ша о́чередь! (*It's your turn!*)

П. Answer the following questions.

1. Где ты живёшь? _____

2. Где живу́т твои́ роди́тели? Бра́тья? Сёстры?

3. Ты хорошо́ зна́ешь твой го́род? _____

4. Ты рабо́таешь? _____

5. Что ты де́лаешь до́ма? Чита́ешь? Пи́шешь? Отдыха́ешь?

6. Ты хорошо́ и́ли пло́хо игра́ешь в ша́хматы?

7. Ты студе́нт (студе́нтка)? Аспира́нт (Аспира́нтка)?

Сочине́ние (*Composition*)

Р. Write a short paragraph (five or six sentences) similar to Elena's letter in exercise **К**, introducing yourself to a new pen pal. Tell where you live, who else lives there, whether or not your parents work, if your brothers/sisters work or are students, and who reads, writes, and so on.

РАБОТА В ЛАБОРАТОРИИ (*Laboratory exercises*)

ДИАЛОГИ (*Dialogues*)

Диалог 1 Что ты де́лаешь? (Asking what someone is doing)

АА. Follow along as you listen to the dialogue.

А. Что ты де́лаешь?
Б. Пишу́ сочине́ние.
А. А Са́ша что де́лает?
Б. Чита́ет газе́ту.

- Now read and repeat aloud in the pause after each phrase.
- Now read the lines for speaker **Б** aloud.
- Now read the lines for speaker **А** aloud.

Rewrite the dialogue so that speaker **А** is talking to an older man and asks (in line 3) about his children, **Са́ша** and **Да́ша**.

А. _____
Б. _____
А. _____
Б. _____

Диалог 2 Где вы живёте? (Asking where someone lives)

ББ. Follow along as you listen to the dialogue.

А. Вы живёте в Москве́?
Б. Нет, в Санкт-Петербу́рге. А вы?
А. Я живу́ в Но́вгороде.
Б. В Но́вгороде? Мои́ роди́тели то́же живу́т в Но́вгороде.

- Now read and repeat aloud in the pause after each phrase.
- Now read the lines for speaker **Б** aloud.
- Now read the lines for speaker **А** aloud.

How would the last line read if it were the speaker's sister who also lived in Novgorod?

_____

АУДИРОВАНИЕ (*Listening comprehension*)

ВВ. You will hear a series of questions. For each one, choose the most appropriate answer from the list below. The first one has been done for you.

1. _____ Отдыха́ю.
2. _____ В Филаде́льфии.
3. _____ Нет, сочине́ние.
4. _____ Нет, пиани́стка.
5. _____ Да, но интере́сная.
6. __а__ Не зна́ю.
7. _____ Журна́л.

88 Уро́к 3, Часть пе́рвая

Name_____ Date_____ Class_____

ГГ. Ве́рно и́ли неве́рно? (*True or false?*) You will hear a series of statements, each telling that a certain city is located in a certain country. Each sentence contains the Russian word **нахо́дится,** which means *is located*. Decide if the statements are true (**в** = **ве́рно**) or false (**н** = **неве́рно**). (If you're not sure where these cities are, try to find them on a map.)

ОБРАЗЕЦ: *You hear:* Рим нахо́дится в Норве́гии.
          You circle: **н** (because Rome is in Italy, not in Norway)

1. в н
2. в н
3. в н
4. в н
5. в н
6. в н
7. в н
8. в н

ДД. Listen to the speaker's description of his family and what the individual members are doing. Match the people below with the activity. The first one has been done for you.

1. __д__ Mom and Dad   а. writing a composition
2. _____ brother Tom   б. working
3. _____ brother Mark   в. resting
4. _____ sister Erin   г. reading a book
5. _____ Grandma   ~~д. playing chess~~
6. _____ Grandpa   е. writing a letter
7. _____ the speaker   ж. reading a magazine

ГОВОРЕ́НИЕ (*Speaking drills*)

ЕЕ. **Assimilation of prepositions.** Listen to and repeat each of the following prepositional phrases after the speaker. Indicate in writing whether you hear the sound [в] or [ф] for the preposition **в**.

ОБРАЗЕЦ: в Кана́де   [ф]

1. в Таила́нде   [ ]
2. в Герма́нии   [ ]
3. в Сиби́ри   [ ]
4. в Росси́и   [ ]
5. в Брази́лии   [ ]
6. в Норве́гии   [ ]
7. в Калифо́рнии [ ]
8. в Португа́лии [ ]

ЖЖ. You will hear a series of questions. Answer each according to the cued response below.

ОБРАЗЕЦ: *You hear:* Где живёт Анна? В Бостоне?
You see: (New York)
You say: Нет, она живёт в Нью-Йорке.

1. (reading a book)
2. (in Moscow)
3. (composition)
4. (book)
5. (playing chess)

33. How would you ask the following questions using the most common Russian word order?

ОБРАЗЕЦ: *You hear:* Where does Boris live?
You say: Где живёт Борис?

1. What is Vova reading?
2. What is he reading?
3. Where does Olya live?
4. Where does she live?
5. What is she doing?
6. What is Sveta doing?
7. Where does Misha work?
8. Where does he work?

Name_____ Date_____ Class_____

ЧАСТЬ ВТОРАЯ
Сосе́д симпати́чный?

РАБО́ТА ДО́МА (*Homework*)

ПИСЬМО́ (*Written exercises*)

Понима́ние те́кста

А. Review the reading on page 94 of the textbook. Below is a list of adjectives that the speakers use to talk about their surroundings. Match the adjectives to the nouns they describe. Some adjectives will be used more than once, and some nouns will require more than one descriptive word. All adjectives are given in their dictionary form. Be sure to change the endings to correctly modify the nouns. The first one has been done for you.

| большо́й | но́вый | све́тлый | ста́рый |
| и́мпортный | отли́чный | симпати́чный | |

1. ____и́мпортный____ стол
2. _____ дива́н
3. _____ кварти́ра
4. _____ , _____ ко́мната
5. _____ кре́сло
6. _____ ла́мпы
7. _____ , _____ , _____ ме́бель
8. _____ сосе́д
9. _____ сту́лья

Accusative case of nouns

Б. Write the subject and the direct object of each sentence in the appropriate column.

	SUBJECT	DIRECT OBJECT
ОБРАЗЕ́Ц: Erin is reading a book.	Erin	book
Ма́ша пи́шет письмо́.	Ма́ша	письмо́
1. Ann wants to buy a new car.	_____	_____
2. Diane loves cookies.	_____	_____
3. Bill gave me a job.	_____	_____
4. Anton wrote his parents a letter.	_____	_____
5. I am building a house.	_____	_____
6. Ма́ма пи́шет статью́.	_____	_____

	SUBJECT	DIRECT OBJECT
7. Андрей и Вова знают его.	_____	_____
8. Ты меня понимаешь?	_____	_____
9. Она читает книгу.	_____	_____
10. Что пишет Алик?	_____	_____

Б. In the following sentences, indicate whether the underlined word is in the Nominative or Accusative case.

	NOMINATIVE	ACCUSATIVE
ОБРАЗЕЦ: Это моя <u>мама</u>.	X	_____
1. Маша сейчас пишет <u>статью</u>.	_____	_____
2. Это твоя <u>статья</u>?	_____	_____
3. <u>Статью</u> пишет Витя.	_____	_____
4. Ты знаешь <u>Машу</u>?	_____	_____
5. <u>Наташу</u> я знаю, а <u>Машу</u> нет.	_____	_____
6. <u>Машу</u> знает <u>Антон</u>.	_____	_____
7. Какая интересная <u>книга</u>!	_____	_____
8. Кто читает <u>книгу</u>?	_____	_____
9. <u>Книгу</u> читает Вика.	_____	_____
10. Книгу читает <u>Вика</u>.	_____	_____

Г. Now construct some of your own sentences. First use the cued words in **А** to make an exclamation about the object. Then in **Б** ask something about it, conjugating the cued verb to agree with the subject. Notice that in line **А**, the given noun is the subject. In line **Б**, the same noun is the direct object. Each underscore indicates a missing letter — except for one which will remain blank. Which one is it?

ОБРАЗЕЦ: интересн_ _ / книга!   Какая интересная книга!

Федя / читать / книг_?   Федя читает книгу?

1. **А.** интересн_ _ / газета!   _____

   Б. Нина / читать / газет_?   _____

2. **А.** трудн_ _ / тема!   _____

   Б. ты / понимать / тем_?   _____

3. **А.** плох_ _ / журнал!   _____

   Б. студенты / читать / журнал_? _____

4. **А.** неинтересн_ _ / письмо!   _____

   Б. кто / писать / письм_?   _____

5. **А.** оригинальн_ _ / статья!   _____

   Б. вы / писать / стать_?   _____

92   Урок 3, Часть вторая

Name _____ *Date* _____ *Class* _____

Д. Complete each sentence with the correct form of the noun in parentheses.

1. Кака́я неинтере́сная _____ ! (кни́га)
2. Студе́нты понима́ют _____ . (аспира́нтка)
3. Кни́гу чита́ет _____ . (ма́ма)
4. Э́то наш симпати́чный _____ . (сосе́д)
5. _____ зна́ют А́ллу Ива́новну. (аспира́нты)
6. Э́то и́мпортная _____ . (ла́мпа)
7. Джон хорошо́ понима́ет _____ . (статья́)
8. Мы не зна́ем _____ . (Татья́на Ви́кторовна)
9. Со́ня пи́шет _____ . (сочине́ние)

Е. Write five logical sentences from the words in the box below. Use each word only once. You will not need to change the form of any of the words. A sample sentence has been done for you.

мы	игра́ет	статью́	интере́сная
о́чень	му́зыка	студе́нты	хоро́шая
кака́я	статья́	~~аспира́нт~~	~~не понима́ет~~	Ве́ру Никола́евну
зна́ют	чита́ем	джаз	~~студе́нтку~~	Ве́ра Никола́евна

ОБРАЗЕ́Ц: <u>Аспира́нт не понима́ет студе́нтку.</u>

1. _____
2. _____
3. _____
4. _____
5. _____

Adverbs related to adjectives

Ж. Your classmates want to know not only what your family does, but how they do it. Choose from the words in the box and revise what you have told them. You must first, however, change the endings on the words so that they are adverbs.

| оригина́льный |
| хоро́ший |
| плохо́й |
| неплохо́й |

ОБРАЗЕЦ: Дéдушка игрáет в шáхматы. <u>Дéдушка плóхо игрáет в шáхматы.</u>

1. Моя́ сестрá — журналистка. Онá пи́шет.

2. Мáма — пианистка. Онá игрáет клáссику.

3. Отéц игрáет джаз, но он не музыкáнт.

4. Брат знáет Москвý.

5. Бáбушка знáет сосéдку.

Expressing opinions: *It's easy!*

3. Combine either **как** or **э́то** with one of the words below to express your opinion about the following situations. In many instances, there is more than one possibility.

        легкó   хорошó   ужáсно   трýдно   интерéсно

ОБРАЗЕЦ: Your sister lost one of your mother's favorite earrings.
<u>Э́то ужáсно!</u>

1. Your father did well in the stock market and is giving you some of the profits.

2. Your classmate tells you she was asked out by a guy she has liked for a long time.

3. You find out that you and your roommate have the same birth dates.

Use only **э́то** for situations 4 through 7.

4. Your classmate says she's taking a class in quantum physics.

5. Someone asks you how to say hello in Russian.

6. Someone tells you about a serious flood near your hometown.

7. Your brother wants to learn to drive a car.

Name_____ Date_____ Class_____

Перевод (*Translation*)

И. Translate the following dialogue into Russian.

"What is your father doing?"
"He's writing an article."
"What's the topic?"
"The topic is not hard: 'What students read.'"

_____

_____

_____

_____

Повторение — мать учения (*Practice makes perfect*)

К. Following is a summary of the reading of Part 2. Fill in the blanks with words that maintain the context of the reading. You will have to change the form of some of the words. Do not use any of the words more than once.

Вот квартира шесть. Здесь _____¹	диван
Силины. Наталья Ивановна и Лена _____².	дома
Лена _____³ на балконе.	жить
Их квартира _____⁴ и	импортный
_____.⁵ Их _____⁶	мебель
новая, _____.⁷ Только (*only*)	новый
_____⁸ старый.	светлый
	читать

Ситуации (*Situations*)

Л. How would you . . .

1. ask a classmate if she's writing a composition?

   _____

2. tell somebody that you're writing a letter?

   _____

3. tell your professor that she writes well?

   _____

4. ask your classmates if they know Moscow well?

   _____

5. tell somebody that you don't know California (**Калифóрния**) very well?

_____

6. ask a classmate if she reads the newspaper?

_____

Вáша óчередь! (*It's your turn!*)

M. Answer the following questions.

1. Вáша (*your family's*) мéбель нóвая? Стáрая?

_____

2. Вáша мéбель америкáнская? Импортная?

_____

3. Вáша квартúра хорóшая? Большáя? Свéтлая?

_____

4. Что ты читáешь дóма? Газéты? Журнáлы? Кнúги?

_____

5. Ты хорошó знáешь Вашингтóн? Чикáго? Сан-Франциско?

_____

6. Ты пúшешь сочинéния? Пúсьма? Статьú?

_____

Сочинéние (*Composition*)

H. Write a short paragraph (five or six sentences) about your apartment/house or your dorm room. Do you have a large apartment/house? How about your room? Is it light? What kind of furniture do you have? Is it old? new? American? imported?

_____
_____
_____
_____
_____

РАБОТА В ЛАБОРАТОРИИ (*Laboratory exercises*)

ДИАЛОГИ (*Dialogues*)

Диалог 1 Ты рабóтаешь? (Asking about someone's occupation)

AA. Follow along as you listen to the dialogue.

А. Ты рабóтаешь?
Б. Нет, я не рабóтаю, я студéнтка. А ты тóже студéнт? Или ты рабóтаешь?
А. Я рабóтаю. В цúрке.
Б. В цúрке?! Как интерéсно! А что ты там дéлаешь?
А. Это секрéт.

96 Урóк 3, Часть вторáя

Name_____ Date_____ Class_____

- Now read and repeat aloud in the pause after each phrase.
- Now read the lines for speaker **Б** aloud.
- Now read the lines for speaker **А** aloud.

What do the two people do for a living?

_____

Диалог 2 Это на́ша но́вая кварти́ра (Showing a new apartment)

ББ. Follow along as you listen to the dialogue.

А. Вот, Ри́та, э́то на́ша но́вая кварти́ра. Кварти́ра хоро́шая: больша́я и све́тлая. А тут балко́н.
Б. О́чень хоро́шая кварти́ра. И балко́н большо́й.
А. А э́то наш но́вый телеви́зор. Ме́бель, как ви́дишь, ста́рая, а телеви́зор но́вый. О́чень хорошо́ рабо́тает!
Б. Како́й большо́й экра́н (*screen*)!

- Now read and repeat aloud in the pause after each phrase.
- Now read the lines for speaker **Б** aloud.
- Now read the lines for speaker **А** aloud.

What if things were just the opposite in speaker **А**'s apartment? How would the dialogue read if the apartment, for example, were small and dark (**тёмный**), the television were old, didn't work well, and so on?

А. _____
Б. _____
А. _____
Б. _____

АУДИ́РОВАНИЕ (*Listening comprehension*)

ВВ. Listen carefully to the speaker's questions and put an **X** by the most appropriate response.

ОБРАЗЕ́Ц: Что ты чита́ешь?   _____ Статья́.
                              ___X___ Кни́гу.
                              _____ Газе́та.

1. _____ Ве́ру.
   _____ Та́ню.
   _____ Ма́ша.

2. _____ Плохо́й.
   _____ Хоро́ший.
   _____ Непло́хо.

3. _____ Кни́га.
   _____ Статья́.
   _____ Статью́.

4. _____ Рабо́таю.
   _____ Чита́ешь.
   _____ Гуля́ете.

5. _____ В Калифо́рнии.
   _____ Калифо́рнию.
   _____ Калифо́рния.

6. _____ Статью́.
   _____ Статья́.
   _____ Газе́ту.

ГГ. In the following conversation, listen for the specific information indicated and fill in as much as you can. The first answer has been given.

WOMAN   MAN

Name _____ Ирина _____   Name _____

Friend's name _____   Friend's name _____

City _____   City _____

Friend's city _____   Friend's city _____

ДД. Check the adjectives that apply to the furniture in Elena Petrovna's apartment. One of the answers has been given for you.

	TABLE	CHAIRS	COUCH	ARMCHAIR	TELEVISION
New					
Old					
Imported	X				
Not imported					

ГОВОРЕНИЕ (*Speaking drills*)

EE. Answer the speaker's questions according to the cued answer.

ОБРАЗЕЦ: *You hear:*   Что ты де́лаешь?
           You see: (*reading a book*)
           You say: Чита́ю кни́гу.

1. (*a book*)   4. (*no, resting*)
2. (*playing chess*)   5. (*an article*)
3. (*no, not imported*)   6. (*no, old*)

ЖЖ. Using the cued adverbs, revise each of the speaker's sentences by telling how the person does what he does.

ОБРАЗЕЦ: *You hear:*   Ива́н зна́ет Санкт-Петербу́рг.
           You see: (*well*)
           You say: Ива́н хорошо́ зна́ет Санкт-Петербу́рг.

1. (*not badly*)   4. (*creatively*)
2. (*well*)   5. (*poorly*)
3. (*poorly*)

33. How would you express the following?

ОБРАЗЕЦ: *You hear and see:*   (*How awful!*)
           You say: Как ужа́сно!

1. (*That's good!*)   4. (*How original!*)
2. (*How interesting!*)   5. (*That's not easy!*)
3. (*That's awful!*)   6. (*That's interesting!*)

Name_____ Date_____ Class_____

ЧАСТЬ ТРЕТЬЯ
Домашнее задание

РАБОТА ДОМА (*Homework*)

ПИСЬМО (*Written exercises*)

Понимание текста

А. Review the reading on page 103 of the textbook and complete the following sentences accordingly.

1. Лёна идёт _____
2. Вова читает _____
3. Вова слушает _____
4. Вова пишет _____
5. Его любимый композитор — _____
6. Билли Джоэл — замечательный _____
7. Мусоргский — русский _____

Going places: Verbs of motion and destinations

Б. Match each question on the left with the correct answer on the right. One of the answers has been given for you.

1. _____ Мария, куда ты идёшь?   а. ~~Он идёт в магазин.~~
2. _____ Мама и папа идут на балет?   б. Они едут во Владимир.
3. __а__ Куда идёт Вадим?   в. Мы идём на концерт.
4. _____ Анна и Дима, куда вы идёте?   г. Нет, в Иркутск.
5. _____ Куда едут Кругловы?   д. Я еду в Тулу.
6. _____ Володя, куда ты едешь?   е. Я иду в ресторан.
7. _____ Вы едете в Новосибирск?   ж. Нет, в театр.

В. Create your own sentences using the verbs **идти** and **ехать** telling where these people are going. Use the following suggestions or make up some of your own.

PERSON		DESTINATION	
моя мать	тётя	на стадион	в Аризону
мой отец	дядя	в университет	во Флориду
мои родители	мой друг	в парк	в консерваторию
мой брат / мои братья	мои соседи	в театр	на концерт
моя сестра / мои сёстры	я	в Новосибирск	в Санкт-Петербург
дедушка и бабушка	мы	на работу	домой

Урок 3, Часть третья

ОБРАЗЕЦ: <u>Мой брат Ро́берт идёт в магази́н.</u>

1. _____
2. _____
3. _____
4. _____
5. _____
6. _____
7. _____

Г. Referring to the pictures below, make up sentences telling where each person is going.

Ми́ша и Ма́ша   Ивано́вы   студе́нты

Ла́ра и То́ля   Со́ня и Бо́ря   На́стя   Ната́лья Серге́евна

ОБРАЗЕЦ: <u>Ми́ша и Ма́ша иду́т в консервато́рию.</u>

1. _____
2. _____
3. _____
4. _____
5. _____
6. _____

Don't over-"do" it

Д. How would you translate the following sentences from Russian into English or from English into Russian? Pay close attention to the English use of the helping verb *to do* and the lack of a helping verb in Russian.

Name_____ Date_____ Class_____

ОБРАЗЕЦ: Вы зна́ете А́ню?   <u>Do you know Anya?</u>
Does he write articles?   <u>Он пи́шет статьи́?</u>

1. Ты слу́шаешь джаз? _____
2. Где вы живёте? _____
3. Я не игра́ю в ша́хматы. _____
4. Мы не зна́ем, куда́ он идёт. _____
5. Do you read magazines? _____
6. What are you doing? _____
7. Do you understand the article? _____
8. Where do you work? _____

Giving and soliciting opinions

E. How would you ask somebody's opinion about the following activities? How might you answer the same question? You may agree or disagree!

ОБРАЗЕЦ: (*living in New York—interesting*)
<u>Как по-ва́шему, жить в Нью-Йо́рке интере́сно?</u>
<u>Да, по-мо́ему, это интере́сно.</u> *or* <u>Нет, по-мо́ему, это неинтере́сно.</u>

1. (*writing compositions—easy*)
   _____
   _____

2. (*listening to jazz—interesting*)
   _____
   _____

3. (*working on a farm* [**на фе́рме**]—*difficult*)
   _____
   _____

4. (*reading newspapers—interesting*)
   _____
   _____

5. (*writing articles—difficult*)
   _____
   _____

6. (*doing homework—easy*)
   _____
   _____

Уро́к 3, Часть тре́тья

Перево́д (*Translation*)

Ж. Translate the following dialogue into Russian.

"Hi, Seryozha! Where are you going?"
"To the library. And you?"
"I'm going to the post office."

_____

_____

_____

Повторе́ние — мать уче́ния (*Practice makes perfect*)

3. Following is a summary of the reading of Part 3. Fill in the blanks with words that maintain the context of the reading. You will have to change the form of some of the words. Do not use any of the words more than once.

Во́ва до́ма. Он _____¹ дома́шнее зада́ние. Он _____² му́зыку и _____³ статью́. Его́ _____⁴ компози́тор — Би́лли Джо́эл. Это _____⁵ америка́нский компози́тор и пиани́ст. Ле́на то́же слу́шает _____.⁶ Она́ слу́шает, как _____⁷ Са́ша Кругло́в. Это не рок, а _____⁸ му́зыка, Му́соргский.	де́лать замеча́тельный игра́ть класси́ческий люби́мый му́зыка слу́шать чита́ть

Name_____ Date_____ Class_____

Ситуа́ции (*Situations*)

И. How would you ...

1. ask a classmate where he's going (walking)?
   _____

2. tell somebody that you are going to Canada?
   _____

3. tell somebody that you are going to a concert?
   _____

4. ask your classmates if they are going to Vologda (**Во́логда**)?
   _____

5. tell somebody that you are doing your homework?
   _____

6. tell somebody that Tchaikovsky is a marvelous Russian composer?
   _____

Ва́ша о́чередь! (*It's your turn!*)

К. Answer the following questions.

1. Ты слу́шаешь джаз? Рок? Ка́нтри?
   _____

2. Ты де́лаешь дома́шнее зада́ние?
   _____

3. Кто твой люби́мый компози́тор?
   _____

4. Ты сего́дня идёшь в университе́т (*university*)?
   _____

5. Куда́ ты сего́дня идёшь? _____

Сочине́ние (*Composition*)

Л. Write a short paragraph (five or six sentences) about your family. Imagine that everybody is leaving after having gathered for a family reunion. Where is everybody going now? And you?

_____
_____
_____
_____

РАБОТА В ЛАБОРАТОРИИ (*Laboratory exercises*)

ДИАЛОГИ (*Dialogues*)

Диалог 1 Домашнее задание (Discussing a homework assignment)

АА. Follow along as you listen to the dialogue.

А. Привет, Андрей! Что ты делаешь?
Б. Домашнее задание.
А. Какое?
Б. Физику.
А. Задание большое?
Б. Большое и трудное.

- Now read and repeat aloud in the pause after each phrase.
- Now read the lines for speaker **Б** aloud.
- Now read the lines for speaker **А** aloud.

1. What is Andrei doing? _____

2. What does he think of it? _____

Диалог 2 Куда вы едете? (Asking where someone is traveling to)

ББ. Follow along as you listen to the dialogue.

Three friends meet in a train station.

А. Привет, Аня! Привет, Коля! Куда вы едете?
Б. Саша, привет! Мы едем в Вологду. Наш дядя там работает.
А. Вологда! Это красивый город.
В. Очень красивый. А ты куда едешь?
А. Я? Я еду в Кострому. Там живёт моя бабушка.
Б. Кострома! Как интересно! Наша бабушка тоже там живёт!

- Now read and repeat aloud in the pause after each phrase.
- Now read the lines for speaker **Б** aloud.
- Now read the lines for speaker **А** aloud.

Rewrite the dialogue so that speakers **Б** and **В** (**Аня** and **Коля**) are going to **Пермь,** where their aunt works, and speaker **А** (**Саша**) is going to **Пенза**, where his parents live.

А. _____
Б. _____
А. _____
В. _____
А. _____
Б. _____

Name_____ Date_____ Class_____

АУДИРОВАНИЕ (*Listening comprehension*)

ВВ. Listen carefully to the speaker and match who is going to which place. The first one has been done for you.

ОБРАЗЕЦ: Са́ша идёт на концерт.

1. _____ Ivan and Andrei
2. _____ children
3. _____ Petya
4. _____ Valya
5. __и__ Sasha
6. _____ Masha
7. _____ Sonya
8. _____ Vasilii Dmitrievich
9. _____ parents
10. _____ Dasha

а. to Arkhangelsk
б. to the drugstore
в. to work
г. to the stadium
д. to the theater
е. to Kostroma
ж. to the store
з. to school
и. to a concert
к. to the kitchen

ГГ. You will hear a series of questions. Choose the most appropriate answer for each number.

ОБРАЗЕЦ: *You hear:* Алла, куда́ ты е́дешь?

You check: _____ Я иду́ на концерт.

__X__ Я е́ду в Сара́тов.

_____ Ты е́дешь в Ту́лу.

1. _____ Он е́дет в Вашингто́н.
   _____ Они́ иду́т на рабо́ту.
   _____ Они́ е́дут в Чика́го.

2. _____ Мы идём в консервато́рию.
   _____ Они́ иду́т на стадио́н.
   _____ Вы идёте в апте́ку.

3. _____ Я иду́ в магази́н.
   _____ Он идёт на концерт.
   _____ Он е́дет на рабо́ту.

4. _____ Мы идём на балко́н.
   _____ Ты идёшь в ку́хню.
   _____ Я иду́ в спа́льню.

5. _____ Они́ е́дут в Ки́ев.
   _____ Я е́ду в Му́рманск.
   _____ Вы е́дете в Ирку́тск.

6. _____ Я иду́ в теа́тр.
   _____ Вы идёте на рабо́ту.
   _____ Он идёт на концерт.

ДД. Two professors meet and discuss what the American exchange students are doing. Listen to their dialogue and tell in English what each person is doing.

ОБРАЗЕЦ: Brian and James *are doing their homework.*

1. Steve and Brandon _____
2. Alan _____
3. Chris _____
4. Nate and Damon _____
5. Kelly _____
6. Sara and Erin _____

ГОВОРЕНИЕ (*Speaking drills*)

ЕЕ. Using the cued items, tell where each person is going.

ОБРАЗЕЦ: You hear: (*to the theater*)
          You see: Наташа
          You say: Наташа идёт в театр.

1. Юля
2. соседи
3. Николай Васильевич
4. музыканты
5. его родители
6. Вася

ЖЖ. Answer each question with the cued verb.

ОБРАЗЕЦ: You hear: Что делает Вова?
          You see: (*reading a book*)
          You say: Он читает книгу.

1. (*listening to music*)
2. (*playing chess*)
3. (*taking a walk*)
4. (*writing an article*)
5. (*resting*)
6. (*doing her homework*)

33. How would you talk about your favorite things?

ОБРАЗЕЦ: You hear and see: (*musician—Billy Joel*)
          You say: Мой любимый музыкант — Билли Джоэл.

1. (*composer—Tchaikovsky*)
2. (*music—jazz*)
3. (*city—Seattle*)
4. (*book—Anna Karenina*)
5. (*newspaper—New York Times*)

Name _____ Date _____ Class _____

ЧАСТЬ ЧЕТВЁРТАЯ
Наш микрорайо́н

РАБО́ТА ДО́МА (*Homework*)

ПИСЬМО́ (*Written exercises*)

Понима́ние те́кста

А. True or false? All of the following statements about the reading on pages 112–113 of the textbook are false. Rewrite them correctly.

1. Джим е́дет в университе́т.

   _____

2. За́втра прилета́ют теннисисты.

   _____

3. Илья́ Ильи́ч пло́хо игра́ет в футбо́л.

   _____

4. Илья́ Ильи́ч о́чень хорошо́ зна́ет микрорайо́н.

   _____

5. Ма́ленькая по́чта далеко́, больша́я ря́дом.

   _____

6. По́чта — нале́во, апте́ка — напра́во, его́ (*Ilya Ilyich's*) дом — то́же напра́во.

   _____

Playing a sport

Б. Tell about who's who in the world of American sports. First try to do the exercise without peeking, but if you don't know who's who, even through the process of elimination, look at the end of this exercise for the sport that each person plays or used to play. A couple of these players may have retired and no longer play professionally, but chances are, they still play!

бейсбо́л гольф
америка́нский футбо́л
те́ннис
хокке́й баскетбо́л

ОБРАЗЕЦ: Джо Монга́на игра́ет в америка́нский футбо́л.

1. Та́йгер Вудз _____

2. Серёна Уи́льямс _____

3. Дэн Море́но _____

4. Андре́ А́гасси _____

5. Ма́йкл Джо́рдан _____

6. Уэ́йн Гре́цки _____

7. Сэ́мми Со́са _____

1. golf, 2. tennis, 3. American football, 4. tennis, 5. basketball, 6. hockey, 7. baseball

Word study: и, а, но

В. Combine the following sentences using **и**, **а**, or **но**.

ОБРАЗЕЦ: Мы живём в Москве́. Они́ живу́т в Санкт-Петербу́рге.

Мы живём в Москве́, а они́ живу́т в Санкт-Петербу́рге.

1. Го́род о́чень ма́ленький. Там хоро́шая по́чта и больши́е магази́ны.
_____

2. Их дочь живёт и рабо́тает в Во́логде. Их сын живёт и рабо́тает в Но́вгороде.
_____

3. За́втра мы е́дем в Бо́стон. На́ши сосе́ди то́же е́дут в Бо́стон.
_____

4. Роди́тели гуля́ют. Де́ти игра́ют в волейбо́л.
_____

5. На́дя чита́ет журна́л. Ве́ра то́же чита́ет журна́л.
_____

6. Мы лю́бим игра́ть в футбо́л. Мы не лю́бим игра́ть в волейбо́л.
_____

Subordinate clauses with где, кто, что, почему, как

Г. Your Russian host mother is asking you about the photos you just had developed. As you look at them you realize these are not the pictures you took and that the camera shop must have given you someone else's pictures by mistake. How will you answer your host mother's questions?

ОБРАЗЕЦ: Who lives here? Я не зна́ю, кто здесь живёт.

1. Who is this? _____

2. What are they doing? _____

Name_____ Date_____ Class_____

3. What is his name? _____

4. Where is she going? (*She's in a car.*)
   _____

5. Why is she going (*in the car*), but he's not?
   _____

6. Where do they work? _____

Д. Complete each of the sentences below with **где, кто, что, почему́,** or **как**.

ОБРАЗЕ́Ц: Я зна́ю, ____где____ живу́т Медве́девы.

1. Я не зна́ю, _____ его́ зову́т. Но я зна́ю, _____ её зову́т Га́ля.

2. Ты зна́ешь, _____ рабо́тает Алексе́й Ива́нович?

3. Вы зна́ете, _____ э́то зада́ние тако́е (*such a*) тру́дное?

4. Мы зна́ем, _____ пи́шет статью́. Мы зна́ем, _____ статью́ пи́шет Ви́ка.

5. Вы зна́ете, _____ идёт в консервато́рию?

6. Я зна́ю, _____ ба́бушка и де́душка. Я зна́ю, _____ они́ до́ма. Но я не зна́ю, _____ они́ де́лают.

Е. Below is a short interview with a woman named Mitrofanova taken from the Russian magazine *Yes!* Answer the questions that follow the article.

Уро́к 3, Часть четвёртая

1. How would you translate the title of the article?

   _____

2. What specific questions might a reporter ask Mitrofanova as a follow-up to this title?

   _____
   _____

3. Within the article are six subheadings. You know enough Russian to figure out what each one means. Write the English translation across from the appropriate Russian subheading.

   In a romantic situation
   On vacation (= while resting)
   When driving (= in the car)
   In the morning

   а. Утром _____

   б. В машине _____

   в. На отдыхе _____

   г. С друзьями _____*With friends*_____

   д. В романтической обстановке _____

   е. Перед сном _____*Before sleep*_____

4. Now see if you can find what kind of music Mitrofanova listens to on each of these particular occasions. The types of music are listed below. Match them to the appropriate occasion. You will have to use one answer twice.

   nothing
   Italian music, such as the singer Eros Ramazotti
   the radio
   whatever – Turkish ethnic music when in Turkey, for example
   the songs of singer Zemfira

   а. Утром _____

   б. В машине _____

   в. На отдыхе _____

   г. С друзьями _____

   д. В романтическом обстановке _____

   е. Перед сном _____

Перевод (*Translation*)

Ж. Translate the following dialogue into Russian.

"Do you happen to know where there's a grocery store around here?"
"It's not far. There it is, on the right."

_____
_____

Name_____ Date_____ Class_____

Повторе́ние — мать уче́ния (*Practice makes perfect*)

3. Following is a summary of the reading of Part 4. Fill in the blanks with words that maintain the context of the reading. You will have to change the form of some of the words. Do not use any of the words more than once.

Илья́ Ильи́ч пло́хо зна́ет их _____.¹	где
Он не зна́ет, _____² магази́н, апте́ка и по́чта.	далеко́
Но Степа́н Евге́ньевич зна́ет. Он зна́ет, _____³	дом
по́чта напра́во и что апте́ка _____.⁴	ма́ленький
Он зна́ет, что больша́я по́чта _____,⁵	нале́во
а _____⁶ ря́дом. Он зна́ет,	остано́вка
где _____⁷ авто́буса. И он зна́ет,	райо́н
где их но́вый _____.⁸	что

Ситуа́ции (*Situations*)

И. How would you . . .

1. tell somebody that you play tennis but not well?
   _____

2. tell somebody that your sister plays basketball and your brother plays soccer?
   _____

3. ask a stranger if she knows where the stadium is?
   _____

4. tell somebody that you know who is reading the magazine?
   _____

5. tell somebody that the post office is on the left and the (grocery) store is on the right?
   _____

6. tell somebody that the large drugstore is far away and the small one is close by?
   _____

Ва́ша о́чередь! (*It's your turn!*)

К. Answer the questions below.

1. Ты игра́ешь в те́ннис? В футбо́л? В баскетбо́л? Ты хорошо́ игра́ешь?

   _____

2. Твои́ роди́тели (бра́тья, сёстры) игра́ют в волейбо́л? В гольф? В хокке́й?

   _____

3. Ты зна́ешь, где магази́н «Проду́кты»? Э́то большо́й магази́н?

   _____

4. Апте́ка бли́зко? Далеко́? А по́чта?

   _____

5. Где рабо́тает твой оте́ц (твоя́ мать)?

   _____

6. Твой дом далеко́ (*from the university*) или бли́зко?

   _____

Сочине́ние (*Composition*)

Л. Write a short paragraph (five or six sentences) about the area in which you live (**райо́н**). Is it a nice area? Do you know where the post office, drugstore, and so on are? Are they near or far? Are they large or small? Do you know where the gym is? Do you play basketball (or volleyball, etc.) there? What sports do you play? What do your friends play? Do you play well or poorly?

_____

_____

_____

_____

_____

Name_____ Date_____ Class_____

Fun with grammar! Case review

M. Fill in the blanks of the following sentences with the appropriate case endings. Not all blanks, however, will have an ending. Then enter the words into the crossword puzzle below to help check your spelling. The letter-number combinations (e.g., **г12**) at the end of each sentence indicate the location of the word or words in the puzzle. The first letter and number are for the first word and so on. Note that **г** is for **горизонта́ль**, or horizontal; **в** is for **вертика́ль**, or vertical.

1. Вы игра́ете в ша́хмат_____? (г5)

2. Куда́ ты идёшь? В поликли́ник_____? (г9)

3. Ми́ша хорошо́ игра́ет в баскетбо́л_____. (в6)

4. Ве́ра чита́ет газе́т_____. (в4)

5. Э́то мо_____ но́в_____ ме́бел_____. (в13) (г16) (в11)

6. Мо_____ брат_____ е́дет в Москв_____. (в17) (в15) (в14)

7. Ты игра́ешь в те́ннис_____? (г12)

8. На́дя пи́шет сочине́ни_____ и́ли стать_____? (в8) (г18)

9. Тво_____ сестр_____ идёт на конце́рт_____? (г19) (в2) (в10)

10. Ваш_____ де́душк_____ слу́шает рок-му́зык_____? (в3) (г7) (в1)

РАБОТА В ЛАБОРАТОРИИ (*Laboratory exercises*)

ДИАЛОГИ (*Dialogues*)

Диалог 1 Вы не зна́ете, где...? (Asking for directions)

АА. Follow along as you listen to the dialogue.

А. Вы не зна́ете, где по́чта?
Б. Вот она́, нале́во.
А. А магази́н?
Б. Магази́н напра́во.
А. Спаси́бо.
Б. Пожа́луйста.

- Now read and repeat aloud in the pause after each phrase.
- Now read the lines for speaker **Б** aloud.
- Now read the lines for speaker **А** aloud.

Rewrite the dialogue so that speaker **А** first asks about the store and then about the post office.

А. _____
Б. _____
А. _____
Б. _____
А. _____
Б. _____

Диалог 2 А где по́чта? (Asking about locations)

ББ. Follow along as you listen to the dialogue.

А. Ты уже́ зна́ешь наш микрорайо́н?
Б. Да.
А. Остано́вка авто́буса далеко́?
Б. Нет, она́ ря́дом.
А. А где по́чта?
Б. По́чта далеко́.
А. А магази́ны? Они́ то́же далеко́?
Б. Нет, магази́ны ря́дом.

- Now read and repeat aloud in the pause after each phrase.
- Now read the lines for speaker **Б** aloud.
- Now read the lines for speaker **А** aloud.

What three things does speaker **А** ask about? Where are they located? Write your answers in English.

	WHAT?	WHERE?
1.	_____	_____
2.	_____	_____
3.	_____	_____

Name_____ Date_____ Class_____

АУДИРОВАНИЕ (*Listening comprehension*)

ВВ. Listen to Boris tell about his very athletic family. Who plays what? The first two have been marked for you.

	брат	сестра́	оте́ц	мать	ба́бушка	де́душка
баскетбо́л	X	X	____	____	____	____
волейбо́л	____	____	____	____	____	____
гольф	____	____	____	____	____	____
те́ннис	____	____	____	____	____	____
хокке́й	____	____	____	____	____	____
ша́хматы	____	____	____	____	____	____

ГГ. Listen to the questions and choose the most appropriate answer for each from the list below.

ОБРАЗЕ́Ц: Вы зна́ете, где по́чта?

1. _____ Нет, ма́ленькая.
2. _____ Зна́ю. Его́ зову́т Фе́дя.
3. _____ Да, непло́хо.
4. _____ Нет, он далеко́.
5. __Об.__ Зна́ю, она́ ря́дом.
6. _____ Напра́во.
7. _____ Са́ша зна́ет.

ДД. Listen to the speaker's question and decide to whom she is most likely talking. Check the appropriate column. For some numbers you may check more than one category.

ОБРАЗЕ́Ц: Куда́ ты идёшь? В шко́лу?

	A FRIEND OR CHILD	AN OLDER PERSON	MORE THAN ONE PERSON
ОБРАЗЕ́Ц:	X	____	____
1.	____	____	____
2.	____	____	____
3.	____	____	____
4.	____	____	____
5.	____	____	____
6.	____	____	____
7.	____	____	____
8.	____	____	____

Уро́к 3, Часть четвёртая

ГОВОРЕНИЕ (*Speaking drills*)

ЕЕ. Repeat the following **и́ли** questions after the speaker. Pay close attention to the speaker's intonation.

1. Пе́тя игра́ет в баскетбо́л и́ли в футбо́л?
2. Её зову́т Да́ша и́ли Ма́ша?
3. Что Ва́ся чита́ет — газе́ту и́ли журна́л?
4. Где вы живёте — в Москве́ и́ли в Санкт-Петербу́рге?
5. Страви́нский — э́то америка́нский компози́тор или ру́сский?
6. Где магази́н — нале́во и́ли напра́во?

ЖЖ. How would you ask your classmate if she knows the following?

ОБРАЗЕЦ: *You hear and see:*   where the school is
　　　　　　You say:　　　　　Ты зна́ешь, где шко́ла?

1. who that is
2. where the theater is
3. what the neighbors are doing
4. where the Maiorovs live
5. where Mila is going (walking)
6. what day it is today

33. Tell what sport each of the following people plays.

ОБРАЗЕЦ: *You hear and see:*   your brother—basketball
　　　　　　You say:　　　　　Мой брат игра́ет в баскетбо́л.

1. your neighbor—soccer
2. your sister—volleyball
3. your brothers—American football
4. your father—golf
5. your mother—tennis
6. your uncle—hockey

Name_____ Date_____ Class_____

ВЫ ГОВОРИТЕ ПО-РУССКИ?

УРОК 4

ЧАСТЬ ПЕРВАЯ
У нас ужа́сные пробле́мы

РАБОТА ДОМА

ПИСЬМО

Понима́ние те́кста

A. The following statements about the reading on page 128 of the textbook are false. The building manager, Silin, was obviously having trouble remembering who complained about what. Rewrite the sentences so that they correctly represent the neighbors' complaints.

1. У профе́ссора Петро́вского невозмо́жно закры́ть о́кна.

   _____

2. У профе́ссора Петро́вского нет ва́нны.

   _____

3. У Алекса́ндры Никола́евны нет ду́ша.

   _____

4. У Татья́ны Дми́триевны есть вода́.

   _____

5. Пол у них хоро́ший. Сте́ны у них неплохи́е.

   _____

6. У Алекса́ндры Никола́евны то́же невозмо́жно закры́ть о́кна.

   _____

Possession (*to have*): У тебя́ есть телеви́зор?

Б. Your classmates want to know what you and your family members have. What questions might you anticipate? Use pronouns in your questions to ask about the items in parentheses.

ОБРАЗЕЦ: When asking about your brother (**маши́на**):

У него́ есть маши́на?

1. When asking about you (**мотоци́кл**):

2. When asking about you (**гита́ра**):

3. When asking about your sister (**компью́тер**):

4. When asking about your brother (**телеви́зор**):

5. When asking about your parents (**пылесо́с**):

6. When asking about your grandparents (**балко́н**):

7. When asking about all of you (**стира́льная маши́на**):

8. When asking about all of you (**микроволно́вая печь**):

В. How would you answer each of the questions in exercise **Б** affirmatively?

ОБРАЗЕЦ: Да, у него́ есть маши́на.

1.
2.
3.
4.
5.
6.
7.
8.

Name_____ Date_____ Class_____

Genitive of nouns: *Missing, lacking* = <нет + Genitive>

Г. You grabbed your **рюкзáк** without checking it this morning and you find that you don't have what you need for the day. Tell your classmate what you are missing.

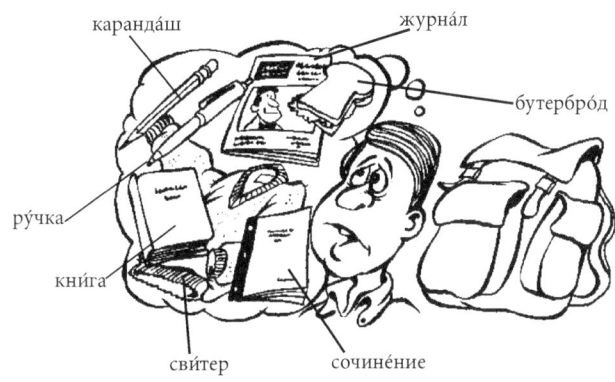

(карандáш, журнáл, бутербрóд, рýчка, кнúга, свúтер, сочинéние)

ОБРАЗЕЦ: <u>Карандашá нет.</u>

1. _____
2. _____
3. _____
4. _____
5. _____
6. _____

Д. Use the following words to describe your dorm room as pictured below. What do you have? What don't you have? You will not use all the words given.

ВÁША КÓМНАТА

~~стол~~   пóлка
~~стул~~   лáмпа
будúльник   пылесóс
дивáн   телефóн
крéсло   телевúзор
кровáть   тóстер
мúксер   холодúльник

ОБРАЗЕЦ: <u>У меня́ есть стол. У меня́ нет стýла.</u>

1. _____. _____.
2. _____. _____.
3. _____. _____.
4. _____. _____.
5. _____. _____.

Урок 4, Часть первая   119

E. Your professor is attending a conference and has arranged for Professor Bukharin to take your class. Many students have decided to skip, however. Help Professor Bukharin as he reads names from his list of students. If the student is there, what will he or she say? If the student is absent, how will you respond (using a pronoun) that he or she is not there? Below is the class seating chart. **X** indicates the students who are present. You will not use all the names given.

X Марк	Со́ня	**X** Суса́нна	**X** Ю́ля	**X** Дон
Мари́я	**X** Билл	Са́ра	Ро́берт	**X** Бра́йан
X А́нджела	Э́рик	**X** Кристи́на	Джон	Э́рика

ОБРАЗЕ́Ц: — Билл? — <u>Здесь.</u>

— Са́ра? — <u>Её нет.</u>

1. — Кристи́на? — _____
2. — Со́ня? — _____
3. — Ро́берт? — _____
4. — Э́рик? — _____
5. — Дон? — _____
6. — Э́рика? — _____
7. — Ю́ля? — _____
8. — Бра́йан? — _____
9. — Джон? — _____
10. — Мари́я? — _____

Possession phrases without есть

Ж. To the left is a description of members of Kolya's family. To the right are things that they "have." Choose the most appropriate "possession" for each member and write a second sentence telling what they "have."

ОБРАЗЕ́Ц: Мы живём в Москве́. <u>У нас ма́ленькая кварти́ра.</u>

1. Моя́ сестра́ тала́нтливая актри́са.
   _____

2. Ма́ма и па́па хоро́шие роди́тели.
   _____

3. Ба́бушка — диплома́т.
   _____

4. Де́душка — бизнесме́н.
   _____

5. Мой брат пи́шет статью́.
   _____

а. интере́сная профе́ссия
б. большо́й и краси́вый о́фис
в. интере́сная те́ма
г. хоро́шие де́ти
д. больша́я роль в но́вом фи́льме

120   Уро́к 4, Часть пе́рвая

Name _____ Date _____ Class _____

Перево́д

3. Translate the following dialogue into Russian.

"I have a problem."
"What kind?"
"I have very unpleasant neighbors."
"That's terrible!"

_____
_____
_____
_____

Повторе́ние — мать уче́ния!

И. Following is a summary of the reading in Part 1. Fill in the blanks with words that maintain the context of the reading. You will have to change the form of some of the words. Do not use any of the words more than once.

Профе́ссор Петро́вский, Татья́на Дми́триевна и Алекса́ндра Никола́евна — _____.¹ У них ужа́сные _____.² У них _____³ кварти́ры, но невозмо́жно _____⁴ о́кна, а две́ри _____⁵ закры́ть. _____⁶ ва́нна, но нет _____.⁷ Пол у _____⁸ ужа́сный и о́кна _____.⁹	вода́ есть невозмо́жно но́вый они́ откры́ть пробле́ма сосе́д ужа́сный

Ситуа́ции

К. How would you . . .

1. ask a classmate if she has a guitar?
_____

2. ask your professor if he has a big house?
_____

3. tell somebody that you have an old American car?
_____

4. tell somebody that you don't have a computer?
_____

5. tell your professors that, yes, you *do* have an alarm clock?
_____

Ва́ша о́чередь!

Л. Answer these questions about yourself, using complete sentences.

1. У тебя́ есть душ в кварти́ре (в общежи́тии, в до́ме)?
   _____

2. Кака́я у тебя́ маши́на?
   _____

3. У тебя́ до́ма есть пылесо́с? А ми́ксер? А то́стер?
   _____

4. Кака́я у тебя́ ко́мната?
   _____

5. Како́й у вас (*you and your family*) дом?
   _____

Сочине́ние

М. Write a short paragraph describing your dorm room, apartment, or house. Do you have a large or small room? What furniture do you have in your room? What don't you have? Is there anything that doesn't work well? Anything that is impossible to open or close? What kind of neighbors do you have? Use the preceding exercises to help you come up with specific ideas.

_____
_____
_____
_____
_____

РАБО́ТА В ЛАБОРАТО́РИИ

ДИАЛО́ГИ

Диало́г 1 У меня́ больша́я кварти́ра (Describing an apartment)

АА. Follow along as you listen to the dialogue.

— А. У вас но́вая кварти́ра? Больша́я?
— Б. Да, больша́я и о́чень хоро́шая.
— А. А дом то́же хоро́ший?
— Б. И дом хоро́ший, и сосе́ди хоро́шие.

- Now read and repeat aloud in the pause after each phrase.
- Now read the lines for speaker **Б** aloud.
- Now read the lines for speaker **А** aloud.

Name_____ Date_____ Class_____

The woman in this dialogue likes her apartment and talks positively about it. Rewrite the dialogue as if she were complaining.

А. _____
Б. _____
А. _____
Б. _____

Диалог 2 У меня ужасная проблема (Discussing problems)

ББ. Follow along as you listen to the dialogue.

А. У меня ужасная проблема.
Б. У меня тоже. Какая у вас проблема?
А. У меня нет ванны. А у вас?
Б. У меня есть ванна, но нет душа.
А. Это плохо, но не ужасно.

- Now read and repeat aloud in the pause after each phrase.
- Now read the lines for speaker **Б** aloud.
- Now read the lines for speaker **А** aloud.

What is the name of the room (in Russian) in which these people's problems are located?

_____

АУДИРОВАНИЕ

ВВ. Проблемы, проблемы. A group of senior Russian engineers is moving into a dorm on your campus for a two-week conference. Housing officials have asked you to make a list in English of the problems being reported. The first complaint has been listed for you.

1. *The television doesn't work.*
2. _____
3. _____
4. _____
5. _____
6. _____

ГГ. Что есть? Чего нет? Vera and Petya are discussing Petya's new apartment. Listen to their dialogue and make a list of what Petya has and what he doesn't have. Write **есть** in the blanks to indicate that he has something; write **нет** to indicate that he does not. Put a question mark in the blank if the item was not discussed. If you have written **нет**, change the ending on the given noun so that it correctly expresses *lack of* the item. One answer has been given for you.

_____ балкон   _____ душ   _____ лампа   _____ стул

_____ ванна   _____ кресло   _____ полка   _____ телевизор

  нет дива**а**   _____ кровать   _____ стол   _____ телефон

Урок 4, Часть первая   123

ДД. **Question or statement?** For each item below, first repeat the question after the speaker, then repeat the statement.

1. У него́ есть буди́льник? У него́ есть буди́льник.
2. У неё япо́нская маши́на? У неё япо́нская маши́на.
3. У них нет воды́? У них нет воды́.
4. Там есть лифт? Там есть лифт.
5. Э́то ва́ша ка́рта? Э́то ва́ша ка́рта.
6. У него́ есть маши́на? У него́ есть маши́на.

Now one of each pair will be read aloud. Circle what you hear—question or statement.

ОБРАЗЕЦ: *You hear and circle:* (У него́ есть соба́ка?)

ЕЕ. You will hear a series of questions. Write the letter of the question next to the most appropriate response in the list below. The first one has been done for you.

1. _____ Нет, у меня́ есть то́лько дива́н.
2. _____ Ма́ленький, но хоро́ший.
3. ___а___ Есть, но он не рабо́тает.
4. _____ Нет, италья́нская.
5. _____ Больша́я и краси́вая.

ГОВОРЕНИЕ

ЖЖ. Ask your classmate if he has the following items.

ОБРАЗЕЦ: *You hear and see:* toaster
          You ask: У тебя́ есть то́стер?

1. car
2. pen
3. television
4. lamp
5. alarm clock
6. easy chair

ЗЗ. Now the speaker will ask you if you have the same items. Answer negatively.

ОБРАЗЕЦ: *You hear:* У тебя́ есть то́стер?
          You say: Нет, у меня́ нет то́стера.

ИИ. The speaker will now ask you what kind of an object you have. For each item, answer according to the cued adjective.

ОБРАЗЕЦ: *You hear:* Како́й у тебя́ то́стер?
          You see: old
          You say: У меня́ ста́рый то́стер.

1. American
2. new
3. old
4. not very big
5. new
6. imported

Уро́к 4, Часть пе́рвая

Name _____ Date _____ Class _____

ЧАСТЬ ВТОРАЯ
Внизу́ всё слы́шно

РАБОТА ДОМА

ПИСЬМО

Понима́ние те́кста

А. Что мы зна́ем? Чего́ мы не зна́ем? Use the reading on pages 138–139 of the textbook to determine which of the following statements are fact, and which are only opinions of the speakers. If the statement is a fact, write **да**. If the statement is an opinion, write **нет** and identify the person who expresses the opinion.

1. Са́ша игра́ет мно́го.
   _____

2. Внизу́ всё слы́шно, когда́ Са́ша игра́ет.
   _____

3. Ле́на лю́бит му́зыку.
   _____

4. Са́ша игра́ет рок.
   _____

5. У Во́вы за́втра контро́льная.
   _____

6. Серге́й Петро́вич спит.
   _____

«-ишь» verbs: Basic (говори́ть) type

Б. Following are examples of **-ешь** and **-ишь** verbs. Conjugate the two and note the similarities as well as the differences.

чита́ть	говори́ть
я _____	я _____
ты _____	ты _____
он, она́, оно́ _____	он, она́, оно́ _____
мы _____	мы _____
вы _____	вы _____
они́ _____	они́ _____

1. The **я**-forms of both types of verbs use either the vowel _____ or _____ as the ending.

2. With verbs such as **читать,** the forms for **ты, он, она́, оно́, мы,** and **вы** use the stem vowel _____, whereas with verbs such as **говори́ть,** the same forms use the stem vowel _____.

3. With verbs such as **чита́ть,** the **они́**-form uses either the vowel _____ or _____ in the ending. With verbs such as **говори́ть,** the same form uses either the vowel _____ or _____ in the ending.

В. The verb говори́ть. Which of the following people says what?

~~аспира́нт~~   журнали́ст   тенниси́стка   пиани́сты   студе́нты

ОБРАЗЕЦ: <u>Аспира́нт</u> <u>говори́т</u>, что он пи́шет диссерта́цию.

1. _____ _____, что они́ игра́ют кла́ссику.
2. _____ _____, что он пи́шет статью́.
3. _____ _____, что она́ ка́ждый (*every*) день игра́ет в те́ннис.
4. _____ _____, что за́втра контро́льная.

Г. Different opinions. First repeat what your classmates say, then disagree with them.

ОБРАЗЕЦ: Ты <u>говори́шь</u>, что кварти́ра больша́я, а я <u>говорю́</u>, что она́ ма́ленькая.

1. Ты _____, что те́ма лёгкая, а я _____, что она́ _____.
2. Вы _____, что библиоте́ка далеко́, а мы _____, что она́ _____.
3. Ты _____, что Ната́ша хорошо́ игра́ет в ша́хматы, а я _____, что она́ _____ игра́ет в ша́хматы.
4. Вы _____, что де́душка мно́го гуля́ет, а мы _____, что он _____ гуля́ет.

Stem-changing verbs

Д. Unscramble the following words to make five complete sentences.

Ната́ша	ма́льчики	гро́мко.	спишь
я	ты	говори́т	смо́трят
ви́дите	му́зыку.	люблю́	вы
рюкза́к?	телеви́зор.	на балко́не?	

126   Уро́к 4, Часть втора́я

Name _____ Date _____ Class _____

1. _____
2. _____
3. _____
4. _____
5. _____

Е. The verbs ви́деть and смотре́ть. Fill in the blanks of the following dialogue between mother and son with the correct forms of the verb **ви́деть** or **смотре́ть**. The first one has been done for you.

МА́МА. (*Opening the door of their apartment and hearing loud sounds of TV.*) Ва́ся, ты <u>смо́тришь</u> телеви́зор?

ВА́СЯ. Да.

МА́МА. А что ты _____?

ВА́СЯ. Америка́нский фильм.

МА́МА. Что-что?

ВА́СЯ. (*Loudly.*) Я _____ америка́нский фильм «Вам письмо́» (*You've Got Mail*). Вот Том Хэнкс. А э́то Мэг Ра́йан. _____?

МА́МА. (*Coming to the doorway.*) Да, сейча́с _____. А де́душка и ба́бушка до́ма?

ВА́СЯ. Да, они́ то́же _____ телеви́зор.

БА́БУШКА И
ДЕ́ДУШКА. (*From the far end of the same room.*) Мы тут. Мы то́же _____ телеви́зор.

МА́МА. (*Looking into the room.*) Почему́ вы так далеко́? Вы всё отту́да _____? Па́па, ты хорошо́ _____ субти́тры (*subtitles*)?

БА́БУШКА И
ДЕ́ДУШКА. Мы всё хорошо́ _____. А субти́тры Ва́ся чита́ет вслух (*aloud*). О́чень хоро́ший фильм.

Ж. The verb люби́ть. Who likes to do what? Complete each sentence using one of the words listed here and the appropriate form of the verb **люби́ть**.

соба́ки   журнали́сты   ~~музыка́нт~~   сосе́д   профе́ссор исто́рии

ОБРАЗЕ́Ц: <u>Музыка́нт</u> <u>лю́бит</u> игра́ть джаз.

1. _____ _____ гуля́ть в па́рке.
2. _____ _____ слу́шать ра́дио.
3. _____ _____ чита́ть.
4. _____ _____ писа́ть статьи́.

Уро́к 4, Часть втора́я 127

3. You and your classmates are finding out that you have dissimilar interests. Referring to things they like or like to do, they ask about you. You respond negatively to their questions, adding that you (or you and your friends) like to do something else (as cued below).

ОБРАЗЕЦ:	гулять в центре города
	гулять в парке
балет	смотреть футбол
оперу	смотреть баскетбол
играть в теннис	слушать рок
играть в баскетбол	слушать джаз

ОБРАЗЕЦ: — <u>Ты любишь гулять в центре города?</u>

— <u>Нет, не очень. Я люблю гулять в парке.</u>

1. — Вы _____

— Нет, мы _____

2. — Ты _____

— Нет, я _____

3. — Вы _____

— Нет, мы _____

4. — Ты _____

— Нет, я _____

И. The verb спать. Ужас! Everybody's doing what he or she is supposed to, but sleeping dust falls over the land and fatigue takes over. Who is sleeping where?

| в библиотеке | на концерте | на кухне |
| ~~в комнате~~ | в парке | на стадионе |

ОБРАЗЕЦ: Студент <u>спит в комнате.</u>

1. Бабушка _____

2. Дети _____

3. Я — футболист, и я _____

4. Мы — музыканты, и мы _____

5. Профессор истории _____

К. Complete the sentences, using the following expressions. Use each expression only once. The first one has been done for you.

~~все спят~~	любим играть	ничего не вижу
много спать	смотрю телевизор	говорите очень тихо
не любишь музыку	видишь его	много спит

128   Урок 4, Часть вторая

Name_____ Date_____ Class_____

1. Николай любит работать, когда все спят .
2. Где лампа? Я _____.
3. Мы много играем, потому что _____.
4. Он мало работает и _____.
5. Ты не слушаешь, как Иван играет, потому что _____.
6. Я сегодня не работаю. Я _____.
7. Вы _____.
8. Вот Ваня. Ты не _____?
9. Моя бабушка говорит, что нельзя _____.

Л. Complete the dialogue with the correct forms of the following verbs. The first answer has been given for you.

говорить   видеть   любить   смотреть   спать

АНДРЕЙ.   Какой у вас прекрасный дом!

МАРИНА.   Да, мы очень любим [1] наш дом и наш район.

АНДРЕЙ.   У вас есть балкон?

МАРИНА.   Да, очень большой. Бабушка _____[2] там спать.

Она и сейчас там _____[3].

БАБУШКА. Я не _____![4] Я _____[5] телевизор.

МАРИНА.   Бабушка, а ты нас _____?[6]

БАБУШКА. Где вы? Я вас не _____,[7] но я всё слышу (hear). Вы _____[8] очень громко.

Genitive case: <У + noun>

М. Что у кого. The music teacher has distributed all the musical instruments to various students. Tell her who has which instrument.

скрипка   виолончель   саксофон   труба   контрабас   гитара

~~Марина~~   Коля   Саша   Борис   Олег   Соня

ОБРАЗЕЦ: Скрипка у Марины.

1. _____
2. _____
3. _____
4. _____
5. _____

Урок 4, Часть вторая   129

H. Who would be the most likely to have what?

~~ру́чка~~   па́спорт   скри́пка   буди́льник   холоди́льник   саксофо́н

ОБРАЗЕЦ: (журнали́стка) У журнали́стки есть ру́чка.

1. (скрипа́ч) _____

2. (тури́ст) _____

3. (муж и жена́) _____

4. (студе́нтка) _____

5. (саксофони́ст) _____

Genitive: Noun linkage

О. How would you combine the following words to form the English expressions indicated below? Each phrase will contain a word in the Genitive case.

~~автобус~~   Ива́н   но́мер   сосе́дка   фами́лия   ~~остано́вка~~   сын   телефо́н   продю́сер   фильм   а́дрес   апте́ка   шахматы   дире́ктор   Во́ва   маши́на   клуб   Ка́тя

ОБРАЗЕЦ: bus stop   остано́вка авто́буса

1. phone number _____
2. address of the drugstore _____
3. club director _____
4. film producer _____
5. Ivan's last name _____
6. (my) neighbor's son _____
7. Katya's car _____
8. Vova's chess set _____

П. Answer the following questions as they pertain to you, your family, your work, your country, and so on.

1. У нас до́ма роди́тели ча́сто (*often*) смо́трят телеви́зор. А у вас?
   _____

2. У нас до́ма сосе́ди говоря́т о́чень гро́мко. А у вас?
   _____

3. У нас в университе́те студе́нты не де́лают дома́шнее зада́ние. А у вас?
   _____

130   Уро́к 4, Часть втора́я

Name_____ Date_____ Class_____

4. У нас на работе все пьют (*drink*) кофе. А у вас?
_____

5. У нас в России студенты обычно (*usually*) не работают. А у вас?
_____

6. У нас в России студенты живут в общежитии или дома. А у вас?
_____

Перевод

P. Translate the following dialogue into Russian.

"Do you like jazz?"
"No, I like classical music."
"Who's your favorite composer?"
"Tchaikovsky."

_____
_____
_____
_____
_____

Повторение — мать учения!

С. Following is a summary of the reading in Part 2. Fill in the blanks with words that maintain the content of the reading. You will have to change the form of some of the words. Use each word only once.

| Саша _____¹ играть джаз, _____² и рок, но бабушка _____,³ что он играет _____⁴ и что он играет слишком _____.⁵ Нельзя _____⁶ громко, потому что внизу соседи и всё _____.⁷ Может быть, у них гости. Может быть, у _____⁸ контрольная. Может быть, его отец _____.⁹ | говорить играть классика любить мало слышно спать Вова тихо |

Ситуации

T. How would you . . .

1. ask a classmate if she likes to listen to classical music?
_____

2. tell a classmate that your mother says that (**что**) Quebec (**Квебек**) is a beautiful city?
_____

3. say that Mark has your alarm clock?
_____

4. ask a classmate if he knows the address of the theater?

5. tell your classmate that you have her passport?

6. say that in America students work a lot and sleep a lot?

Ва́ша о́чередь!

У. Answer these questions about yourself, using complete sentences.

1. Что ты лю́бишь де́лать?

2. Каку́ю му́зыку лю́бят америка́нские студе́нты?

3. Ты мно́го спишь? Ты ма́ло спишь?

4. У твои́х (*your*) де́душки и ба́бушки большо́й дом? ма́ленький? но́вый? ста́рый?

5. У вас в Аме́рике сосе́ди говоря́т друг дру́гу (*each other*) «До́брый день»?

Сочине́ние

Ф. Write a short paragraph about either your family or a couple of your friends. Tell what they like and don't like to do. Tell what they have and/or don't have—perhaps interesting work, a nice / big / small / new / old house or apartment, German (**неме́цкий**) / American / Japanese (**япо́нский**) car, and so on.

РАБО́ТА В ЛАБОРАТО́РИИ

ДИАЛО́ГИ

Диало́г 1 А что де́лает...? (Making an inquiry over the phone)

АА. Follow along as you listen to the dialogue.

А. Ми́ша, э́то тётя Ва́ря. Ты что, оди́н (*alone*) до́ма?
Б. Нет, я не оди́н. Ба́бушка, де́душка и ма́ма то́же до́ма.
А. А что де́лает ба́бушка?
Б. Спит.

Name_____ Date_____ Class_____

    А. А де́душка?
    Б. Слу́шает му́зыку.
    А. А ма́ма?
    Б. Ма́ма говори́т, что её нет (*she's not*) до́ма.

- Now read and repeat aloud in the pause after each phrase.
- Now read the lines for speaker **Б** aloud.
- Now read the lines for speaker **А** aloud.

1. Why did the mother tell Misha what she did?

   _____

2. How would the last line read if the father had said it?

   _____

Диало́г 2 Я люблю́ бале́т! (Choosing a performance to attend)

ББ. Follow along as you listen to the dialogue.
(*Looking at a theater schedule.*)

    А. Вот Большо́й теа́тр. За́втра там Му́соргский. «Бори́с Годуно́в».
    Б. Я не люблю́ о́перу.
    А. А вот Музыка́льный теа́тр. Там «Роме́о и Джулье́тта». Бале́т Проко́фьева «Роме́о и Джулье́тта».
    Б. Прекра́сно! Я о́чень люблю́ бале́т!

- Now read and repeat aloud in the pause after each phrase.
- Now read the lines for speaker **Б** aloud.
- Now read the lines for speaker **А** aloud.

In this dialogue, speaker **Б** likes ballet but doesn't like opera. Rewrite the dialogue so that speaker **Б** likes opera but not ballet.

    А. _____
       _____
    Б. _____
    А. _____
    Б. _____

АУДИ́РОВАНИЕ

ВВ. Listen carefully to Lyudmila's description of her family. Write in English what each family member enjoys or doesn't enjoy doing. One answer has been given for you.

1. Her brother Ivan *likes to play soccer.*
2. Her brother Sergei _____
3. Her mother _____
4. Her father _____
5. Her grandmother _____
6. Her grandfather _____

Уро́к 4, Часть втора́я

ГГ. **Keeping up with the Joneses. Keeping up with the Ivanovs?** Your Russian host family is quietly bemoaning the many expensive items that their acquaintances have. Which member of which family has what? Part of the first answer has been given.

1. the Kuznetsovs: *Misha —new television*_____

    *Misha's mom—*_____

    *Misha's dad—*_____

2. the Terekhovs: *Tamara—*_____

    *Tamara's brother—*_____

    *their grandfather—*_____

3. the Sokolovs: *Vladimir Vasilevich—*_____

    *his son (in Moscow)—*_____

    *at his son's university (in St. Petersburg)—*_____

ДД. You will hear a series of questions. Write the letter of the question next to the most appropriate response in the list below. The first one has been done for you.

1. _____ Нет, не очень.   4. _____ Нет, у Миши.

2. _____ У Коли.   5. _____ Прекрасно! Я очень люблю оперу.

3. __a__ Спит.

ГОВОРЕНИЕ

ЕЕ. Explain in Russian what each person is doing.

ОБРАЗЕЦ: *You hear and see:* Nina is playing tennis.
   You say: Нина играет в теннис.

1. Ivan is sleeping.   4. Oleg is writing a letter.
2. Alla is listening to the radio.   5. Tanya is watching television.
3. Masha is reading a magazine.

ЖЖ. You will hear a series of questions. Answer each one affirmatively.

ОБРАЗЕЦ: *You hear and see:* Ты играешь в шахматы?
   You say: Да, я играю в шахматы.

1. Ты много спишь?   4. Ты видишь профессора?
2. Ты играешь в бейсбол?   5. Ты читаешь газету?
3. Ты не очень любишь играть в теннис?

33. You will be asked who has certain items. Answer with the given names.

ОБРАЗЕЦ: *You hear:* У кого японская машина?
   You see: Angela
   You say: У Анджелы.

1. Bill   4. Boris
2. Susanna   5. Alan
3. Sveta

134   Урок 4, Часть вторая

Name_____ Date_____ Class_____

ЧАСТЬ ТРЕТЬЯ
Золоты́е ру́ки

РАБО́ТА ДО́МА

ПИСЬМО́

Понима́ние те́кста

А. Review the reading on pages 148–149 of the textbook and match the items in the left-hand column with the most appropriate completion in the right-hand column.

1. _____ Ле́на
2. _____ Во́ва и Бе́лка
3. _____ Лифт
4. _____ У профе́ссора
5. _____ Инструме́нты
6. _____ Во́ва
7. _____ Джим
8. _____ У Джи́ма
9. _____ Ба́бушка

а. золоты́е ру́ки.
б. есть инструме́нты.
в. немно́го говори́т по-англи́йски.
г. у́чится у профе́ссора Петро́вского.
д. не зна́ет, когда́ Во́ва де́лает дома́шнее зада́ние.
е. говори́т, что Джим ма́стер на все ру́ки.
ж. на по́лке и́ли на столе́.
з. опя́ть не рабо́тает.
и. в ли́фте.

Playing an instrument

Б. Strange family traditions! The Russian family you are staying with is very musical, but they play instruments according to age and size. That is, the youngest person plays the smallest instrument and so on. Listed below are the family members, their ages, and the instruments. Who plays what? The first one has been done for you.

> саксофо́н
> ~~фле́йта~~
> роя́ль
> ту́ба

1. Ма́ша (5)   _Ма́ша игра́ет на фле́йте._
2. Алёша (12) _____
3. ма́ма (34) _____
4. па́па (38) _____

The prepositions «в» and «на»

Б. What is the most appropriate answer to each of the following questions? Place the correct letter in the space provided. The first one has been done for you.

1. __г__ Где спортсмены играют в футбол?   а. в Москве
2. _____ Где живёт президент США?   б. в парке
3. _____ Где гуляют мальчик и собака?   в. на концерте
4. _____ Где живёт президент России?   ~~г. на стадионе~~
5. _____ Где вы слушаете музыку?   д. в Вашингтоне

Г. Can't see! Can't find очки! Help your roommate find her glasses. She's going crazy without them. Suggest some unlikely places where she might not have looked. Remember, they could be in something or on something. Some places may be used more than once.

shelf   bathtub   table   TV   refrigerator   backpack

ОБРАЗЕЦ: Они на столе?

1. _____
2. _____
3. _____
4. _____
5. _____
6. _____

About: < о + Prepositional > (and "buffer consonants")

Д. What do the following groups of people talk about most frequently? Do not use a word more than once.

поликлиника   университет   космос   консерватория   семья
политика   ~~спортзал~~

ОБРАЗЕЦ: Спортсмены говорят о спортзале.

1. Музыканты говорят _____
2. Космонавты говорят _____
3. Президенты говорят _____
4. Бабушка и дедушка говорят _____
5. Профессора говорят _____
6. Врачи говорят _____

Name_____ Date_____ Class_____

Past tense

Е. Fill in the blanks with one of the verbs from the following list. Use each form only once. The first one has been done for you.

читáла	~~смотрéл~~	слýшал
писáла	бы́ли	бы́л	ви́дели
смотрéли		игрáл	Рабóтал

Вчерá я смотрéл ¹ телеви́зор, моя́ мáма _____² газéту, а бáбушка и дéдушка

_____³ в теáтре. Они́ _____⁴ «Мисс Сайгóн». В теáтре они́

_____⁵ моегó дрýга Валéру. Мой пáпа вчерá вéчером _____,⁶ а сестрá

_____⁷ курсовýю рабóту. Мой брат вчерá _____⁸ в баскетбóл, а потóм

_____⁹ дóма и _____¹⁰ рок-мýзыку.

Ж. Say what the following people were doing yesterday.

~~Юра~~ и Ви́тя   Вáня   Нáдя   Óля и Мáша

ОБРАЗЕЦ: Юра читáл статью́.

1. _____
2. _____
3. _____
4. _____

З. Sergei wants to know what his classmates did over the weekend. What does he ask them and how do they answer? The first one has been done for you.

Андрéй   Тáня и Олéг

Ми́ша Са́ша и Ве́ра Лю́ба

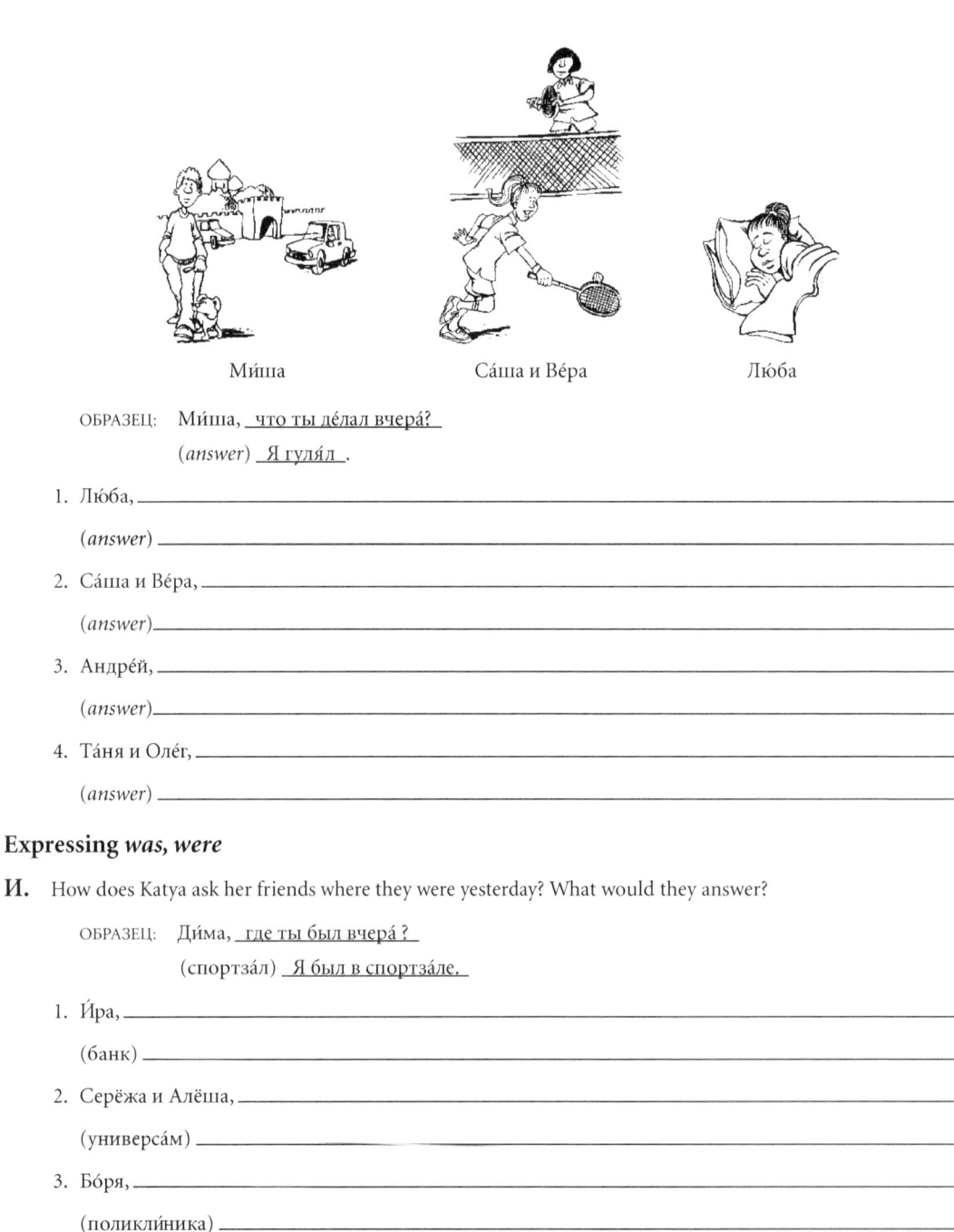

ОБРАЗЕЦ: Ми́ша, _что ты де́лал вчера́?_
           (answer) _Я гуля́л_ .

1. Лю́ба, _____ ?

   (answer) _____ .

2. Са́ша и Ве́ра, _____ ?

   (answer) _____ .

3. Андре́й, _____ ?

   (answer) _____ .

4. Та́ня и Оле́г, _____ ?

   (answer) _____ .

Expressing *was, were*

И. How does Katya ask her friends where they were yesterday? What would they answer?

ОБРАЗЕЦ: Ди́ма, _где ты был вчера́?_
           (спортза́л) _Я был в спортза́ле._

1. И́ра, _____

   (банк) _____

2. Серёжа и Алёша, _____

   (универса́м) _____

3. Бо́ря, _____

   (поликли́ника) _____

4. Фе́дя и Ю́ля, _____

   (кафе́) _____

5. Анто́н, _____

   (по́чта) _____

6. Да́ша, _____

   (библиоте́ка) _____

138   Уро́к 4, Часть тре́тья

Name_____ Date_____ Class_____

К. Below is the title of an article that appeared in the Russian glamour magazine *Лиза*.

> Первая любовь: она была и не была…

1. **Первый** means *first*. You can guess the meaning of the noun **любовь** since you know the verb **любить**. So what does **первая любовь** mean?
   _____

2. How would you translate the complete title of the article?
   _____

3. What do you think it might be about?
   _____
   _____

To speak a language

Л. Write two sentences about each of the following students. Using the cues given, tell where they live and what language they speak.

ОБРАЗЕЦ: Пьер (он) / Париж
Пьер живёт в Париже. Он говорит по-французски.

1. Тómоко (онá) / Óсака _____
   _____

2. Лин Чен (она) / Пекин _____
   _____

3. Курт и Ильзе / Берлин _____
   _____

4. Джина (онá) / Рим _____
   _____

5. Пабло (он) / Мадрид _____
   _____

Урок 4, Часть третья

6. Алан и Сузан / Денвер _____

7. Таня / Кострома _____

Перевод

M. Translate the following dialogues into Russian.

1. "Do you speak English?"
   "A little."
   _____
   _____

2. "Borya, where were you yesterday?"
   "I was playing basketball at the gym. And where were you, Lyuda?"
   "At home. I was doing my homework."
   _____
   _____
   _____

Повторение — мать учения!

H. Following is a summary of the reading in Part 3. Fill in the blanks with words that maintain the context of the reading. You will have to change the form of some of the words. Use each word only once.

Вова и Белка в _____,¹ но лифт не работает. Лифт и вчера не _____.² У _____³ Петровского есть инструменты, и Джим открывает (*opens*) дверь лифта. У Джима _____⁴ руки. Джим американец, но он хорошо _____⁵ по-русски. Он учится в _____.⁶ Вова учится в _____.⁷ Он немного говорит _____.⁸ Он говорит Джиму: Сэнк'ю.	говорить золотой лифт по-английски профессор работать университет школа

Name _____ *Date* _____ *Class* _____

Ситуа́ции

О. How would you . . .

1. ask your Russian host parents if they speak English or Spanish?
   _____

2. ask a classmate if she plays the violin?
   _____

3. tell someone that you watched television yesterday?
   _____

4. ask your classmates what they did yesterday?
   _____

5. tell someone that you don't like to talk about politics (**поли́тика**)?
   _____

6. ask someone if the alarm clock is in the suitcase?
   _____

Ва́ша о́чередь!

П. Answer the following questions about yourself, using complete sentences.

1. Ты игра́ешь на гита́ре? на роя́ле? на саксофо́не?
   _____

2. Ты говори́шь по-неме́цки? по-францу́зски? по-испа́нски?
   _____

3. Где ты был (была́) вчера́?
   _____

4. Ты лю́бишь говори́ть о спо́рте? о поли́тике? о кино́?
   _____

5. Каку́ю му́зыку ты слу́шал (слу́шала) вчера́?
   _____

6. Где ты де́лаешь дома́шнее зада́ние?
   _____

Сочине́ние

Р. Write a short paragraph about your day yesterday. What did you do and where? Certainly you were reading for just a short time—a book? a newspaper? at home? in the library? at a friend's? Did you write something? What language did you speak? Here is a list of verbs to give you some ideas.

говори́ть	игра́ть	чита́ть	писа́ть	быть	ви́деть	смотре́ть
де́лать	понима́ть	гуля́ть	рабо́тать	слу́шать	спать	

_____
_____
_____
_____
_____

РАБОТА В ЛАБОРАТОРИИ

ДИАЛОГИ

Диало́г 1 Как по-ру́сски . . . ? (Asking how to say something in Russian)

АА. Follow along as you listen to the dialogue.

А. Как по-ру́сски *journalist*?
Б. Журнали́ст, журнали́стка.
А. А как по-ру́сски *The journalist is writing an article*?
Б. Журнали́ст (и́ли журнали́стка) пи́шет статью́.
А. Спаси́бо.
Б. Пожа́луйста.

- Now read and repeat aloud in the pause after each phrase.
- Now read the lines for speaker **Б** aloud.
- Now read the lines for speaker **А** aloud.

Rewrite the dialogue so that speaker **А** is asking how to say, "*Students listen to rock music.*"

А. _____
Б. _____
А. _____
Б. _____
А. _____
Б. _____

Name _____ Date _____ Class _____

Диало́г 2 Вы о́чень хорошо́ говори́те по-францу́зски (Discussing knowledge of foreign languages)

ББ. Follow along as you listen to the dialogue.

   А. Вы о́чень хорошо́ говори́те по-францу́зски. Вы жи́ли во Фра́нции?
   Б. Да, я жил там два го́да (*two years*). В Пари́же. Я говори́л то́лько по-францу́зски.
   А. А каки́е ещё языки́ (*what other languages*) вы зна́ете?
   Б. Я непло́хо говорю́ по-италья́нски и по-испа́нски. И (*smiling*) немно́го говорю́ по-ру́сски.

   • Now read and repeat aloud in the pause after each phrase.
   • Now read the lines for speaker **Б** aloud.
   • Now read the lines for speaker **А** aloud.

   1. Is speaker **Б** a male or female? _____
   2. Which two words tell you? _____
   3. What would those two words be if speaker **Б** was of the opposite sex? _____

АУДИ́РОВАНИЕ

ВВ. **What is where?** Listen to the dialogues and match the objects and people to their locations. The first one has been done for you.

   1. __г__ book   а. in the shower
   2. _____ pencil   б. outside
   3. _____ magazine   в. in the elevator
   4. _____ cat   ~~г. on the shelf~~
   5. _____ dog   д. on the balcony
   6. _____ guest   е. in the car
   7. _____ television   ж. on the table
   8. _____ director   з. in the kitchen

ГГ. You will hear several sentences describing four different students—**Ната́лья, Мари́на, Серге́й, Алексе́й.** Listen carefully and decide which student matches each of the descriptions listed. The first one has been done for you.

   1. Who speaks French and Spanish, plays flute and clarinet, and plays basketball? __Ната́лья__
   2. Who speaks French, plays guitar and clarinet, and plays volleyball? _____
   3. Who speaks French, plays guitar and clarinet, and plays basketball? _____
   4. Who speaks French and Spanish, plays flute and guitar, and plays volleyball and basketball?

   _____

ДД. You will hear several sentences telling about Vika's day yesterday and what she plans to do today. Put a **B** (**вчера́**) next to the events that happened yesterday and a **C** (**сего́дня**) next to the events that are happening or are going to happen today. You may need to use both letters for certain events. The first one has been done for you.

1. __B__ read magazines
2. _____ write a term paper
3. _____ attend a lecture
4. _____ go to a concert
5. _____ listen to classical music
6. _____ listen to jazz
7. _____ see a movie
8. _____ watch television
9. _____ play tennis

EE. You will hear a series of questions. Write the letter of the question next to the most appropriate response in the list below.

ОБРАЗЕ́Ц: *You hear:*   У Фе́ди золоты́е ру́ки?
              You mark: #3: Да, он ма́стер на все ру́ки.

1. _____ Он на сту́ле.
2. _____ Нет, по-испа́нски.
3. __Об.__ Да, он ма́стер на все ру́ки.
4. _____ Факульте́т и́ли ка́федра.
5. _____ О Герма́нии.
6. _____ Да, в Берли́не.

ГОВОРЕ́НИЕ

ЖЖ. You will hear a series of questions asking you where certain objects or people are. Answer according to the given cues.

ОБРАЗЕ́Ц: *You hear:*   Где маши́на?
              You see: (in the garage)
              You say: В гараже́.

1. (on the table)
2. (in the backpack)
3. (in the bag)
4. (in the library)
5. (on the couch)

ЗЗ. You will be asked if you are doing certain activities today. Respond negatively, but say that you did them yesterday.

ОБРАЗЕ́Ц: *You hear and see:*   Ты сего́дня игра́ешь на роя́ле?
              You respond: Нет, но я игра́л (игра́ла) на роя́ле вчера́.

1. Ты сего́дня пи́шешь сочине́ние?
2. Ты сего́дня чита́ешь статью́?
3. Ты сего́дня слу́шаешь кла́ссику?
4. Ты сего́дня игра́ешь в баскетбо́л?
5. Ты сего́дня смо́тришь фильм?
6. Ты сего́дня спишь на балко́не?

Name_____ Date_____ Class_____

ИИ. You will again be asked the questions from exercise 33. Again respond that you did that activity yesterday, but add that you are doing the cued activity today.

    ОБРАЗЕЦ: *You hear:*   Ты сегóдня игрáешь на роя́ле?
                    You see: (*played the flute*)
                    You say: Я игрáл (игрáла) на роя́ле вчерá, а сегóдня я игрáю на флéйте.

1. (*write letter*)   4. (*play volleyball*)
2. (*read magazine*)   5. (*watch ballet*)
3. (*listen to jazz*)   6. (*sleep on couch*)

КК. Some of the following people play an instrument. Some play a sport. Tell what each one plays.

    ОБРАЗЕЦ: *You hear and see:*   (*Jim—hockey*)
                    You say: Джим игрáет в хоккéй.

1. (*Angela—cello*)   4. (*Sasha—violin*)
2. (*Jennifer—soccer*)   5. (*Zhenya—basketball*)
3. (*Tom—bass*)   6. (*Alyosha—chess*)

Name_____ Date_____ Class_____

ЧАСТЬ ЧЕТВЁРТАЯ
Очень приятно познакомиться

РАБОТА ДОМА

ПИСЬМО

Понимание текста

А. Review the reading on page 161 of the textbook and answer the following questions.

1. Джим хорошо говорит по-русски?

2. В Москве Джим говорит по-русски. А дома?

3. В доме, где живёт Лена, лифт хорошо работает?

4. На каком факультете учится Лена?

5. Что Джим умеет делать?

6. Где Джим работал, когда он учился?

Double negatives

Б. **Какой ужас!** Your class is experiencing spring fever, and nobody is doing any work! Tell your roommate just how bad the situation is!

ОБРАЗЕЦ: Когда работает Джеф? <u>Джеф никогда не работает.</u>

1. Когда Брайан говорит по-русски?

2. Где работает Диана?

3. Что Джон любит читать?

4. Кто слу́шает ле́кцию?

_____

5. Что говори́т Ли́нда на ле́кции?

_____

Permission and prohibition: *One may/may not*

В. Write the word **нельзя́** or **мо́жно** to show what is logically prohibited or allowed.

ОБРАЗЕ́Ц: На уро́ке ___нельзя́___ спать.

1. В теа́тре _____ кури́ть.

2. _____ кури́ть на у́лице.

3. _____ гро́мко игра́ть на роя́ле, ма́ма спит.

4. _____ игра́ть в футбо́л то́лько на у́лице, а в до́ме _____.

5. На́ши роди́тели ру́сские, и они́ не лю́бят, когда́ мы говори́м по-англи́йски до́ма. У нас

_____ говори́ть то́лько по-ру́сски.

6. До́ма _____ слу́шать му́зыку, когда́ роди́тели смо́трят телеви́зор.

Г. Now make up your own rules for Russian class. List three things you think you should be allowed to do and three things that you should not be allowed to do.

мо́жно

1. _____
2. _____
3. _____

нельзя́

1. _____
2. _____
3. _____

The reflexive verb учи́ться

Д. In which country do the following students study?

в Герма́нии   во Фра́нции   в Ме́ксике   в А́нглии   ~~в Росси́и~~

ОБРАЗЕ́Ц: Са́ша и Та́ня у́чатся в Росси́и.

1. И́льзе _____

2. Пьер и Марго́ _____

3. Хуа́н _____

4. Джон и Мэ́ри _____

5. How would you ask another student where she studies?

_____

Уро́к 4, Часть четвёртая

Name_____ Date_____ Class_____

6. How would you answer if someone asked you the same question?
_____

7. How would you ask a group of students where they study?
_____

8. How would you answer the same question directed to you and your classmates?
_____

To know and *to know how*: знать and уметь

Е. Below is a picture of **Борис** at his apartment building. What do you know about him from the picture? (Note: Begin each sentence with the Russian for *I know that / where / what . . .*)

МОСКВА

ОБРАЗЕЦ: Я знаю, что Борис живёт в Москве.

1. _____
2. _____
3. _____
4. _____
5. _____

Ж. What does **Борис** know how to do?

ОБРАЗЕ́Ц: Бори́с уме́ет чини́ть маши́ны.

1. _____
2. _____
3. _____
4. _____
5. _____

3. Which verb would you choose for the following, **знать** or **уметь**? Fill in the blanks with the appropriate form of the correct verb.

ОБРАЗЕ́Ц: Ты _уме́ешь_ говори́ть по-испа́нски?

1. Ты _____, где мы у́чимся?
2. Ты _____ игра́ть в америка́нский футбо́л?
3. Вы _____ чини́ть лифт?
4. Вы _____, кто там живёт?

Professions and occupations

И. Match each profession on the left with the appropriate description on the right. The first one has been done for you.

1. __и__ актёр
2. ____ скрипа́ч
3. ____ фи́зик
4. ____ шофёр
5. ____ кло́ун
6. ____ гео́лог
7. ____ секрета́рша
8. ____ фото́граф
9. ____ ме́неджер
10. ____ эле́ктрик
11. ____ бро́кер
12. ____ автомеха́ник
13. ____ журнали́стка
14. ____ профе́ссор исто́рии
15. ____ аспира́нтка
16. ____ ма́стер на все ру́ки

а. Он уме́ет чини́ть ла́мпы.
б. Он рабо́тает в университе́те.
в. Он рабо́тает в ци́рке.
г. Он всё уме́ет.
д. Он рабо́тает в фи́рме.
е. У него́ мно́го фотогра́фий.
ж. Она́ пи́шет диссерта́цию.
з. Он игра́ет в орке́стре.
и. ~~Он лю́бит теа́тр.~~
к. Он хорошо́ зна́ет би́ржу.
л. Она́ пи́шет статьи́.
м. Он рабо́тает в лаборато́рии.
н. Он рабо́тает в автосе́рвисе.
о. Она́ де́лает то, что (that which) говори́т дире́ктор.
п. У него́ о́чень хоро́шая маши́на.
р. У него́ есть географи́ческие ка́рты.

Name _____ Date _____ Class _____

Перевод

К. Translate the following dialogue into Russian.

"Do you know how to play chess?"
"Yes, and you?"
"I know, too. And I really like to play chess."

_____
_____
_____

Повторение — мать учения!

Л. Following is a summary of the reading in Part 4. Fill in the blanks with words that maintain the context of the reading. You will have to change the form of some of the words. Use each word only once.

Лена студентка, она _____¹ в университете на _____² журналистики. Она живёт на втором _____.³ Джим аспирант. Он не только хорошо _____⁴ по-русски, но и хорошо _____,⁵ Когда он учился в Америке, он работал в магазине _____,⁶ в автосервисе и на _____.⁷ Он _____⁸ чинить лифты.	биржа говорить понимать уметь учиться факультет электроника этаж

Ситуации

М. How would you . . .

1. say that you don't know anything about sports (**спорт**)?
   _____

2. ask your host parents if they speak English?
   _____

3. ask an acquaintaince if she goes to college?
   _____

4. tell somebody that your major is history?
   _____

5. ask a classmate if he knows how to play chess?
   _____

6. ask a professor if she knows where the math department is?
   _____

Урок 4, Часть четвёртая   151

Ва́ша о́чередь!

H. Answer the following questions, using complete sentences.

1. Ты никогда́ не́ был (не была́) в Вашингто́не? в Чика́го?

   _____

2. У вас в рестора́не мо́жно кури́ть (*smoke*)?

   _____

3. На како́м факульте́те ты у́чишься?

   _____

4. Ты уме́ешь чини́ть маши́ны?

   _____

5. Ты зна́ешь, кто президе́нт ва́шего университе́та?

   _____

Сочине́ние

O. Write a short paragraph about your life at home with your family. What are you allowed or not allowed to do? Be creative! (For example, talk loudly, write on the wall, sleep on the table, play tennis in the house, listen to music when your father/mother is watching TV.) As a result, are there things that you never do?

_____

_____

_____

_____

_____

Name_____ Date_____ Class_____

Fun with grammar! Case review

П. Fill in the blanks of the following sentences with the appropriate case endings. Not all blanks, however, will have an ending. Then enter the words into the crossword puzzle below to help check your spelling. The letter-number combinations (e.g., **г12**) at the end of each sentence indicate the location of the word or words in the puzzle. The first letter and number are for the first word and so on. Note that **г** is for **горизонталь,** or horizontal; **в** is for **вертикаль,** or vertical.

1. У автомеханик_____ неплох_____ машин_____ (*plural*). (г13) (г19) (г10)

2. У Никола_____ нет будильник_____. (в5) (в2)

3. Это квартир_____ Наташ_____? (в14) (в6)

4. Он учится на историческ_____ факультет_____. (в8) (в11)

5. Наш_____ аспирантк_____ играет на саксофон_____. (г17) (г22) (в3)

6. Ты любишь говорить о политик_____? (в18)

7. Наш_____ профессор_____ физик_____ хорошо играет в волейбол_____. (г16) (г9) (г7) (г20)

8. Ты сейчас идёшь в ресторан_____? (г21)

9. Он преподаёт в маленьк_____ школ_____ на наш_____ улиц_____. (в12) (г4) (в15) (в1)

Урок 4, Часть четвёртая   153

РАБОТА В ЛАБОРАТОРИИ

ДИАЛОГИ

Диалог 1 Я не уме́ю игра́ть на виолонче́ли (Discussing musical abilities)

АА. Follow along as you listen to the dialogue.

А. Э́то твоя́ виолонче́ль? Я не зна́ла, что ты игра́ешь на виолонче́ли.
Б. Я не уме́ю игра́ть на виолонче́ли. Э́то виолонче́ль Ната́ши, мое́й (*my*) сестры́.
А. Она́ хорошо́ игра́ет?
Б. Коне́чно! Она́ преподаёт в консервато́рии.
А. Мой брат у́чится в консервато́рии.
Б. Мо́жет быть, моя́ сестра́ его́ зна́ет.

- Now read and repeat aloud in the pause after each phrase.
- Now read the lines for speaker **Б** aloud.
- Now read the lines for speaker **А** aloud.

Rewrite the dialogue so that the characters are talking about the brother Andrei's **саксофо́н**.

А. _____
Б. _____
А. _____
Б. _____
А. _____
Б. _____

Диалог 2 О́чень прия́тно познако́миться (Getting acquainted)

ББ. Follow along as you read the dialogue.

А. Вы здесь живёте?
Б. Да, вот моя́ кварти́ра.
А. Так мы сосе́ди! Меня́ зову́т Мари́я Анто́новна.
Б. А меня́ — Бори́с Васи́льевич. О́чень прия́тно познако́миться.
А. О́чень прия́тно.

- Now read and repeat aloud in the pause after each phrase.
- Now read the lines for speaker **Б** aloud.
- Now read the lines for speaker **А** aloud.

1. How would Maria's brother Ivan have introduced himself?

   _____

2. How would Boris's sister Alla have introduced herself?

   _____

Name_____ Date_____ Class_____

АУДИРОВАНИЕ

ВВ. You are in a crazy, mixed-up town where nothing happens the way you think it should. Listen to the following statements and write down what you are allowed to do and what you are not allowed to do in the following locations. The lists have been started for you.

	NOT ALLOWED TO DO	ALLOWED TO DO
1. in the park	_walk around_	_____
2. in the library	_____	_walk around_
3. at the stadium	_____	_____
4. in the house	_____	_____
5. at work	_____	_____

ГГ. **Who's studying where?** A group of Russian students is studying in the United States. Match their names with the state in which they are studying. The first one has been done for you.

1. _д_ Kolya   а. Colorado
2. ____ Lisa   б. Washington
3. ____ Dasha   в. Iowa
4. ____ Andryusha   г. Arizona
5. ____ Alyosha   д. California
6. ____ Katya   е. Florida
7. ____ Natasha   ж. New York

ДД. You will hear a series of questions. Write the letters of the questions next to the most appropriate response in the list below.

ОБРАЗЕЦ: *You hear:* Ты у́чишься в университе́те?
You mark: #5: Нет, в консервато́рии.

1. ____ Не зна́ю.
2. ____ На факульте́те биоло́гии.
3. ____ Нет, никогда́.
4. ____ Нет, нельзя́.
5. _Об._ Нет, в консервато́рии.
6. ____ Нет, я не уме́ю.

ГОВОРЕНИЕ

ЕЕ. You will be asked if you do a particular activity. For each question, answer that you *never* do that particular activity.

    ОБРАЗЕЦ: *You hear and see:* Ты игра́ешь в ша́хматы?
                      You respond: Нет, я никогда́ не игра́ю в ша́хматы.

1. Ты слу́шаешь кла́ссику?
2. Ты всегда́ рабо́таешь до́ма?
3. Ты всегда́ де́лаешь дома́шнее зада́ние?
4. Ты смо́тришь телеви́зор?
5. Ты понима́ешь, когда́ наш преподава́тель говори́т по-ру́сски?

ЖЖ. You will hear classmates make statements about what is or isn't allowed in their homes. Indicate that the opposite is true at your house.

    ОБРАЗЕЦ: *You hear and see:* У нас до́ма мо́жно игра́ть на саксофо́не.
                      You respond: А у нас до́ма нельзя́ игра́ть на саксофо́не.

1. У нас до́ма мо́жно смотре́ть телеви́зор.
2. У нас до́ма нельзя́ слу́шать рок-му́зыку.
3. У нас до́ма мо́жно кури́ть (*smoke*).
4. У нас до́ма нельзя́ говори́ть гро́мко.
5. У нас до́ма нельзя́ игра́ть на тромбо́не.

33. Say that you know the following facts or know how to do the following activities.

    ОБРАЗЕЦ: *You hear and see:* (*how to fix the car*)
                      You say: Я уме́ю чини́ть маши́ну.
                      You hear and see: (*where Professor Levin lives*)
                      You say: Я зна́ю, где живёт профе́ссор Ле́вин.

1. (*where the drugstore is*)
2. (*what Anton is reading*)
3. (*how to speak French*)
4. (*how to play tennis*)
5. (*who lives in apartment seven*)
6. (*how to play the clarinet*)

Name_____ Date_____ Class_____

ДЖИМ В МОСКВЕ

УРОК 5

ЧАСТЬ ПЕРВАЯ
Мой отéц не миллионéр!

РАБОТА ДОМА

ПИСЬМО

Понимáние тéкста

A. Review the reading on page 178 of the textbook. Then indicate which of the following statements apply to **Вóва** and which to **Джим**. Which might apply to both?

	ВÓВА	ДЖИМ	
1.	_____	_____	Он живёт в Бóстоне.
2.	_____	_____	У негó дóма вездé кнúги.
3.	_____	_____	Егó сестрá лю́бит цветы́.
4.	_____	_____	У негó дóма вездé цветы́.
5.	_____	_____	У негó большáя кóмната.
6.	_____	_____	В Москвé у негó нет машúны.
7.	_____	_____	Он хорошó говорúт по-рýсски.
8.	_____	_____	Там, где он живёт, нет гаражá.
9.	_____	_____	В Москвé он живёт в общежúтии.
10.	_____	_____	У негó в машúне есть рáдио и магнитофóн.

Prepositional case (singular): Adjectives and possessives

Б. Choose an appropriate adjective/noun combination to complete the sentences below.

моя́ ба́бушка	в большо́м го́роде
~~мой брат~~	в на́шем университе́те
но́вый сосе́д	на́ша сосе́дка
мои́ сёстры	~~в но́вом общежи́тии~~
в но́вой ру́сской шко́ле	на́ши роди́тели
в большо́й но́вой кварти́ре	в Моско́вском университе́те

ОБРАЗЕ́Ц: <u>Мой брат</u> живёт <u>в но́вом общежи́тии.</u>

1. _____ рабо́тает _____
2. _____ живу́т _____
3. _____ у́чится _____
4. _____ живёт _____
5. _____ у́чатся _____

В. Answer the following questions, using the words in parentheses.

ОБРАЗЕ́Ц: — Где живу́т Кругло́вы? (наш дом)
— Кругло́вы живу́т <u>в на́шем до́ме.</u>

1. — На како́м этаже́ ты живёшь? (пе́рвый эта́ж)
   —_____

2. — Где живу́т твои́ роди́тели? (ма́ленький го́род)
   —_____

3. — Где дом профе́ссора Ивано́ва? (на́ша у́лица)
   —_____

4. — Где рабо́тает твой оте́ц? (но́вый магази́н)
   —_____

5. — Где живу́т италья́нские студе́нты? (хоро́шее большо́е общежи́тие)
   —_____

6. — Где твои́ кни́ги? (моя́ ко́мната)
   —_____

Name_____ Date_____ Class_____

Г. Alyosha has moved to a new town. His new address is **г. Кривóй Рог, ул. Садóвая, д. 15, кв. 6.** His postcard got wet in the rain, causing some of the letters to wash out. Can you restore them? The first ones have been done for you.

Я живý в Кривóм___ Рóге___ , на Садóвой___ ýлице___ , в дóм_____¹ нóмер 15,

в кварти́р_____² нóмер 6. Я учýсь в университéт_____³ и рабóтаю в кни́жн_____⁴ магази́н_____.⁵

На пéрв_____⁶ этаж_____⁷ дóма есть ресторáн. На втор_____⁸ этаж_____⁹ живёт мой друг.

Он рабóтает в нóв_____¹⁰ библиотéк_____.¹¹ А егó женá рабóтает в университéт_____ ¹²

на наш_____¹³ факультéт_____.¹⁴ О егó женé писáли в газéт_____.¹⁵ У них есть сын, он ýчится в

Амéрик_____,¹⁶ в больш_____¹⁷ университéт_____¹⁸ в Калифóрни_____.¹⁹ В наш_____²⁰

гóрод_____²¹ есть большóй парк. В парк_____ ²² везде́ цветы́. Óчень краси́во!

Noun irregularities: Shifting-stress masculines and masculine prepositional in «-ý»

Д. Below is a list of nouns and prepositional phrases in English. For each, give the equivalent Russian word (Nominative case) and prepositional phrase. Mark the stress for each word.

ОБРАЗЕЦ: street <u>ýлица</u> on the street <u>на ýлице</u> (The stress doesn't change.)

1. room _____ in the room _____
2. garage _____ in the garage _____
3. shelf _____ on the shelf _____
4. floor _____ on the floor _____
5. table _____ on the table _____
6. city _____ in the city _____

Now, go back and circle the number of the nouns whose stresses shift to the end. Put an **X** next to the number of the nouns that take a stressed «-ý» ending in the Prepositional case.

A productive suffix: -овать verbs

Е. A little fun with **-овать** verbs! Following is a list of **-овать** verbs that you have more than likely never seen before. If you sound them out, however, you should be able to guess their meaning because each is comparable to a verb in English. Try to do it without peeking, but if you must, look at the bottom of the page for the English translations. Fill in the blanks with the appropriate form of the correct verb. Remember how to conjugate **-овать** verbs! Use each verb only once.

| критиковáть | интересовáть | игнори́ровать | коллекциони́ровать |
| команд́овать | вальси́ровать | ~~анализи́ровать~~ | артикули́ровать |

ОБРАЗЕЦ: Аспирáнт <u>анализи́рует</u> проблéму.

1. Мой брат óчень лю́бит баскетбóл, а меня́ _____ волейбóл.

2. Я егó хорошó понимáю, когдá он говори́т по-рýсски. Он óчень я́сно (*clearly*)

   _____ словá.

---
to criticize   to interest   to ignore   to collect
to command   to waltz   to analyze   to articulate

Урóк 5, Часть пéрвая   159

3. Мои́ роди́тели о́чень лю́бят му́зыку, осо́бенно (*especially*) му́зыку Ри́харда Штра́уса. Когда́ они́ слу́шают вальс, они́ _____ по (*around*) ко́мнате.

4. Ты _____ фа́кты, а фа́кты нельзя́ игнори́ровать.

5. Профе́ссор Марли́нский о́чень пло́хо чита́ет ле́кции (*gives lectures*). Студе́нты всегда́ _____ его́ ле́кции.

6. Мой де́душка _____ календари́. А что вы _____ ?

7. У нас до́ма _____ ба́бушка. А у вас?

Факульте́ты

Ж. Guess which department the following people are in. Refer to the list of university departments on page 184 of the textbook.

ОБРАЗЕ́Ц: Фёдор о́чень лю́бит фи́зику.
Он у́чится на физи́ческом факульте́те.

1. Васи́лий лю́бит матема́тику.
   _____

2. Ма́ша хорошо́ зна́ет исто́рию.
   _____

3. Андре́й всегда́ говори́т о хи́мии.
   _____

4. Ди́ма и Анто́н лю́бят биоло́гию.
   _____

5. Да́ша и То́ля лю́бят и зна́ют литерату́ру.
   _____

6. Мари́на всегда́ чита́ет статьи́ об эконо́мике.
   _____

160 Уро́к 5, Часть пе́рвая

Name _____ Date _____ Class _____

3. Below is an advertisement for an international university that is recruiting students. Scan through the ad to find answers to the following questions. Answer the first three in English.

> **МЕЖДУНАРОДНЫЙ УНИВЕРСИТЕТ БИЗНЕСА И УПРАВЛЕНИЯ**
> Гос. лицензия № 16-326
>
> объявляет набор студентов на факультеты
>
> **МЕНЕДЖМЕНТА, ПРАВОВЕДЕНИЯ, СОЦИОЛОГИИ, ЭКОНОМИКИ**
>
> Учредители:
> - Университет «Братья Карич», Белград;
> - Социологический ф-т МГУ;
> - Московская государственная юридическая академия;
> - Фонд «Братья Карич», Белград;
> - Институт высшего коммерческого образования, Париж.
>
> Формы обучения:
> *Бакалавриат - 4 года (дневная);*
> *Дополнительное высшее образование - 2 года (вечерняя).*
>
> Учебные планы и технологии образования - по современным мировым стандартам
> Диплом о высшем образовании установленного образца
> *Обучение платное*
> Зарубежная практика входит в стоимость обучения
> *Иногородним предоставляется общежитие*
> Приём документов до 10 августа
> Тестирование с 10 по 15 августа
> **Осуществляет перевод из других вузов**
>
> 119899, Москва, Воробьёвы горы, МГУ,
> Учебный корпус 3, к. 203, 301
> 932-88-64, 939-50-16

1. What are three of the official departments of this university?
   _____

2. Judging by the type of departments, what career would you say the university prepares most of its graduates for?
   _____

3. How many years does it take to complete a baccalaureate degree?
   _____

4. What is the university's street address?
   _____

5. What are the two telephone numbers given for the university?
   _____

To want: **хотеть**

И. You are buying presents for your family members. What do you think they would like? Choose from the pictured items.

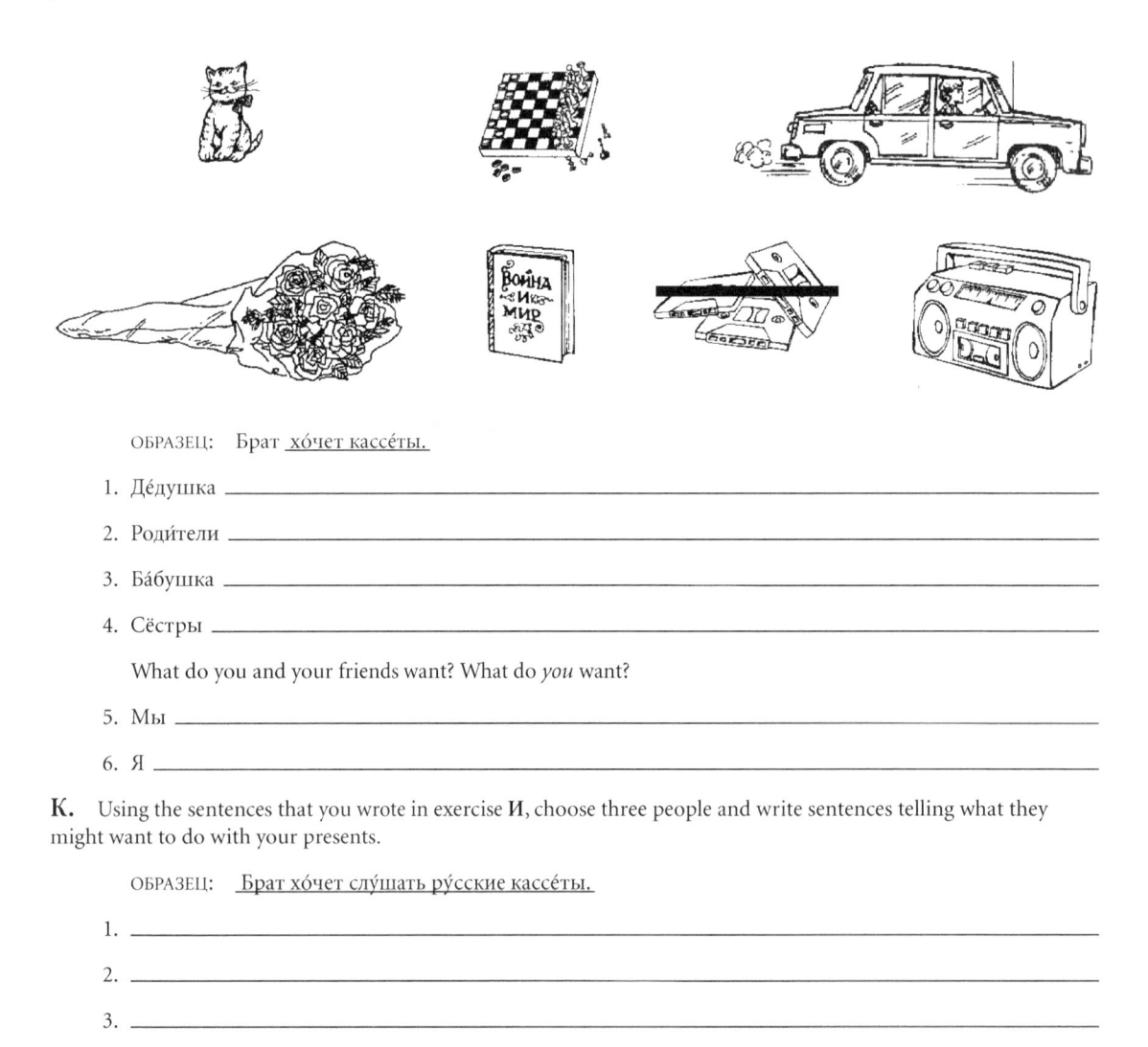

ОБРАЗЕЦ: Брат <u>хо́чет кассе́ты.</u>

1. Де́душка _____
2. Роди́тели _____
3. Ба́бушка _____
4. Сёстры _____

What do you and your friends want? What do *you* want?

5. Мы _____
6. Я _____

К. Using the sentences that you wrote in exercise **И**, choose three people and write sentences telling what they might want to do with your presents.

ОБРАЗЕЦ: <u>Брат хо́чет слу́шать ру́сские кассе́ты.</u>

1. _____
2. _____
3. _____

Name_____ Date_____ Class_____

Перевóд

Л. Translate the following dialogue into Russian.

"What city do you live in?"
"Seattle (Сиэ́тл)."
"What state is it in?"
"Washington."
"Is it a big city?"
"Yes, it's big."

_____
_____
_____
_____
_____
_____

Повторе́ние — мать уче́ния

М. Following is a summary of the reading in Part 1. Fill in the blanks with words that maintain the context of the reading. You will have to change the form of some of the words. You will need to use one of the words twice, but do not use any of the other words more than once.

Джим америка́нец. Он живёт в Бо́стоне. Там у него́ есть маши́на, но нет _____.¹ Он _____² маши́ну на у́лице. В _____³ есть магнитофо́н, и Джим ча́сто слу́шает _____⁴ кассе́ты. В Москве́ у Джи́ма нет _____.⁵ Он живёт в _____,⁶ и университе́т бли́зко. Ко́мната у него́ в общежи́тии _____,⁷ но везде́ кни́ги — на _____,⁸ по́лке, на крова́ти и на _____.⁹	большо́й гара́ж кни́жный маши́на общежи́тие паркова́ть пол ру́сский

Ситуа́ции

Н. How would you...

1. ask someone if he parks his car on your street?

_____

2. ask your classmates if they want to live in a big city?

_____

Уро́к 5, Часть пе́рвая 163

3. ask an acquaintance what she's majoring in?

4. ask your parents if they want to listen to classical music or jazz?

5. tell somebody that you want to study at a small university?

6. tell somebody that your mother works at the new school in your neighborhood?

Ваша очередь!

О. Answer the following questions, using complete sentences.

1. На каком факультете ты учишься?

2. У тебя есть машина? Где ты паркуешь её?

3. В каком городе ты хочешь жить?

4. Что ты хочешь делать сегодня вечером?

5. У тебя в комнате есть книги? Где они?

6. Ты учишься в большом университете? в маленьком?

Сочинение

П. Write a short paragraph (five or six sentences) about your life at the university. Ideas: At what kind of a university do you study? large? small? good? expensive? What is your major? What is your favorite subject? Do you live in a dorm or an apartment? What is it like? Do you have a car?

Name _____ Date _____ Class _____

РАБОТА В ЛАБОРАТОРИИ

ДИАЛОГИ

Диалог 1   Где ты учишься? (Asking where someone studies)

АА. Follow along as you listen to the dialogue.

А. Вова, на каком факультете учится твоя сестра?
Б. На факультете журналистики.
А. А где ты учишься?
Б. В школе.
А. А где твоя школа?
Б. На нашей улице.

- Now read and repeat aloud in the pause after each phrase.
- Now read the lines for speaker **Б** aloud.
- Now read the lines for speaker **А** aloud.

Who is older, **Вова** or his sister? How do you know?

_____

Диалог 2   Ты знаешь, где...? (Clarifying directions)

ББ. Follow along as you listen to the dialogue.

А. Ты знаешь, где Тверская улица?
Б. Да, конечно. В центре.
А. У тебя есть карта Москвы?
Б. Да, вот она. Смотри, вот Тверская.
А. Но это улица Горького!
Б. Нет, это Тверская. Тверская — это очень старое название (*name*). Потом это была улица Горького, а сейчас — опять Тверская!

- Now read and repeat aloud in the pause after each phrase.
- Now read the lines for speaker **Б** aloud.
- Now read the lines for speaker **А** aloud.

Rewrite the dialogue so that speaker **А** is trying to find a downtown Moscow area called **площадь** (*square*) **Ногина**. Its original and current name is **Китай-город**.

А. _____

Б. _____

А. _____

Б. _____

А. _____

Б. _____

АУДИРОВАНИЕ

ВВ. **На каком факультете ты учишься?** Listen as the following university students tell what their majors are. Then indicate who is studying what by placing the letter of the department next to the appropriate student.

ОБРАЗЕЦ: — Фе́дя, на како́м факульте́те ты у́чишься?
— На географи́ческом.

Об. ___ж___ Fedya   а. Physics

1. _____ Marina   б. Philology (Languages and Literatures)

2. _____ Tanya   в. Philosophy

3. _____ Yura   г. Chemistry

4. _____ Petya   д. Sociology

5. _____ Dima   е. Economics

6. _____ Masha   ~~ж. Geography~~

     з. History

ГГ. You will hear a series of sentences, each containing a verb whose infinitive ends in **-овать**. You may not be familiar with all of the verbs, but you can probably guess their meanings. Circle the letter of the translation that corresponds to the Russian sentence.

ОБРАЗЕЦ: *You hear*   Студе́нты критику́ют профе́ссора Гайда́ра.
           You see: а. Students cram for Professor Gaidar's exam.
                     б. Students criticize Professor Gaidar.
                     в. Students are crazy about Professor Gaidar.
           You circle: (б.) Students criticize Professor Gaidar.

1. а. Japan has many experts in sumo wrestling.

    б. Japan experiences economic difficulties.

    в. Japan exports electronics.

2. а. Are you interested in classical music?

    б. Are you interning at a music school?

    в. Do you intend to study classical music?

3. а. The professor isn't an artist, and it's difficult to tell what his drawings are of.

    б. The professor articulates his words poorly, and it isn't easy to understand him.

    в. The professor's speciality is artillery that is especially difficult to fire.

4. а. The students are recovering from a new strain of the flu.

    б. The students are recruiting residents for the new dorm.

    в. The students recommend the new dorm.

5. а. The music appeals to the composer.

    б. The musicians applaud the composer.

    в. The musicians approve the new composition.

166   Уро́к 5, Часть пе́рвая

Name_____ Date_____ Class_____

ДД. For each question that you hear, choose the most appropriate answer from the list below. Do not use an answer more than once.

ОБРАЗЕЦ: You hear: Вы хоти́те игра́ть в ша́хматы?
          You choose: д. Да, хоти́м.

Об. __д__   а. Нет, мы хоти́м жить в Мичига́не.
1. _____   б. В Моско́вском университе́те.
2. _____   в. Нет, я хочу́ купи́ть маши́ну.
3. _____   г. Со́ня хо́чет.
4. _____   ~~д. Да, хоти́м.~~
5. _____   е. Нет, я хочу́ игра́ть в ша́хматы.

ГОВОРЕНИЕ

ЕЕ. Answer each of the following questions according to the cued response. Use a prepositional phrase with «в» or «на».

ОБРАЗЕЦ: You hear: Где ты парку́ешь маши́ну?
          You see: (On our street.)
          You say: На на́шей у́лице.

1. (At the new drugstore.)
2. (In our dormitory.)
3. (On the bookshelf.)
4. (On the fourth floor.)
5. (At our university.)

ЖЖ. You will hear a series of sentences. Rephrase each one with the verb **хоте́ть** (*to want*) plus the appropriate infinitive phrase.

ОБРАЗЕЦ: You hear and see: Са́ша игра́ет рок-му́зыку.
          You say: Са́ша хо́чет игра́ть рок-му́зыку.

1. Ва́ся чита́ет журна́л.
2. Да́ша парку́ет маши́ну в гараже́.
3. Андрю́ша говори́т по-италья́нски.
4. О́ля живёт в Ирку́тске.
5. То́мас у́чится в Сан-Франци́ско.
6. Ли́за слу́шает му́зыку.

33. What do you, your friends, and family want to buy?

ОБРАЗЕЦ: You hear and see: Sandra, radio
          You say: Са́ндра хо́чет купи́ть ра́дио.

1. Mike, cassettes
2. mother, toaster
3. we, computer
4. Sam and Bill, chess set
5. I, jeans
6. parents, refrigerator

ЧАСТЬ ВТОРАЯ
Ходя́чая энциклопе́дия!

РАБО́ТА ДО́МА

ПИСЬМО́

Понима́ние те́кста

А. Each of the following statements about the reading in Part 2 is false. Review the reading on page 189 of the textbook and rewrite the sentences correctly. A simple **не** is not enough!

1. В про́шлом году́ Илья́ Ильи́ч Петро́вский был в Росси́и.
   _____

2. У Ильи́ Ильича́ плоха́я библиоте́ка.
   _____

3. Кни́ги у него́ то́лько в гости́ной.
   _____

4. У него́ есть ста́рые кассе́ты. _____

5. Илья́ Ильи́ч хорошо́ зна́ет Санкт-Петербу́рг.
   _____

6. Он роди́лся в Москве́. _____

7. Илья́ Ильи́ч — плохо́й гид. _____

Accusative case: Pronouns

Б. You and a classmate are comparing notes and find that you have a lot in common. Respond to her statements according to the example. Note: The verb in the answers is at the end of the sentence and the pronoun precedes it.

ОБРАЗЕ́Ц: — Я ча́сто чита́ю журна́л «Тайм».
— <u>Я то́же его́ ча́сто чита́ю.</u>

1. — Я зна́ю Людми́лу Анто́новну Росто́ву. — _____
2. — Я люблю́ му́зыку «Битлз». — _____
3. — Я люблю́ Санкт-Петербу́рг. — _____
4. — Я люблю́ фи́льмы Хичко́ка. — _____
5. — Я хорошо́ по́мню Суса́нну и А́нну. — _____
6. — Я хорошо́ зна́ю Чика́го. — _____

Б. You are being told about or introduced to people you already know. Tell the speaker that you remember the person(s) in question.

ОБРАЗЕЦ:　— Нас зову́т Ри́та и А́ня.　— Я <u>вас хорошо́ по́мню.</u>

1. — Её зову́т Ли́я.　　　　　　　　　　— Я _____
2. — Её зову́т Ле́на. Его́ зову́т Ми́ша.　— Мы _____
3. — Нас зову́т Ли и Бра́йан.　　　　　— Мы _____
4. — Меня́ зову́т Ви́ка.　　　　　　　　— Я _____
5. — Меня́ зову́т Ната́лья Степа́новна.　— Мы _____

6. How would you ask another student if she remembers you?

_____

7. A certain professor met you and your family in the States. How would you ask her if she remembers you all?

_____

Accusative case: Animate masculine nouns

Г. You are pointing out various people in the local library. Your classmate responds that she doesn't see them. Note: The possessive adjective **мой** or **наш** does not need to be repeated in the classmate's response.

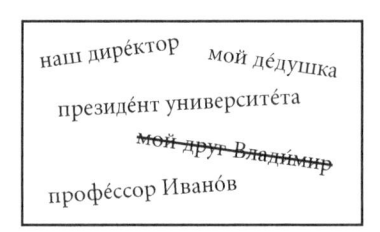

> наш дире́ктор　　мой де́душка
> президе́нт университе́та
> ~~мой друг Влади́мир~~
> профе́ссор Ивано́в

ОБРАЗЕЦ:

— <u>Вон мой друг Влади́мир.</u>　　　　— <u>Где? Я не ви́жу Влади́мира.</u>

1. — _____　— _____
2. — _____　— _____
3. — _____　— _____
4. — _____　— _____

Д. Using the picture below, describe whom or what you see as you look out the window of your home.

Name_____ Date_____ Class_____

ОБРАЗЕЦ: <u>Я ви́жу библиоте́ку.</u>

1. _____
2. _____
3. _____
4. _____
5. _____
6. _____

Reflexive verbs: Past tense forms

Е. It's always interesting to learn about the heritage of other people and tell about your own. Using the verbs **роди́ться, учи́ться,** and **познако́миться** and the words in the boxes (or your own variations), tell about your grandparents and parents — (**А.**) where they were born, (**Б.**) where they studied, and (**В.**) where they met. Two of the blanks have been filled in for you.

А. РОДИ́ТЬСЯ

| ~~в Ита́лии~~ в Росси́и |
| в Калифо́рнии |
| в Нью-Йо́рке |
| в Герма́нии в Кана́де |

Б. УЧИ́ТЬСЯ

| в Моско́вском университе́те |
| в Петербу́ргском университе́те |
| ~~в Га́рварде (Harvard)~~ |
| в Ста́нфордском университе́те |
| в Моско́вской консервато́рии |
| в юриди́ческом институ́те |

В. ПОЗНАКО́МИТЬСЯ

| на экску́рсии |
| на вы́ставке |
| в кафе́ |
| в авто́бусе |

1. А. Ба́бушка <u>родила́сь в Ита́лии.</u>   Де́душка _____

   Б. Ба́бушка _____   Де́душка <u>учи́лся в Га́рварде.</u>

   В. Они́ _____

2. А. Ма́ма _____   Па́па _____

   Б. Ма́ма _____   Па́па _____

   В. Они́ _____

Verbs of motion: ходи́ли куда́ = бы́ли где

Ж. You are telling your Russian professor where you and your friends have been during a recent trip to Russia. You use the verb **быть,** but she asks you questions using the verbs **ходи́ть** and **е́здить** to confirm that she heard you properly. What does she say? Note: Remember that when used with **быть,** the prepositions «в» and «на» will require the Prepositional case because they show location. When used with **ходи́ть** or **е́здить,** however, they show direction and require the Accusative case.

Уро́к 5, Часть втора́я   171

ОБРАЗЕЦ: Мы бы́ли на рок-концéрте.
Вы ходи́ли на рок-концéрт?

1. Мы бы́ли на по́чте. _____
2. Я был (была́) в библиотéке. _____
3. Мы бы́ли в Кремлé. _____
4. Мы бы́ли во Влади́мире. _____
5. Я был (была́) в поликли́нике. _____
6. Мы бы́ли в Санкт-Петербу́рге. _____
7. Я был (была́) на стадио́не. _____
8. Мы бы́ли в клу́бе. _____

Перево́д

3. Translate the following dialogue into Russian.

"When I was in Washington I saw the president."
"You saw the president? But when did you go to Washington?"
"Last year."
"Do you know that I was born in Washington?"

_____
_____
_____
_____

Повторéние — мать учéния

И. Following is a summary of the reading in Part 2. Fill in the blanks with words that maintain the context of the reading. You will have to change the form of some of the words. You will need to use one of the words twice, but do not use any of the other words more than once.

Профéссор Илья́ Ильи́ч Петро́вский был у Джи́ма в _____¹ в Бо́стоне. У Ильи́ Ильича́ _____² библиотéка. Кни́ги у него́ везде́, да́же в пере́дней и в _____³. У него́ есть не _____⁴ кни́ги, но и _____⁵ ка́рты. Илья́ Ильи́ч _____⁶ гид. Он _____⁷ не в Москвé, а на Кавка́зе, но он о́чень хорошо́ зна́ет у́лицы и _____⁸ Москвы́.	замеча́тельный пло́щадь роди́ться ста́рый то́лько туалéт университéт

172 Уро́к 5, Часть втора́я

Name_____ Date_____ Class_____

Ситуа́ции

К. How would you ...

1. tell a Russian professor, whom you met several years earlier, that you remember her well?
   _____

2. tell a classmate that you are listening to the opera *Rigoletto* and ask her if she knows it?
   _____

3. tell somebody that you went to Tula yesterday?
   _____

4. tell somebody that you went to a concert yesterday?
   _____

5. ask your classmate whether she knows the student Sergei Pavlov?
   _____

6. say that last year you studied at a large university, but now you study at a small one?
   _____

7. ask your classmate if she understands Professor Nikolaev well?
   _____

Ва́ша о́чередь!

Л. Answer the questions that are asked of you.

1. Где ты роди́лся (родила́сь)? _____

2. Где познако́мились твои́ роди́тели?
   _____

3. Ты вчера́ ходи́л (ходи́ла) в библиоте́ку? в теа́тр? на по́чту? в магази́н?
   _____

4. Ты е́здил (е́здила) в Нью-Йо́рк? в Вашингто́н? в Чика́го? в Сан-Франци́ско?
   _____

5. Ты всегда́ понима́ешь профе́ссора Миро́нова, когда́ он говори́т по-ру́сски?
   _____

6. Э́то твой сосе́д? Как его́ зову́т? Ты его́ хорошо́ зна́ешь?
   _____

7. Ты слу́шаешь рок-му́зыку? Ты её лю́бишь?
   _____

Сочине́ние

M. Write a short paragraph (five or six sentences) about your grandparents. Ideas: Where were they born? Where did they live and study? Did they go to college? Do you know them well? What do they like to do?

_____
_____
_____
_____
_____
_____

РАБО́ТА В ЛАБОРАТО́РИИ

ДИАЛО́ГИ

Диало́г 1 «Ма́стер и Маргари́та» (Discussing a writer)

AA. Follow along as you listen to the dialogue.

    А. Джон, где ты был вчера́?
    Б. Я ходи́л на вы́ставку «Ру́сская кни́га». Там бы́ли кни́ги Булга́кова.
    А. Ты лю́бишь Булга́кова?
    Б. Да, я о́чень люблю́ «Ма́стера и Маргари́ту».
    А. Ты чита́л Булга́кова по-ру́сски?
    Б. Ну что ты! По-англи́йски, коне́чно!

- Now read and repeat aloud in the pause after each phrase.
- Now read the lines for speaker **Б** aloud.
- Now read the lines for speaker **А** aloud.

Rewrite the dialogue so that speaker **Б** is talking about the books «**Защи́та Лу́жина**» (The Defense) and «**Лоли́та**» by the Russian writer Vladimir Nabokov.

    А. _____
    Б. _____
    А. _____
    Б. _____
    А. _____
    Б. _____

Name_____ Date_____ Class_____

Диалог 2 Вы не зна́ете, где . . . ? (Finding a certain place)

ББ. Follow along as you listen to the dialogue.

    А. Вы не зна́ете, где Пионе́рские пруды́ (пруд = *pond*)?
    Б. Э́то ста́рое назва́ние. Сейча́с э́то Патриа́ршие пруды́.
    А. А где они́?
    Б. Они́ в друго́м райо́не, в це́нтре.
    А. Спаси́бо.

- Now read and repeat aloud in the pause after each phrase.
- Now read the lines for speaker **Б** aloud.
- Now read the lines for speaker **А** aloud.

1. Why might speaker **A** not have been able to find the location that he was looking for on a map?
   _____

2. Where is it located? _____

АУДИРОВАНИЕ

ВВ. You will hear a series of questions. Circle the letter of the correct response.

    ОБРАЗЕЦ: *You hear:* Я люблю́ Стэ́йнбека. А ты?
               You see: а. Я её то́же люблю́.
                           б. Я его́ то́же люблю́.
                           в. Я их то́же люблю́.
               You circle: (б.) Я его́ то́же люблю́.

1. а. Да, я её хорошо́ зна́ю.
   б. Да, я его́ хорошо́ зна́ю.
   в. Да, я их хорошо́ зна́ю.

2. а. Да, я её о́чень хорошо́ зна́ю.
   б. Да, я его́ о́чень хорошо́ зна́ю.
   в. Да, я их о́чень хорошо́ зна́ю.

3. а. Коне́чно, я вас хорошо́ по́мню.
   б. Коне́чно, я её хорошо́ по́мню.
   в. Коне́чно, я их хорошо́ по́мню.

4. а. Нет, я её не люблю́.
   б. Нет, я его́ не люблю́.
   в. Нет, я их не люблю́.

5. а. Ну что вы, я вас хорошо́ по́мню.
   б. Ну что вы, я его́ хорошо́ по́мню.
   в. Ну что вы, я их хорошо́ по́мню.

6. а. Нет, я её не понима́ю.
   б. Нет, я его́ не понима́ю.
   в. Нет, я их не понима́ю.

ГГ. You will hear a series of sentences about people's pasts. Match the person with what happened and the place.

ОБРАЗЕЦ: Ба́бушка родила́сь в Герма́нии.

Об. __ж__ Grandma   а. was born in Mississippi.

1. _____ Uncle Vanya and Aunt Anya   б. met in Paris.

2. _____ Nastya   в. was born in France.

3. _____ Brother   г. met at the university.

4. _____ Grandma and Grandpa   д. studied in the math department.

5. _____ Uncle   е. studied at Moscow University.

6. _____ Aunt   ~~ж. was born in Germany.~~

7. _____ Vova   з. studied at University of Colorado.

ДД. Read through the following questions, listen to the dialogue, and then circle the letter of the most appropriate answers.

1. This dialogue probably occurred

    а. on a city street.

    б. in a store.

    в. in a rural area.

2. The woman wants to find

    а. some music by Tchaikovsky.

    б. Tchaikovsky Street.

    в. the Tchaikovsky Concert Hall.

3. The place she wants is now called

    а. Tverskaya Street.

    б. the Bolshoi Theater.

    в. Novinsky Boulevard.

4. The place is

    а. straight ahead.

    б. to the right.

    в. to the left.

5. The place she wants is

    а. not far away.

    б. far away.

    в. in another part of the city.

Name_____ Date_____ Class_____

ГОВОРЕНИЕ

ЕЕ. Respond to the speaker's statements by saying that you, too, do the same thing. Substitute a pronoun for the direct object.

ОБРАЗЕЦ: *You hear and see:*   Я люблю журнал «Спортс иллюстрейтед».
           You say: Я его тоже люблю.

1. Я знаю Марию Николаевну.
2. Я хорошо помню Вадима Леонидовича и Татьяну Александровну.
3. Я люблю молоко.
4. Я часто читаю газету «Нью-Йорк таймс».
5. Я хорошо помню профессора Михайлова.

ЖЖ. How would you say that you know the following people, places, or things well?

ОБРАЗЕЦ: *You hear and see:*   (the president of the university)
           You say: Я хорошо знаю президента университета.

1. (*San Francisco*)   4. (*Vermont*)
2. (*the director of the school*) 5. (*Natasha*)
3. (*the [female] neighbor*)   6. (*Bill and Tom*)

ЗЗ. The speaker will ask you where you were yesterday. In each instance, answer using the verb **ходить** or **ездить** and the cued destination.

ОБРАЗЕЦ: *You hear:*   Где ты был (была) вчера?
           You see: (*post office*)
           You answer: Я ходил (ходила) на почту.

1. (*concert*)   4. (*university*)
2. (*Kostroma* [*a town not far from Moscow*])   5. (*Vladimir* [*a town not far from Moscow*])
3. (*store*)   6. (*theater*)

Name_____ Date_____ Class_____

ЧАСТЬ ТРЕТЬЯ
Би́знес по-моско́вски

РАБО́ТА ДО́МА

ПИСЬМО́

Понима́ние те́кста

А. First review the reading on pages 201–202 of the textbook. Then match each beginning sentence on the left with its appropriate continuation on the right.

1. Дом, где живёт профе́ссор, но́вый _____   а. есть рези́новые сапоги́.
2. Ле́на не мо́жет купи́ть _____   б. пла́тят пятьсо́т рубле́й.
3. У профе́ссора, Ле́ны и Са́ши _____   г. получа́ют сапоги́ беспла́тно.
4. Нет _____   в. ждёт друг Ви́ктора.
5. У Ви́ктора _____   д. пробле́мы.
6. На авто́бусной остано́вке _____   е. а асфа́льта нет.
7. Профе́ссор, Ле́на и Са́ша _____   ж. разме́ра Ле́ны и Са́ши.
8. Краси́вые де́вушки _____   з. рези́новые сапоги́.

Intensifiers: так, тако́й

Б. Your classmates are telling you what their siblings and parents are interested in. You respond that your siblings and parents have very different interests. Use the intensifier **так** to show what your classmates might have said to prompt your response.

ОБРАЗЕ́Ц: — <u>Мой брат так лю́бит игра́ть в баскетбо́л!</u>

— Пра́вда (*Really*)? А мой брат лю́бит игра́ть в футбо́л.

1. — _____!

— Пра́вда? А мои́ роди́тели зна́ют матема́тику о́чень пло́хо.

2. — _____!

— Пра́вда? А моя́ мать не хо́чет покупа́ть (*to buy*) маши́ну.

3. — _____!

— Пра́вда? А моя́ сестра́ хо́чет учи́ться в консервато́рии.

4. — _____!

— Пра́вда? А мои́ бра́тья игра́ют в ша́хматы о́чень хорошо́.

B. Show how much you like or dislike the following items by writing an intensified statement about each. Following are some adjectives you can choose from.

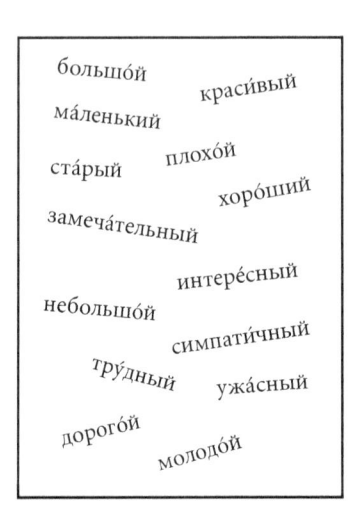

большо́й
краси́вый
ма́ленький
ста́рый плохо́й
хоро́ший
замеча́тельный
интере́сный
небольшо́й
симпати́чный
тру́дный
ужа́сный
дорого́й
молодо́й

ОБРАЗЕЦ: (Нью-Йо́рк / го́род!) <u>Нью-Йо́рк тако́й интере́сный го́род!</u>

1. (Джо Монта́на / футболи́ст) _____!
2. (Чайко́вский / компози́тор) _____!
3. (профе́ссор [*You fill in the name!*] / преподава́тель) _____!
4. («по́рше» / маши́на) _____!
5. («фольк649сва́ген» / маши́на) _____!
6. (Га́рвард / университе́т) _____!
7. (пу́дель / соба́ка) _____!

To be able: мочь

Г. What is it that each of these people *can't* do because of adverse circumstances or because a needed item is missing? Choose from the activities listed below.

слу́шать му́зыку   гуля́ть в па́рке   писа́ть курсову́ю
~~смотре́ть телеви́зор~~   купи́ть рези́новые сапоги́   игра́ть

ОБРАЗЕЦ: Мы <u>не мо́жем смотре́ть телеви́зор</u>. У нас нет телеви́зора.

1. Лари́са и Мари́на _____

   У них нет магнитофо́на.

2. Я _____. В магази́не нет моего́ разме́ра.

3. Бори́с _____. Библиоте́ка закры́та (*closed*).

4. Де́вушки _____. Пого́да (*weather*) плоха́я.

5. Я _____ до́ма. У меня́ нет роя́ля.

Name_____ Date_____ Class_____

Genitive singular: Adjectives and possessives

Д. A small-town student is complaining about his town and university. A big-city student responds by bragging about his. What might the small-town student have said in order to elicit the following responses of the big-city student?

ОБРАЗЕЦ: А. У нас в городе <u>нет большого спортзала</u>.

Б. А у нас очень большой спортзал.

1. А. У нас в университете нет _____

   Б. А у нас очень интересная студенческая газета.

2. А. У нас в городе нет _____

   Б. А у нас есть симфонический оркестр.

3. А. В городе нет _____

   Б. А у нас очень большой стадион.

4. А. В городе нет _____

   Б. А у нас есть драматический театр.

5. А. У нас в университете нет _____

   Б. А у нас очень хорошая библиотека.

6. А. (*Use the singular.*) В университете нет _____

   Б. А у нас есть новые общежития.

7. А. (*Use the singular.*) В городе нет _____

   Б. А у нас есть очень хорошие рестораны.

Е. Who has what? Use the following adjective-noun combinations to identify who would be most likely to have what.

моя мама   наш автомеханик   наша новая студентка
мой друг   наш историк   ~~наша преподавательница~~

ОБРАЗЕЦ: У <u>нашей преподавательницы</u> дорогой рояль.

1. У _____ есть карты Москвы и Санкт-Петербурга.
2. У _____ новый холодильник.
3. У _____ есть брат и сестра.
4. У _____ есть большой рюкзак.
5. У _____ старая машина.

<от + Genitive>

Ж. If you lived in the town shown on the map, how would you answer these questions about the location of various places in relationship to each other? Use the expressions **бли́зко от, далеко́ от,** and **недалеко́ от.** Use a variety of combinations of buildings.

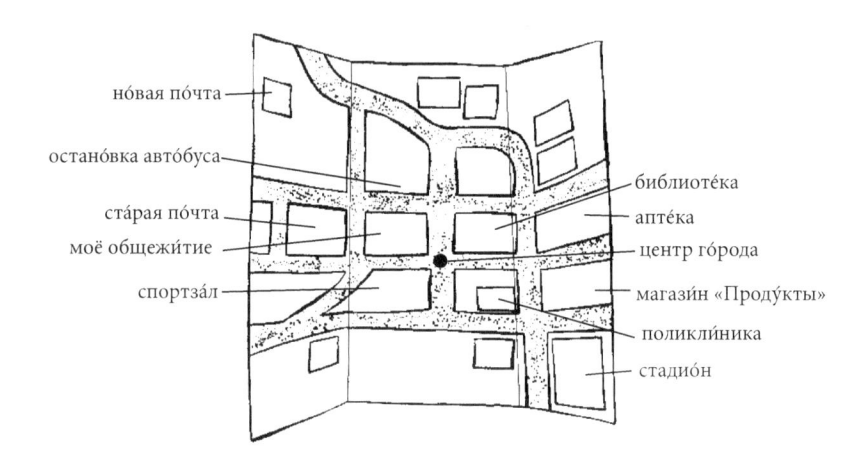

ОБРАЗЕ́Ц: Где нахо́дится (*is located*) ста́рая по́чта?

Ста́рая по́чта недалеко́ от це́нтра го́рода.

1. А но́вая по́чта? _____
2. А твоё общежи́тие? _____
3. А библиоте́ка? _____
4. А стадио́н? _____
5. А поликли́ника? _____
6. А спортза́л? _____

3. Graduation presents! Following is a list of people and the gifts they have sent you for graduation. Tell who gave you what.

~~кни́ги~~   ~~сестра́~~
шокола́д   моя́ люби́мая тётя
цветы́   мой сосе́д
кассе́ты   мой ста́рый друг
буди́льник   мой профе́ссор матема́тики
ва́за   ба́бушка
маши́на   оте́ц

ОБРАЗЕ́Ц: Кни́ги — от сестры́.

1. _____
2. _____
3. _____

Name_____ Date_____ Class_____

4. _____
5. _____
6. _____

Перево́д

И. Translate the following dialogue into Russian.

"How's it going?"
"Not too well. I have a terrible problem."
"What kind of problem?"
"I want to buy new boots, but they don't have my size."

_____
_____
_____
_____

Повторе́ние — мать уче́ния

К. Following is a summary of the reading in Part 3. Fill in the blanks with words that maintain the context of the reading. You will have to change the form of some of the words. You will need to use one word three times and another word twice. Do not use any of the other words more than once.

Ле́на не _____¹ купи́ть

рези́новые сапоги́. Нет её _____².

И Са́ша и Илья́ Ильи́ч то́же не _____³

их купи́ть.

    У Ви́ктора есть план. Он говори́т, «Я _____⁴

помо́чь. Ка́ждое у́тро я жду _____⁵ здесь.

Я даю́ вам сапоги́. На _____⁶ остано́вке ждёт

мой друг. Вы отдаёте (*give back*) сапоги́ и _____⁷

пятьсо́т рубле́й». Ви́ктор говори́т, что _____⁸

де́вушки получа́ют сапоги́ _____⁹

и что Ле́на о́чень _____.¹⁰

беспла́тно
вы
мочь
разме́р
авто́бусная
плати́ть
краси́вый

Уро́к 5, Часть тре́тья

Ситуа́ции

Л. How would you ...

1. say that you really [*don't use* **о́чень**] like to speak Russian?

2. say that your uncle is a really [*don't use* **о́чень**] nice person?

3. ask a classmate if he can sleep when his neighbors are listening to rock (music)?

4. ask your host father if he can read when the children are playing?

5. say that you don't have a car?

6. ask a classmate if his father has a map of old Moscow?

7. tell somebody that the flowers and chocolate are from your (female) neighbor?

8. ask a stranger if the library is not far from the center of town?

Ва́ша о́чередь!

М. Answer the questions that are asked of you.

1. Твой дом (твоя́ кварти́ра) бли́зко от университе́та?

2. От кого́ ты получа́ешь пи́сьма?

3. Что ты хо́чешь де́лать, но не мо́жешь?

4. Ты мо́жешь чита́ть, когда́ твои́ сосе́ди слу́шают му́зыку?

5. Недалеко́ от тебя́ есть хоро́ший рестора́н?

6. У тебя́ в кварти́ре есть кни́жная по́лка?

Name_____ Date_____ Class_____

Сочине́ние

Н. Write a short paragraph (five or six sentences) about somebody with whom you live or are close to (friend, neighbor, brother, sister). What kind of a person is he? What does he do that you really like or don't like? Are there things that you can't do when he is talking, listening to music, and so on? Remember to stick with vocabulary that you know!

_____
_____
_____
_____
_____

РАБО́ТА В ЛАБОРАТО́РИИ

ДИАЛО́ГИ

Диало́г 1 Кака́я грязь! (Expressing dismay)

АА. Follow along as you listen to the dialogue.

   А. Кака́я грязь (*mud*)!
   Б. Да, кошма́р! Дом но́вый, а асфа́льта нет.
   А. У нас то́же но́вый дом и то́же нет асфа́льта.
   Б. Да, э́то ужа́сная пробле́ма.

   • Now read and repeat aloud in the pause after each phrase.
   • Now read the lines for speaker **Б** aloud.
   • Now read the lines for speaker **А** aloud.

Suppose you've moved into a new apartment where the phone is not yet working. Rewrite the dialogue accordingly. The first line has been done for you.

   А. Како́й у́жас!
   Б. _____
   А. _____
   Б. _____

Диало́г 2 Где мо́жно купи́ть...? (Asking where to buy things)

ББ. Follow along as you listen to the dialogue.

   А. Вы не зна́ете, где мо́жно купи́ть рези́новые сапоги́?
   Б. Вот наш магази́н. Там есть рези́новые сапоги́.
   А. Все разме́ры?
   Б. Не зна́ю. Мой разме́р у них есть. Мо́жет быть, ваш то́же есть.

   • Now read and repeat aloud in the pause after each phrase.
   • Now read the lines for speaker **Б** aloud.
   • Now read the lines for speaker **А** aloud.

   1. What is speaker **А** trying to buy? _____

   2. What does speaker **Б** ask about the store? _____

АУДИРОВАНИЕ

ВВ. Which statement would most likely follow the sentence that you hear? Circle the letter of the correct statement.

ОБРАЗЕЦ: *You hear:*   Где моя ру́чка?
              You see: а. Я не могу́ спать.
                          б. Я не могу́ купи́ть су́мку.
                          в. Я не могу́ де́лать дома́шнее зада́ние.
            You circle: (в.) Я не могу́ де́лать дома́шнее зада́ние.

1. а. Вы не мо́жете помо́чь?

   б. Вы не мо́жете здесь жить?

   в. Вы не мо́жете спать?

2. а. Я не могу́ ду́мать.

   б. Я не могу́ ждать его.

   в. Я не могу́ купи́ть но́вую кассе́ту.

3. а. Они́ не мо́гут де́лать дома́шнее зада́ние.

   б. Они́ не мо́гут спать.

   в. Они́ не мо́гут жить на четвёртом этаже́ в до́ме, где нет ли́фта.

4. а. Мы сейча́с не мо́жем игра́ть в баскетбо́л.

   б. Мы сейча́с не мо́жем слу́шать рок-му́зыку.

   в. Мы сейча́с не мо́жем чита́ть журна́л.

5. а. Я не могу́ смотре́ть телеви́зор, когда́ ты рабо́таешь.

   б. Я не могу́ купи́ть проездно́й.

   в. Я не могу́ спать, когда́ ты смо́тришь телеви́зор.

ГГ. Your host parents are leaving you and a younger brother home alone for several days and want to make sure you are prepared for any emergency. One of the host parents writes several telephone numbers down, then tells you whom they are for—in a different order, of course. Place the letter of the telephone number next to the person it belongs to.

    ОБРАЗЕЦ: Но́мер телефо́на тёти А́ни 374-89-63.

Об. __в__ Aunt Anya's   а. 176-45-20

1. _____ Uncle Anton's   б. 376-17-82

2. _____ the mother's friend Vika   ~~в. 374-89-63~~

3. _____ the director of the school   г. 209-58-01

4. _____ the family's doctor   д. 294-38-37

5. _____ the neighbor   е. 483-69-29

6. _____ the director of the American program   ж. 251-90-28

ДД. You will hear a paragraph in which members of your host family tell you where places are located in relationship to their home. Check the appropriate column for each place. The first place has been marked for you.

Name_____ Date_____ Class_____

	NEAR	FAR
1. university	X	
2. post office		
3. drugstore		
4. gym		
5. stadium		
6. downtown		
7. subway		
8. Italian restaurant		

ГОВОРЕНИЕ

ЕЕ. Change the statements that you hear to statements expressing intensity. Be sure to use intonation appropriate for an exclamation!

ОБРАЗЕЦ: *You hear and see:* Он симпатичный человек.
You say: Он такой симпатичный человек!

1. Это интересная статья.
2. Он замечательный врач.
3. Это чистое общежитие.
4. Это дорогие джинсы.
5. Она красивая девушка.
6. Это старый дом.

ЖЖ. Your flight has been delayed and you and your family are stuck at the airport for several hours. What can you all do?

ОБРАЗЕЦ: *You hear and see:* (*brother, do homework*)
You say: Мой брат может делать домашнее задание.

1. (*we, listen to Russian cassettes*)
2. (*the children, play chess*)
3. (*my father, read plays of Chekhov*)
4. (*I, write letters*)
5. (*my mother, sleep*)

33. How would you express the following noun phrases in Russian?

ОБРАЗЕЦ: *You hear and see:* (*my brother's dog*)
You say: собака моего брата

1. our neighbor's car
2. my grandmother's apartment
3. my sister's classmates
4. the old musician's piano
5. the Russian literature instructor
6. the math department's phone number

Name _____ Date _____ Class _____

ЧАСТЬ ЧЕТВЁРТАЯ
Отли́чная мысль

РАБОТА ДОМА

ПИСЬМО

Понима́ние те́кста

А. Review the reading on pages 211–212 of the textbook. How would you complete each of the following statements?

1. Отца́ Та́ни зову́т _____
2. Он ста́рый друг _____
3. Официа́нт рекоменду́ет _____
4. В январе́ у отца́ Та́ни _____
5. Джим живёт в _____
6. Та́ня живёт у _____
7. Та́ня и её подру́га Све́та и́щут _____

Punctuation: Uses of the dash

Б. How would you write the following in Russian?

ОБРАЗЕ́Ц: Paolo is an Italian. <u>Па́оло — италья́нец.</u>

1. Tomiko is a Japanese (woman). _____
2. My brother is a businessman. _____
3. Alan is the son of my doctor. _____
4. My aunt is a movie star. _____
5. I am an American (a Canadian) student. _____

Pointing out and distinguishing things: э́то vs. э́тот

В. Friends are helping you move. Point out some of the major items that are yours.

ОБРАЗЕ́Ц: (television) <u>Э́то мой телеви́зор.</u>

1. (table) _____
2. (couch) _____
3. (armchair) _____
4. (lamp) _____
5. (microwave oven) _____
6. (mixer) _____

When it comes to some of the items, however, you must be a bit more precise. One or more of your roommates have a similar item, and you want to be sure that your friends pack *your* things. Not only do you point out the items that are yours, but you also point out those that are not.

ОБРАЗЕЦ: (*telephone*) <u>Это не мой телефо́н, а вот э́тот телефо́н мой.</u>

1. (*toaster*) _____
2. (*cassettes*) _____
3. (*radio*) _____
4. (*map*) _____
5. (*alarm clock*) _____
6. (*chairs*) _____

Contrasting similar items: э́тот, тот

Г. Contrast the persons or things in the following sentences using э́тот/тот, э́та/та, э́то/то, э́ти/те. For the adjectives with an asterisk, form the opposite by adding **не** at the front of the adjective, as with краси́вый/некраси́вый.

ОБРАЗЕЦ: <u>Э́тот</u> университе́т но́вый, а <u>тот ста́рый.</u>

1. _____ статья́ больша́я, а _____
2. _____ журна́лы плохи́е, а _____
3. _____ сосе́д *симпати́чный, а _____
4. _____ упражне́ние *тру́дное, а _____
5. _____ челове́к ста́рый, а _____
6. _____ маши́на *дорога́я, а _____

Accusative case: Adjectives and possessives

Д. Your host family teases you about being much too vague in the information you share with them. They are repeatedly asking "what kind of" or "which one." Expand on your statements by adding logical adjectives or possessives. Refer to the box in exercise **B** in Part 3, or see exercise 6 on page 217 of the textbook, if you have trouble thinking of different adjectives.

ОБРАЗЕЦ: Билл ча́сто получа́ет <u>интере́сные</u> пи́сьма от сестры́ и бра́та.

1. Вчера́ я купи́ла _____ кре́сло.
2. В теа́тре мы ви́дели _____ дру́га.
3. Мы чита́ем _____ статью́ о ру́сской исто́рии.
4. Я люблю́ чита́ть _____ детекти́вы.
5. Та́ня всегда́ слу́шает _____ му́зыку.
6. Я пло́хо понима́ла _____ сосе́да.
7. В на́шем го́роде есть _____ музе́й.

190 Уро́к 5, Часть четвёртая

Name_____ Date_____ Class_____

E. You just received some money from home! Which items do you want to buy? Again, you may refer to the box in exercise **B** in Part 3 (or see exercise 6 on page 217 of the textbook) for ideas for adjectives. However, you are not limited to these!

ОБРАЗЕЦ: — Какую кассету ты хочешь купить?

— <u>Я хочу купить русскую кассету.</u>

1. — Какую лампу ты хочешь купить?

   — _____

2. — Какие часы ты хочешь купить?

   — _____

3. — Какую собаку ты хочешь купить?

   — _____

4. — Какой магнитофон ты хочешь купить?

   — _____

5. — Какой торт ты хочешь купить?

   — _____

6. — Какие кассеты ты хочешь купить?

   — _____

Clause links: который

Ж. As a child you probably learned about the house that Jack built. Here is an adapted Russian version of it. Insert the correct form of **который** (**которая, которое, которые**) in each of the blanks. The first blank has been filled in for you.

Вот дом, <u>который</u> построил (*built*) Джек. А это молодой аспирант, _____¹ живёт в доме, _____² построил Джек. А это статьи, _____³ пишет аспирант, _____⁴ живёт в доме, _____⁵ построил Джек. А это соседка, _____⁶ читает статьи, _____⁷ пишет аспирант, _____⁸ живёт в доме, _____⁹ построил Джек. А это директор, _____¹⁰ знает соседку, _____¹¹ читает статьи, _____¹² пишет аспирант, _____¹³ живёт в доме, _____¹⁴ построил Джек.

З. You are at the pet market in Moscow, looking for a dog to buy. Below are some of the dogs that you see. For each one, tell whether or not you would want that dog. Use a **который** clause.

ОБРАЗЕЦ: Эта собака любит играть.

Эта собака даёт лапу (*paw* ["*shakes hands*"]).

Эта собака не смотрит на меня.

Урок 5, Часть четвёртая

Эта собáка весь день спит.

Эта собáка чáсто лáет (barks).

ОБРАЗЕ́Ц: Я хочу́ собáку, котóрая лю́бит игрáть.
or   Я не хочу́ собáку, котóрая лю́бит игрáть.

1. _____
2. _____
3. _____
4. _____

Round-trip and habitual travel: ходи́ть, éздить

И. Combine the given words to tell where each person goes. For the first group of sentences, use **ходи́ть**; for the second group, use **éздить**. Choose the correct preposition to go with each destination — either «**в**» or «**на**».

ОБРАЗЕ́Ц: (ходи́ть) бáбушка / магази́н / кáждое у́тро

Бáбушка хóдит в магази́н кáждое у́тро.

ходи́ть

1. мои́ друзья́ / университéт / кáждый день

_____

2. мы / рéдко / ресторáн

_____

3. я / рабóта / кáждый день

_____

4. Áня / библиотéка / кáждый вéчер

_____

5. мои́ роди́тели / чáсто / концéрты

_____

éздить

1. моя́ семья́ / Ки́ев / кáждый год

_____

2. мы / чáсто / Чикáго

_____

192   Урóк 5, Часть четвёртая

Name_____ Date_____ Class_____

3. я / ре́дко / Санкт-Петербу́рг

_____

4. Кругло́вы / Герма́ния / ка́ждый год

_____

5. Скотт / ча́сто / Росси́я

_____

К. Below is a map of places frequented by the Velichkin family. Describe where the individual family members go. This time you will have to decide whether to use **ходи́ть** or **е́здить**. For the purposes of this exercise, let's say that the parents and kids probably walk to locations 2 kilometers away or less. The grandparents, however, resort to riding the bus for anything beyond 500 meters. Remember to add «в» or «на» according to the destination.

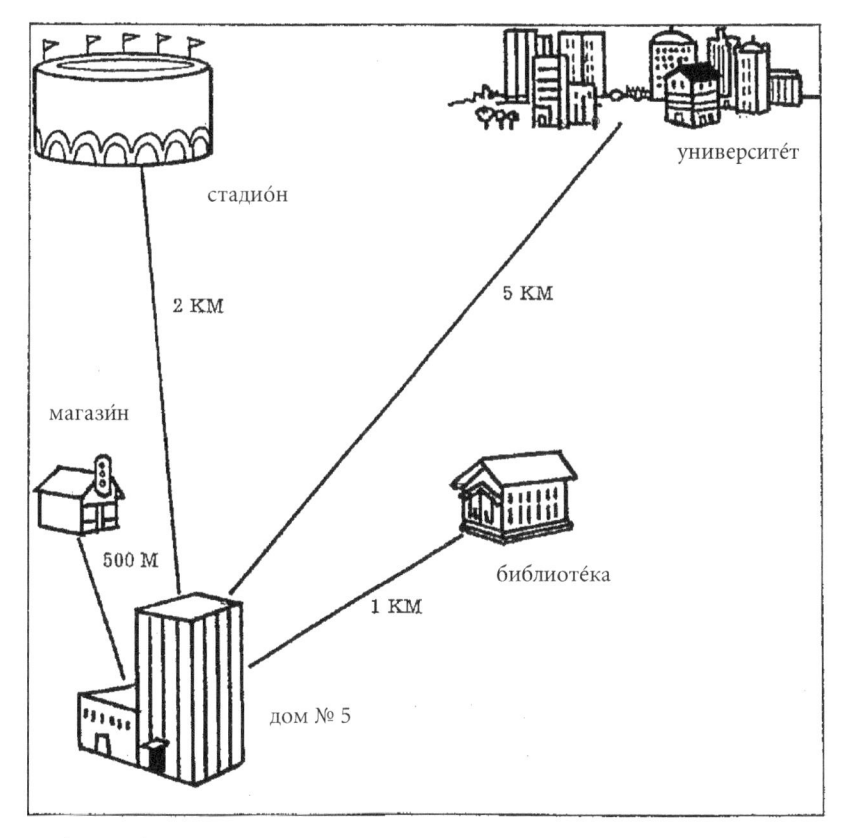

стадио́н

2 КМ

университе́т

5 КМ

магази́н

500 М

библиоте́ка

1 КМ

дом № 5

ОБРАЗЕЦ: А́лик и О́ля / библиоте́ка / ка́ждый день
        А́лик и О́ля хо́дят в библиоте́ку ка́ждый день.

1. А́лик / университе́т / ка́ждый день

_____

2. роди́тели / ча́сто / магази́н

_____

3. я / стадио́н / ка́ждую сре́ду

_____

4. бабушка и дедушка / библиотека / каждое воскресенье

   _____

5. дедушка / редко / стадион

   _____

6. я / университет / каждый вторник

   _____

7. мы / магазин / каждую субботу

   _____

Перевод

Л. Translate the following dialogue into Russian.

"Is that your grandmother?"
"No, that woman is my brother's teacher."
"Is your grandmother here?"
"Yes, she's over there—the woman who's reading the magazine."

_____

_____

_____

_____

Повторение — мать учения

М. Following is a summary of the reading in Part 4. Fill in the blanks with words that maintain the context of the reading. You will have to change the form of some of the words. Use each word only once.

Мы в кафе _____¹ от университета. Мы видим Джима, Илью Ильича и Таню. Джим — аспирант _____², а Таня — дочь его _____³ друга, Андрея Викторовича Жилинского. Андрей Викторович живёт в Петербурге и редко _____⁴ в Москву. Официант Тани, Джима и Ильи Ильича — _____⁵ парень, _____⁶ открывает бутылку. Илья Ильич заказывает (*orders*) _____⁷ воду, Таня и Джим заказывают кофе, _____⁸ пирожное (*pastry*) и _____⁹ торт.	ездить Илья Ильич который миндальный (*almond*) минеральный недалеко старый тот шоколадный (*chocolate*)

194   Урок 5, Часть четвёртая

Name_____ Date_____ Class_____

Ситуа́ции

H. How would you ...

1. tell somebody that this is your apartment?

2. tell somebody that this car is yours?

3. tell somebody that this book is interesting but that one is not (interesting)?

4. tell somebody that you want to buy postcards, toothpaste, and shampoo?

5. tell somebody that you saw the nice American guy who studies at Moscow (**Моско́вский**) university?

6. ask your classmate if she goes to the library every day?

7. ask your professor if she often travels to Uzbekistan?

Ва́ша о́чередь!

O. Answer the questions that are asked of you.

1. Э́тот рюкза́к твой и́ли мой?

2. Каки́е кни́ги ты лю́бишь чита́ть?

3. Каку́ю му́зыку ты лю́бишь слу́шать?

4. Ты хорошо́ зна́ешь студе́нта, кото́рый е́здил в Ирку́тск?

5. Ты ча́сто хо́дишь в рестора́н?

6. Ты ча́сто е́здишь в Нью-Йо́рк?

Уро́к 5, Часть четвёртая

Сочинéние

П. Write a short paragraph (about five or six sentences) about your life this quarter/semester as a student. Ideas: Do you go to the library frequently? What kind of books are you reading? Are you writing any term papers? Do you often go to a café or restaurant? Which particular person also goes?

_____
_____
_____
_____
_____
_____

Fun with grammar! Case review

P. Fill in the blanks of the following sentences with the appropriate case endings. Not all blanks, however, will have an ending. Then enter the words into the crossword puzzle below to help check your spelling. The letter-number combinations (e.g., **г12**) at the end of each sentence indicate the location of the word or words in the puzzle. The first letter and number are for the first word and so on. Note that **г** is for **горизонтáль,** or horizontal; **в** is for **вертикáль,** or vertical.

1. Здесь нет хорóш_____ аптéк_____. (в8) (в18)
2. Мúша живёт на четвёрт_____ этаж_____. (г20) (в15)
3. Ты знáешь мо_____ (*my*) преподавáтел_____? (в5) (в6)
4. Онá купúла óчень интерéсн_____ кнúг_____. (г22) (г2)
5. Где мо_____ (*my*) рюкзáк_____? Ты _____ (*it*) не вúдишь? (в13) (в10) (в4)
6. Кудá ты идёшь? В библиотéк_____? (в16)
7. Пётр óчень хорошó игрáет на контрабáс_____. (в2)
8. У наш_____ сосéд_____ нóвая машúна. (г3) (в7)
9. О как_____ óпер_____ вы говорúте? (г14) (г9)
10. Это замечáтельн_____ стать_____. Ты _____ (*it*) читáла? (г12) (г17) (в21)
11. Я в_____ (*you*) плóхо понимáю. (в1)
12. Вот дирéктор наш_____ общежúти_____. (г11) (г19)

196 Урóк 5, Часть четвёртая

Name _____ Date _____ Class _____

[Crossword puzzle grid with numbered squares: 1, 2, 3, 4, 5, 6, 7, 8, 9, 10, 11, 12, 13, 14, 15, 16, 17, 18, 19, 20, 21, 22]

РАБОТА В ЛАБОРАТОРИИ

ДИАЛОГИ

Диалог 1 Что бу́дете зака́зывать? (Ordering food)

AA. Follow along as you listen to the dialogue.

ОФИЦИА́НТ. Что бу́дете зака́зывать?
ТО́ЛЯ. Ва́ля, что бу́дем зака́зывать? Что ты хо́чешь?
ВА́ЛЯ. Я хочу́ шокола́дный торт.
ТО́ЛЯ. Но ты же на дие́те!
ВА́ЛЯ. Я была́ вчера́ на дие́те. Я не могу́ быть на дие́те ка́ждый день!

- Now read and repeat aloud in the pause after each phrase.
- Now read the lines for **То́ля** aloud.
- Now read the lines for **Ва́ля** aloud.

1. Why is the man surprised to hear that the woman wants chocolate cake?
   _____

2. How does she justify it? _____

Диалог 2 Вы ча́сто е́здите туда́? (Discussing travel)

ББ. Follow along as you listen to the dialogue.

(*Two acquaintances run into each other on the train to St. Petersburg.*)

А. Вале́рий Петро́вич! Вы то́же е́дете в Петербу́рг на конфере́нцию?
Б. В Петербу́рг, но не на конфере́нцию.
А. Вы ча́сто е́здите туда́?
Б. Да, у меня́ там сын. А вы, ка́жется, живёте в Петербу́рге?
А. Жил. Сейча́с я живу́ в Москве́. Но я то́же ча́сто е́зжу в Петербу́рг. У меня́ там ста́рые друзья́ — ведь я там учи́лся.

- Now read and repeat aloud in the pause after each phrase.
- Now read the lines for speaker **Б** aloud.
- Now read the lines for speaker **А** aloud.

Imagine that the two speakers meet as they are walking up to the university campus. Rewrite the first three lines so that speaker **А** is asking about a concert at the university.

А. _____
Б. _____
А. _____

АУДИ́РОВАНИЕ

ВВ. How would you translate into English what the speaker says?

ОБРАЗЕ́Ц: Э́та кни́га моя́.

    а. _____ That's my book. (naming something)

    б. __X__ That book is mine. (distinguishing one book from other books)

1. а. _____ That's a pretty skirt. (naming something)

   б. _____ That skirt is pretty. (distinguishing one skirt from other skirts)

2. а. _____ This is a nice (good) library. (naming something)

   б. _____ This library is nice (good). (distinguishing one library from other libraries)

3. а. _____ This is my radio. (naming something)

   б. _____ This radio is mine. (distinguishing one radio from other radios)

4. а. _____ That's my dorm. (naming something)

   б. _____ That dorm is mine. (distinguishing one dorm from other dorms)

5. а. _____ That's our garage. (naming something)

   б. _____ That garage is ours. (distinguishing one garage from other garages)

6. а. _____ These are your cassettes. (naming something)

   б. _____ These cassettes are yours. (distinguishing one set of cassettes from other sets)

7. а. _____ That's expensive chocolate. (naming something)

   б. _____ That chocolate is expensive. (distinguishing one type of chocolate from other types)

Name_____ Date_____ Class_____

ГГ. Which adjective has the correct grammatical ending for the question you hear?

ОБРАЗЕЦ: Какой торт ты хо́чешь купи́ть?

   а. _____ Дороги́е.

   б. __X__ Дорого́й.

   в. _____ Дорого́го.

1. а. _____ Япо́нский.
 б. _____ Япо́нскую.
 в. _____ Япо́нского.

2. а. _____ Рези́новые.
 б. _____ Рези́новый.
 в. _____ Рези́новое.

3. а. _____ В италья́нский.
 б. _____ В италья́нском.
 в. _____ В италья́нское.

4. а. _____ Недорого́й.
 б. _____ Недорого́е.
 в. _____ Недорогу́ю.

5. а. _____ Ру́сскую.
 б. _____ Ру́сского.
 в. _____ Ру́сский.

6. а. _____ Хоро́ший и недорого́й.
 б. _____ Хоро́шего и недорого́го.
 в. _____ Хоро́шую и недорогу́ю.

ДД. The speaker is describing various people to you, using **кото́рый** clauses. Match the two things he says about each person.

ОБРАЗЕЦ: Сосе́д, кото́рый живёт на тре́тьем этаже́, о́чень симпати́чный.

Об. __д__ The neighbor is very nice.

1. _____ The American speaks Russian very well.   а. They are always late.
2. _____ We have students in our group.   б. We bought them.
3. _____ Do you know that girl?   в. He's opening the door.
4. _____ Who is that guy?   г. He's parking the car.
5. _____ Where are the books?   д. ~~He lives on the third floor.~~
6. _____ The young man is our neighbor.   е. She plays the piano very well.
     ж. She lives in our dorm.

Уро́к 5, Часть четвёртая   199

ГОВОРЕНИЕ

ЕЕ. Contrast the following items, using **этот/тот, эта/та, это/то, эти/те**.

ОБРАЗЕЦ: *You hear and see:* (a nice neighbor and a not so nice one)
You say: Этот сосед симпатичный, а тот несимпатичный.

1. (an expensive car and a not so expensive one)
2. (a big house and a small one)
3. (an old dorm and a new one)
4. (an old waiter and a young one)
5. (a pretty city and a not so pretty one)
6. (a good play and a bad one)

ЖЖ. Add the cued adjective to the sentences you hear. Pay attention to the endings!

ОБРАЗЕЦ: *You hear:* Я читаю книгу.
You see: (interesting)
You say: Я читаю интересную книгу.

1. (difficult)
2. (new)
3. (inexpensive)
4. (imported)
5. (different)
6. (interesting)

33. How would you say that a person often goes to a certain place? Use the verbs **ходить** and **ездить**. Remember, if you're talking about going to a concert, school, or restaurant, use **ходить**.

ОБРАЗЕЦ: *You hear and see:* (I, the library)
You say: Я часто хожу в библиотеку.

1. (I, Тула [a town])
2. (my parents, concerts)
3. (we, Саратов [a town])
4. (I, the post office)
5. (grandma, the outpatient clinic)
6. (we, restaurant)

Name _____ Date _____ Class _____

НОВЫЕ СОСЕДИ, НОВЫЕ ДРУЗЬЯ

УРОК 6

ЧАСТЬ ПЕРВАЯ

«Ты» и «вы»

РАБОТА ДОМА

ПИСЬМО

Понимáние тéкста

А. To which characters do the descriptions on the right apply? Review the visuals and reading on pages 229–231 of the textbook, then write the letter of the descriptions next to the appropriate person.

1. _____ Сáша
2. _____ Лéна
3. _____ Вóва
4. _____ Кóля
5. _____ учи́тельница му́зыки Сáши

а. Ему́ пять лет.
б. говори́т, как учи́тельница
в. игрáл Гéршвина
г. хóчет знать, скóлько лет Бéлке
д. говори́т, что прелю́д Гéршвина — замечáтельная му́зыка
е. некульту́рный
ж. у́чится на вторóм ку́рсе
з. óчень стрóгая
и. у́чится в шестóм клáссе
к. ду́мает, что онá краси́вая

Dative case

Б. Identify the direct and indirect objects in each sentence below. Underline the direct object with a single line and the indirect object with a double line. Remember that the indirect object in English can be expressed with the preposition *for* or *to*. Remember also that a direct or indirect object in Russian can go at the beginning of a sentence, as required by context.

ОБРАЗЕЦ: I read *the book* *to my brother*.

1. Did you give your cousin the magazines?
2. We wrote a long letter to our professor.
3. Aren't you going to send a card to Grandma and Grandpa?
4. Throw Mike the ball!
5. What did you buy for your host family?
6. Мы отдаём Андрею его книгу.
7. — Что ты купил маме и папе?

    — Маме я купил тостер, а папе — торт.
8. Статьи она читает бабушке, а пьесу Чехова — дедушке.
9. Ты говоришь ему «ты»?
10. Молодой человек продаёт машину соседу.

Б. Oleg is a super salesperson—the kind who can get people to buy what they don't need. Use the people and items in the boxes below (or make up your own) to show some of his unusual sales.

молодая девушка
наша строгая преподавательница
несимпатичный миллионер
твоя красивая соседка
наш новый директор
русский автомеханик
молодая скрипачка
старый официант
американский саксофонист
~~моя бабушка~~

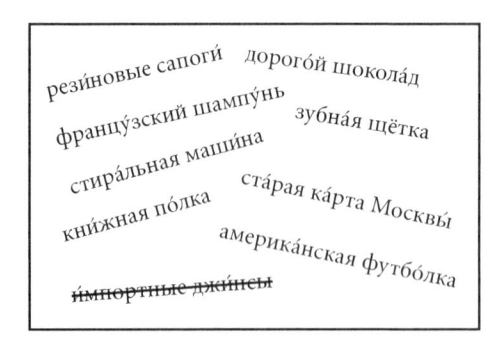

резиновые сапоги   дорогой шоколад
французский шампунь   зубная щётка
стиральная машина
книжная полка   старая карта Москвы
американская футболка
~~импортные джинсы~~

ОБРАЗЕЦ: <u>Олег продаёт моей бабушке импортные джинсы.</u>

1. _____
2. _____
3. _____
4. _____
5. _____
6. _____

Г. Replace the underlined words with the correct form of the Nominative or Dative pronoun.

ОБРАЗЕЦ: <u>Елена</u> читает <u>брату</u> книгу. → <u>Она</u> читает <u>ему</u> книгу.

1. <u>Виктор</u> отдаёт <u>Лене</u> кассеты.

_____

202   Урок 6, Часть первая

Name_____ Date_____ Class_____

2. Воло́дя говори́т Та́не и Ви́ке «ты».
   _____

3. Ната́лья Ива́новна говори́т Ми́ше, что она́ лю́бит му́зыку Чайко́вского.
   _____

4. Мари́на продаёт маши́ну Ди́ме и А́не.
   _____

5. Ви́ка пи́шет письмо́ профе́ссору Петро́ву.
   _____

6. Ты хо́чешь купи́ть Татья́не Дми́триевне цветы́?
   _____

Telling your age: Ско́лько тебе́ лет? (and cardinal numerals through 49)

Д. Your host brother is showing you some pictures of his family. How would you ask him how old the individual family members were at the time the pictures were taken?

ОБРАЗЕЦ: — Э́то моя́ ма́ма.
— Ско́лько лет твое́й ма́ме на э́той фотогра́фии?

1. — Э́то моя́ жена́.
   — _____?

2. — Э́то моя́ сестра́.
   — _____?

3. — Э́то её муж.
   — _____?

4. — Э́то его́ де́душка.
   — _____?

5. — Э́то мой брат.
   — _____?

6. — Э́то моя́ ба́бушка.
   — _____?

7. — Э́то наш ста́рый друг, Бо́ря.
   — _____?

Уро́к 6, Часть пе́рвая

E. Below are the portraits of two related families—Dmitri's grandfathers, aunts, uncles, and cousins. Use these portraits to answer the following questions. Don't forget: When a person's age is given, that person's name must appear in the Dative case. For this exercise do not include last names in your answers.

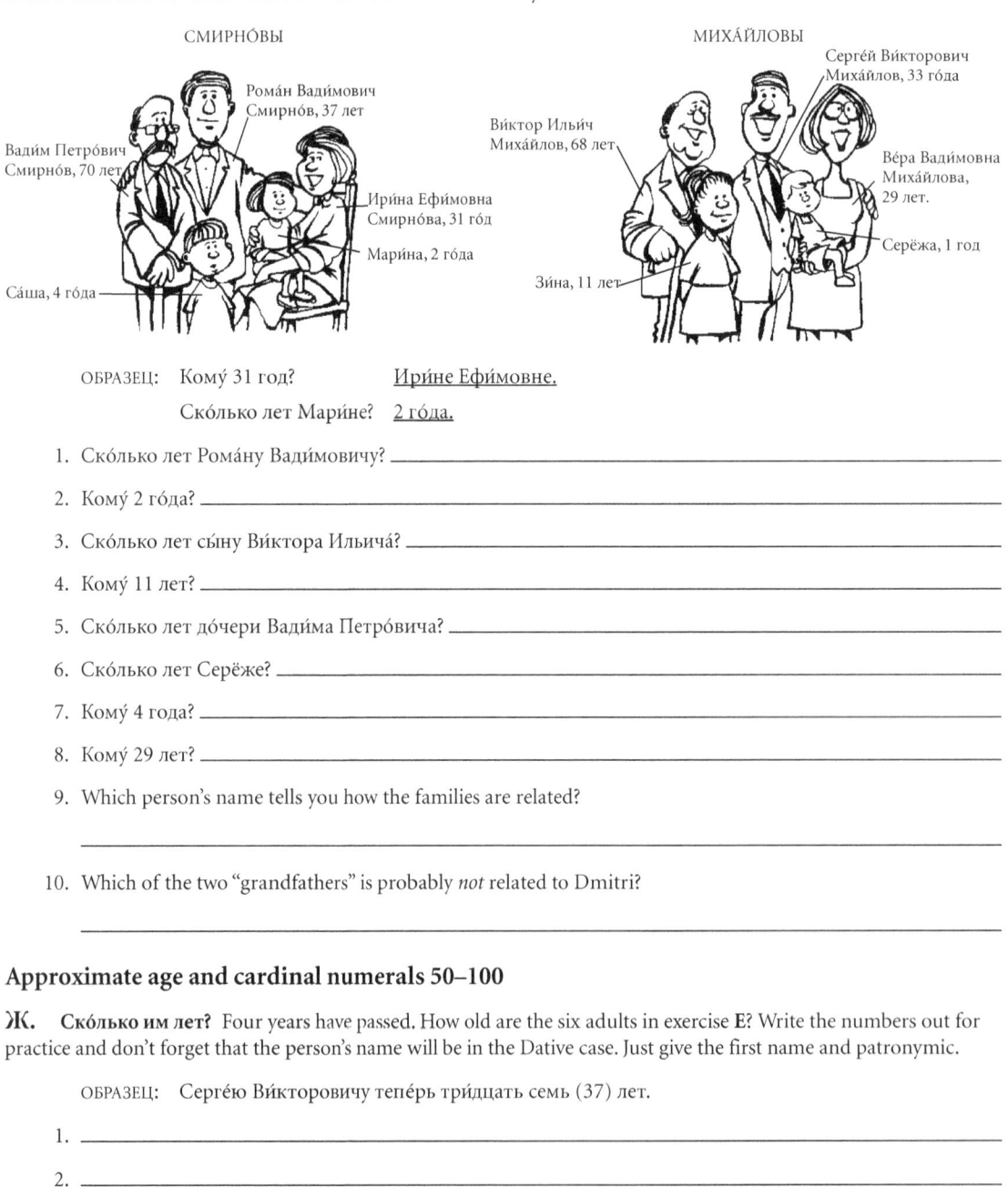

СМИРНО́ВЫ

Вади́м Петро́вич Смирно́в, 70 лет
Рома́н Вади́мович Смирно́в, 37 лет
Ири́на Ефи́мовна Смирно́ва, 31 год
Мари́на, 2 го́да
Са́ша, 4 го́да

МИХА́ЙЛОВЫ

Ви́ктор Ильи́ч Миха́йлов, 68 лет
Серге́й Ви́кторович Миха́йлов, 33 го́да
Ве́ра Вади́мовна Миха́йлова, 29 лет.
Серёжа, 1 год
Зи́на, 11 лет.

ОБРАЗЕ́Ц: Кому́ 31 год? <u>Ири́не Ефи́мовне.</u>

Ско́лько лет Мари́не? <u>2 го́да.</u>

1. Ско́лько лет Рома́ну Вади́мовичу? _____
2. Кому́ 2 го́да? _____
3. Ско́лько лет сы́ну Ви́ктора Ильича́? _____
4. Кому́ 11 лет? _____
5. Ско́лько лет до́чери Вади́ма Петро́вича? _____
6. Ско́лько лет Серёже? _____
7. Кому́ 4 го́да? _____
8. Кому́ 29 лет? _____
9. Which person's name tells you how the families are related?
_____

10. Which of the two "grandfathers" is probably *not* related to Dmitri?
_____

Approximate age and cardinal numerals 50–100

Ж. Ско́лько им лет? Four years have passed. How old are the six adults in exercise **E**? Write the numbers out for practice and don't forget that the person's name will be in the Dative case. Just give the first name and patronymic.

ОБРАЗЕ́Ц: Серге́ю Ви́кторовичу тепе́рь три́дцать семь (37) лет.

1. _____
2. _____
3. _____
4. _____
5. _____

204 Уро́к 6, Часть пе́рвая

Name_____ Date_____ Class_____

3. Below are several members of Zina's family and the year in which she thinks they were born. Assuming it is now the year 2005, approximately how old is each person?

ОБРАЗЕЦ: Марина Игнатьевна, *around* 1940

<u>Я думаю, что ей лет 65.</u>

1. Сергей Валентинович, *around* 1935 _____
2. Мария Матвеевна, *around* 1950 _____
3. Иван Гаврилович, *around* 1965 _____
4. Виталий, *around* 1980 _____
5. Даша, *around* 1990 _____

И. **Fun with numbers!** Connect the dots on the following picture and you will see a favorite toy of Russian children. Follow the order of numbers as given below. The first two dots have been connected for you.

пятьдесят семь	пятьдесят	шестьдесят	сорок семь
сорок два	тридцать один	двадцать два	девяносто шесть
девяносто пять	шестьдесят восемь	семьдесят пять	двадцать
восемьдесят три	тридцать шесть	восемнадцать	пятьдесят один
двенадцать	сорок пять	тридцать девять	девятнадцать
двадцать шесть	девяносто семь	шестьдесят три	семьдесят три
семьдесят четыре	восемьдесят пять	восемьдесят восемь	пятьдесят семь

Перевод

К. Translate the following dialogue into Russian.

"Are you doing your homework?"
"No, I'm writing a letter to my brother."
"Where does he live?"
"In Arizona."
(*Pointing to a nearby picture.*) "Is that him in the picture?"
"Yes, but here he's only twelve years old and now he's twenty-four."

_____
_____
_____
_____
_____
_____
_____

Повторе́ние — мать уче́ния

Л. Following is a summary of the reading in Part 1. Fill in the blanks with words that maintain the context of the reading. You will have to change the form of some of the words. Use each word only once.

Ле́на Си́лина и Са́ша Кругло́в студе́нты. Они́ говоря́т _____[1] «ты». Са́ша у́чится на второ́м _____.[2] Во́ва, брат Ле́ны, ещё у́чится в шко́ле, в шесто́м _____.[3] Во́ва то́же хо́чет говори́ть _____[4] «ты», но Ле́на ду́мает, что э́то _____.[5] Пото́м Во́ва ви́дит Ко́лю. _____[6] то́лько пять лет. Во́ва говори́т, что Ко́ля до́лжен говори́ть _____[7] «вы». Ко́ля хо́чет знать, ско́лько лет _____[8] Во́вы.	друг дру́гу Ко́ля класс курс некульту́рно он Са́ша соба́ка

Ситуа́ции

М. How would you . . .

1. tell somebody that you want to buy your mother some flowers?
_____

2. ask your classmate if he is writing a letter to Anton?
_____

3. tell your father that you bought him a book?
_____

Name_____ Date_____ Class_____

4. ask the neighbor's child how old he is?
   _____

5. tell somebody that you think Uncle Misha is 52 years old?
   _____

6. tell somebody that your music teacher is about 50 years old?
   _____

7. tell somebody that your brother is a freshman (first-year student in college)?
   _____

Ва́ша о́чередь!

Н. Answer the questions that are asked of you.

1. Что ты купи́л (купи́ла) ма́ме на день рожде́ния?
   _____

2. Что ты купи́л (купи́ла) па́пе на день рожде́ния?
   _____

3. Кому́ ты хо́чешь купи́ть ру́сский сувени́р?
   _____

4. Ско́лько тебе́ лет?
   _____

5. Ско́лько лет твое́й сестре́?
   _____

6. Ско́лько лет твоему́ бра́ту?
   _____

7. На како́м ты ку́рсе?
   _____

Сочине́ние

О. A rich relative just sent you some money, and you want to buy your family and friends some nice presents. Write a short paragraph (five or six sentences) about what you would buy for whom and tell why. For example, maybe you want to buy your mother some new cassettes because she likes to listen to music.

_____
_____
_____
_____
_____

РАБОТА В ЛАБОРАТОРИИ

ДИАЛОГИ

Диалог 1 Ско́лько лет твоему́ дру́гу? (Discussing age)

АА. Follow along as you listen to the dialogue.

А. Ско́лько лет твоему́ дру́гу?
Б. Два́дцать три.
А. Где он у́чится?
Б. В университе́те.
А. На како́м факульте́те?
Б. На хими́ческом.
А. А на како́м ку́рсе?
Б. На второ́м.

- Now read and repeat aloud in the pause after each phrase.
- Now read the lines for speaker **Б** aloud.
- Now read the lines for speaker **А** aloud.

Rewrite the dialogue so that speaker **А** is asking the questions of you. Answer truthfully—or give yourself the perfect age! The first line is given for you.

А. Ско́лько тебе́ лет?

Б. _____

А. _____

Б. _____

А. _____

Б. _____

А. _____

Б. _____

Диалог 2 Ей то́лько оди́ннадцать лет (Discussing age)

ББ. Follow along as you listen to the dialogue.

А. Твоя́ сестра́ о́чень краси́вая.
Б. Она́ то́же так ду́мает.
А. Ско́лько ей лет?
Б. Она́ ещё ма́ленькая, ей то́лько оди́ннадцать лет.
А. А тебе́ ско́лько?
Б. Мне уже́ четы́рнадцать!

- Now read and repeat aloud in the pause after each phrase.
- Now read the lines for speaker **Б** aloud.
- Now read the lines for speaker **А** aloud.

1. How old is speaker **Б**'s sister? _____

2. How old is speaker **Б**? _____

3. What do the words **то́лько** and **уже́** indicate about speaker **Б**'s attitude?

_____

Name_____ Date_____ Class_____

АУДИРОВАНИЕ

ВВ. Listen to the sentences and identify what was done and to or for whom.

ОБРАЗЕЦ: Я купи́ла ба́бушке краси́вые цветы́.

	кому́	что
I bought	_grandmother_	_pretty flowers_
1. I usually read	_____	_____
2. The parents bought	_____	_____
3. Olya is writing	_____	_____
4. I bought	_____	_____
5. We gave	_____	_____
6. Fedya bought	_____	_____

ГГ. Match the people in the left-hand column with their appropriate age on the right.

ОБРАЗЕЦ: Мое́й тёте со́рок во́семь лет.

Об. __в__ aunt   а. 51
1. _____ mother   б. 68
2. _____ father   ~~в. 48~~
3. _____ brother   г. 9
4. _____ sister   д. 47
5. _____ uncle   е. 73
6. _____ grandfather   ж. 19
7. _____ grandmother   з. 49
8. _____ dog   и. 12

ДД. Listen to the following paragraph about Misha and answer the questions below in English.

ОБРАЗЕЦ: What is Misha's last name? _Golubev_

1. What is Misha's major? _____
2. What year is he in? _____
3. Where does he live? _____
4. How old is he? _____
5. What kind of music does Misha like? _____
6. Which sports does he like? _____

ГОВОРЕНИЕ

EE. Using the cues in parentheses, say that you would like to buy something for a certain person.

ОБРАЗЕЦ: *You hear and see:* (*my grandfather, a chess set*)
You say: Я хочу́ купи́ть моему́ де́душке ша́хматы.

1. (*my brother, an alarm clock*)
2. (*my sister, pastries*)
3. (*my friend, poodle*)
4. (*my [female] friend, a blouse*)
5. (*my aunt, a cake*)
6. (*my uncle, a suitcase*)

ЖЖ. Say the age of each of the following people.

ОБРАЗЕЦ: *You hear and see:* (Га́ля; 22)
You say: Га́ле два́дцать два го́да.

1. (Ва́ня; 13)
2. (Тама́ра Кири́ловна; 41)
3. (Зи́на; 6)
4. (Бори́с; 24)
5. (Никола́й Леони́дович; 57)
6. (Лю́да; 33)
7. (Васи́лий Ви́кторович; 90)

33. Say that each of the following people is *approximately* the age given.

ОБРАЗЕЦ: *You hear and see:* (Све́та; 5)
You say: Све́те лет пять.

1. (Серге́й Никола́евич; 60)
2. (А́лла Миха́йловна; 45)
3. (Да́ша; 15)
4. (Ве́ра Никола́евна; 50)
5. (Анато́лий Алекса́ндрович; 75)
6. (И́горь; 25)

Name_____ Date_____ Class_____

ЧАСТЬ ВТОРАЯ
Вы сдаёте комнату?

РАБОТА ДОМА

ПИСЬМО

Понимание текста

А. Review the reading on pages 241–242 of the textbook. Then see if you can complete the following sentences with the name of the correct characters. You may need to change the case endings of the names for a couple of the sentences.

Илья Ильич   Таня
Татьяна Дмитриевна   Света
сын Татьяны Дмитриевны   Джим
Татьяна Дмитриевна и её сын

1. _____ сдаёт комнату.

2. Тане сказал о комнате _____.

3. У _____ только один стол.

4. _____ очень любят книги.

5. _____ сейчас в армии.

6. Фамилия _____ — Лебедева,

   фамилия _____ — Жилинская.

7. _____ — сосед Татьяны Дмитриевны.

8. _____ учится на историческом факультете.

9. _____ учится в медицинском институте, на втором курсе.

10. Студенты очень любят _____.

Liking something: (мне) нравится...

Б. A classmate is asking you about your preferences. Indicate whether you like or dislike the things your classmate asks about. Remember that **нравится** indicates that the subject is singular whereas **нравятся** indicates that the subject is plural.

ОБРАЗЕЦ: — Тебе нравятся фильмы Стивена Спилберга?
          — <u>Нет, мне не нравятся фильмы Стивена Спилберга.</u>

1. — Тебе нравится рок-музыка?

   — _____

2. — Тебе нравится твой университет?

   — _____

Урок 6, Часть вторая   211

3. — Тебе нравятся немецкие (*German*) машины?
   — _____

4. — Тебе нравится классическая музыка?
   — _____

5. — Тебе нравятся романы (*novels*) Стивена Кинга?
   — _____

6. — Тебе нравятся японские компьютеры?
   — _____

7. — Тебе нравится жить в этом городе?
   — _____

8. — Тебе нравится говорить по-русски?
   — _____

B. How would you say that the following people like the following things or like to do the following activities?

ОБРАЗЕЦ: Митя; новый книжный шкаф

Мите очень нравится новый книжный шкаф.

1. мой друг; читать о русской истории
   _____

2. наша соседка; наши новые картины
   _____

3. этот парень; яичница
   _____

4. моя подруга; пьесы Чехова
   _____

5. мы; хозяйка
   _____

6. они; фотография
   _____

Name_____ Date_____ Class_____

Нра́виться and люби́ть

Г. The sentences below express a liking of a thing or an activity. Rewrite them so that the feeling expressed is either stronger (if the original sentence uses **нра́виться**, rewrite it with **люби́ть**) or less strong (if the original sentence uses **люби́ть**, rewrite it with **нра́виться**).

ОБРАЗЕЦ: Ей нра́вится рок-му́зыка.
Она́ лю́бит рок-му́зыку.

1. Мне нра́вятся истори́ческие фи́льмы.
_____

2. Ты лю́бишь му́зыку Проко́фьева?
_____

3. Нам о́чень нра́вится Сан-Франци́ско.
_____

4. Вы лю́бите фи́льмы Кли́нта И́ствуда?
_____

5. Он лю́бит сыр «рокфо́р».
_____

6. Им о́чень нра́вится гуля́ть в па́рке.
_____

Verbs: The future *will, will be*

Д. Following is a chart of your activities for Saturday. Your friends are trying to arrange a get-together and want to know what you will be doing at certain times. Tell them!

8.00 утра́ (A.M.)	до́ма
9.00	до́ма
10.00	на рабо́те
11.00	на рабо́те
12.00	на рабо́те
1.00 дня (P.M.)	в кафе́
2.00	игра́ть в те́ннис
3.00	до́ма
4.00	в библиоте́ке
5.00	в библиоте́ке
6.00 ве́чера (P.M.)	в рестора́не
7.00	смотре́ть телеви́зор
8.00	смотре́ть телеви́зор

ОБРАЗЕЦ: 3.00 дня: <u>Я бу́ду до́ма.</u>

1. 2.00 дня: _____
2. 7.00 ве́чера: _____
3. 4.00 дня: _____
4. 11.00 утра́: _____
5. 1.00 дня: _____
6. 6.00 ве́чера: _____
7. 8.00 утра́: _____

E. Use the words or phrases in the box below to answer the following questions or make up logical variations of your own.

```
         в университе́те
               смотре́ть фильм «Эрин Бро́кович»
   игра́ть в футбо́л          в теа́тре
         в Сара́тове    гуля́ть в па́рке
                  де́лать дома́шнее зада́ние
       в общежи́тии
              на рабо́те
```

ОБРАЗЕЦ: Где вы бу́дете за́втра ве́чером? <u>За́втра ве́чером мы бу́дем в теа́тре.</u>

1. Что твой брат бу́дет де́лать за́втра у́тром?
   _____

2. Где ты бу́дешь в сре́ду?
   _____

3. Что Лёна бу́дет де́лать сего́дня ве́чером?
   _____

4. Где твои́ роди́тели бу́дут в суббо́ту и в воскресе́нье?
   _____

5. Что мы бу́дем де́лать в понеде́льник ве́чером?
   _____

6. Где ты бу́дешь жить в Москве́?
   _____

Name_____ Date_____ Class_____

Nouns ending in -ция/-сия

Ж. Following is a list of Russian cognates ending in **-ция**. Match them with their English counterpart. The first one is done for you.

1. __л__ абстра́кция   а. activization
2. _____ абсо́рбция   б. administration
3. _____ адапта́ция   в. annotation
4. _____ администра́ция   г. amplification
5. _____ аккумуля́ция   д. accumulation
6. _____ акклиматиза́ция   е. absorption
7. _____ активиза́ция   ж. ammunition
8. _____ аллитера́ция   з. adaptation
9. _____ амплифика́ция   и. amputation
10. _____ ампута́ция   к. acclimatization
11. _____ амуни́ция   л. ~~abstraction~~
12. _____ аннота́ция   м. alliteration

Command forms (Imperatives)

З. Which would be the most logical command for the following situations?

[box containing: слу́шайте, помоги́те, чита́йте, говори́те, игра́йте, смотри́те, ~~пиши́те~~]

ОБРАЗЕЦ: У вас нет моего́ а́дреса? Вот ру́чка. <u>Пиши́те!</u>

1. Мой компью́тер не рабо́тает. Я не зна́ю, что де́лать. _____!
2. Ничего́ не слы́шно. _____ гро́мко!
3. Почему́ вы спи́те на уро́ке? _____!
4. Это неинтере́сная статья́. Не _____ её.
5. Это ужа́сный фильм. Не _____ его́.

И. Rewrite the same commands using the **ты** form.

ОБРАЗЕЦ: <u>Пиши!</u>

1. _____!
2. _____ гро́мко!
3. _____!
4. Не _____ её.
5. Не _____ его́.

Перевóд

К. Translate the following dialogue into Russian.

"Where are you living?"
"Not far from the university."
"Do you like your apartment?"
"Very much. And I also like my new neighbors."

_____

_____

_____

_____

Повторéние — мать учéния

Л. Following is a summary of the reading in Part 2. Fill in the blanks with words that maintain the context of the reading. You will have to change the form of some of the words. Use each word only once.

Татья́на Дми́триевна _____¹ ко́мнату. Э́то ко́мната её сы́на, _____² сейча́с в а́рмии. В ко́мнате есть крова́ти, сту́лья, кни́жные по́лки, шкаф. Там то́лько нет _____³. Ко́мната о́чень нра́вится _____⁴ и _____⁵. Им нра́вится и _____⁶. Та́ня у́чится в университе́те на _____⁷ факульте́те. Свéта у́чится в медици́нском _____⁸ и рабо́тает на _____⁹ по́мощи.	институ́т истори́ческий кото́рый Свéта сдава́ть ско́рая стол Та́ня хозя́йка

Ситуáции

М. How would you . . .

1. tell somebody that you like watching serious movies?

_____

2. ask your professor if she likes the music of Eric Clapton?

_____

3. say that when you live (=will be living) in Moscow, you will speak only Russian?

_____

_____

Name _____ Date _____ Class _____

4. ask a classmate when she will be at the library tomorrow?
   _____

5. say that unfortunately you don't know what you'll be doing tomorrow?
   _____

6. ask your family to please talk quietly, that grandfather is sleeping?
   _____

7. tell your classmate that you like to play jazz?
   _____

Ва́ша о́чередь!

Н. Answer the questions that are asked of you.

1. Тебе́ нра́вится класси́ческая му́зыка?
   _____

2. Тебе́ нра́вится говори́ть по-ру́сски?
   _____

3. Ты лю́бишь ходи́ть в рестора́ны? в теа́тр?
   _____

4. Где ты бу́дешь за́втра ве́чером?
   _____

5. Когда́ ты бу́дешь де́лать дома́шнее зада́ние? Сего́дня ве́чером? За́втра у́тром?
   _____

6. Где ты бу́дешь жить, когда́ ты бу́дешь в Росси́и?
   _____

Сочине́ние

О. Write a short paragraph (five or six sentences) about the likes and dislikes of your family and/or friends. Ideas: What kind of music do they like? What sports do they like to play or watch? What else do they like to do?

_____
_____
_____
_____
_____

РАБОТА В ЛАБОРАТОРИИ

ДИАЛОГИ

Диалог 1 Какую музыку ты любишь? (Expressing likes and dislikes)

АА. Follow along as you listen to the dialogue.

А. Тебе нравится эта музыка?
Б. Совсем не нравится.
А. А какую музыку ты любишь?
Б. Я люблю классику.

- Now read and repeat aloud in the pause after each phrase.
- Now read the lines for speaker **Б** aloud.
- Now read the lines for speaker **А** aloud.

Rewrite the dialogue so that the speakers are talking about cake rather than music. How would speaker **Б** say that he really likes chocolate (**шоколадный**) cake? Make any necessary changes.

А. _____
Б. _____
А. _____
Б. _____

Диалог 2 Это бесплатно! (Discussing living arrangements)

ББ. Follow along as you listen to the dialogue.

А. Ты живёшь далеко от университета?
Б. Далеко, но зато у меня хорошая квартира. Двухкомнатная.
А. Это, наверно, очень дорого?
Б. Нет, это бесплатно: это квартира моего дяди. Он сейчас в Англии, а мы живём в его квартире.
А. Кто «мы»?
Б. Я и его собака.
А. Теперь я понимаю, почему это бесплатно!

- Now read and repeat aloud in the pause after each phrase.
- Now read the lines for speaker **Б** aloud.
- Now read the lines for speaker **А** aloud.

How would you say, "Now I understand why it's expensive!"

_____

218 Урок 6, Часть вторая

Name_____ Date_____ Class_____

АУДИРОВАНИЕ

ВВ. Identify who likes what or whom in each of the following statements. Remember that word order does not necessarily indicate a word's grammatical role in the sentence.

ОБРАЗЕЦ: Бори́су нра́вятся фи́льмы Ба́рбры Стре́йзанд.

WHO?	likes	WHAT/WHOM?
Boris		_Barbra Streisand movies_

1. _____ _____
2. _____ _____
3. _____ _____
4. _____ _____
5. _____ _____
6. _____ _____
7. _____ _____
8. _____ _____

ГГ. Below is a chart of your day's activities, similar to the one in exercise Д. The speaker wants to know when you will be at certain locations or doing certain things. Fill in the blank with the correct time.

ОБРАЗЕЦ: Когда́ вы бу́дете в библиоте́ке? ___3.00___

10.00	в университе́те
11.00	в университе́те
12.00	в столо́вой
1.00	игра́ть в ша́хматы
2.00	гуля́ть в па́рке
3.00	в библиоте́ке
4.00	смотре́ть фильм «Дра́кула»
5.00	смотре́ть фильм «Дра́кула»
6.00	на стадио́не
7.00	в рестора́не
8.00	в клу́бе

1. _____
2. _____
3. _____
4. _____
5. _____
6. _____
7. _____

ДД. For each of the sentences that you hear, choose the most appropriate continuation from the list below.

ОБРАЗЕЦ: Почему́ вы опа́здываете?

1. _____ Говори́те по-англи́йски!
2. _____ Де́ти, спи́те!
3. _____ Слу́шай!
4. _____ Игра́й!
5. _____ Пиши́!
6. __Об.__ Извини́те!
7. _____ Помоги́те, пожа́луйста!

ГОВОРЕНИЕ

ЕЕ. You will hear a series of statements using the verb **люби́ть** and expressing a strong feeling for a thing or activity. Rephrase the sentence with the verb **нра́виться** to express a less strong feeling.

ОБРАЗЕЦ: *You hear and see:* Мы лю́бим Кана́ду.
You say: Нам нра́вится Кана́да.

1. Я люблю́ смотре́ть ста́рые фотогра́фии.
2. Ты лю́бишь детекти́вы?
3. Он лю́бит Москву́.
4. Они́ лю́бят бале́т.
5. Она́ лю́бит игра́ть в ша́хматы.
6. Вы лю́бите пье́сы Че́хова?

ЖЖ. Use the cued words to say that certain people will be at certain places or doing certain things tomorrow evening.

ОБРАЗЕЦ: *You hear and see:* (Igor; writing a term paper)
You say: За́втра ве́чером И́горь бу́дет писа́ть курсову́ю.

1. (*Lyuda; watching television*)
2. (*the students; at the stadium*)
3. (*Maksim; at the theater*)
4. (*we; writing letters*)
5. (*I; playing basketball*)

33. Tell the following people to do certain things. Use the cued words.

ОБРАЗЕЦ: *You hear and see:* (*Tanya; to speak loudly*)
You say: Та́ня, говори́ гро́мко!

1. (*the children; to sleep*)
2. (*Sonya; to read the article*)
3. (*Mike and Jim; to write to you*)
4. (*Vika and Nadya; to play in the park*)
5. (*Lyuba; to think of Montana*)

ЧАСТЬ ТРЕТЬЯ
На́ша по́чта

РАБО́ТА ДО́МА

ПИСЬМО́

Понима́ние те́кста

А. Review the reading on pages 252–253 of the textbook and match the sentence halves below.

1. Ба́бушка ждёт _____
2. Почтальо́н отдаёт Илье́ Ильичу́ _____
3. На конве́рте _____
4. А́дрес у Ильи́ Ильича́ _____
5. Почтальо́н отдаёт ба́бушке _____
6. Кругло́вы получа́ют _____
7. Си́лины получа́ют _____
8. Сосе́ди отдаю́т _____

а. «Изве́стия».
б. письмо́ и две пе́нсии.
в. «Моско́вские но́вости».
г. краси́вые ма́рки.
д. друг дру́гу газе́ты.
е. два письма́ и бандеро́ль.
ж. в записно́й кни́жке.
з. почтальо́на.

Addressing envelopes

Б. You are in St. Petersburg and want to send New Year's greetings to people you know in other Russian cities. Follow the model on page 254 in the textbook and write the following addresses on each envelope.

1. Matrosov, Ivan, Lesnaya ul., d. 25, kv. 8, Moskva, 129405

2. Petrovskaya, Marina Petrovna, Novaya ul., d. 2, korp. 46, kv. 125, Vologda, 234675
   (The correct form for this last name will be **Петровской.**)

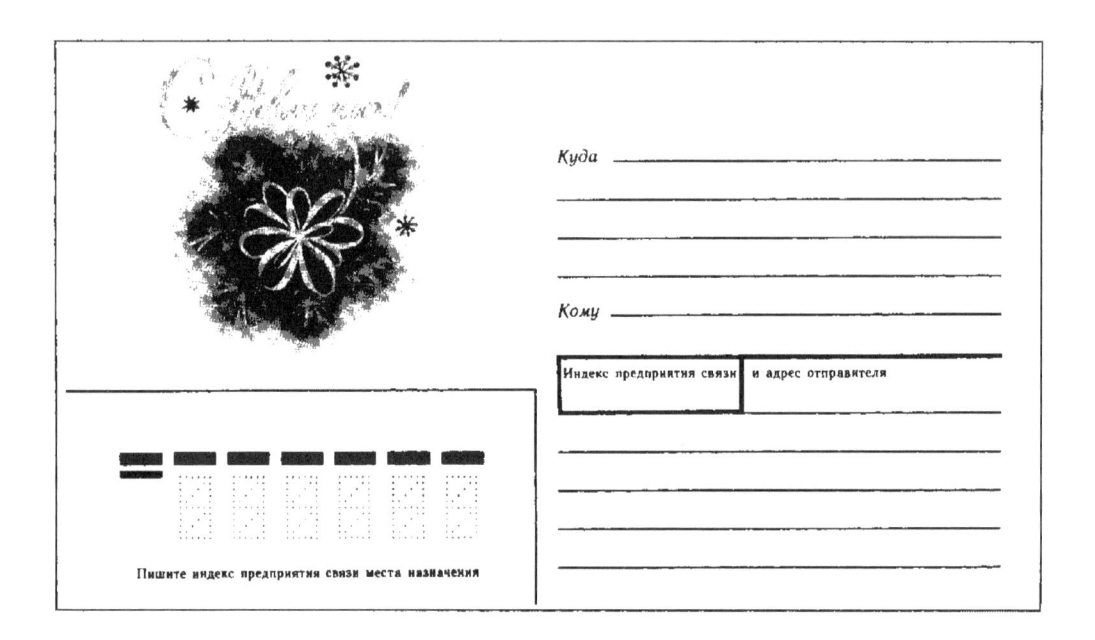

3. Novikov, Anton Dmitrievich, Universitetskaya ul, d. 43, kv. 5, Samara, 458903

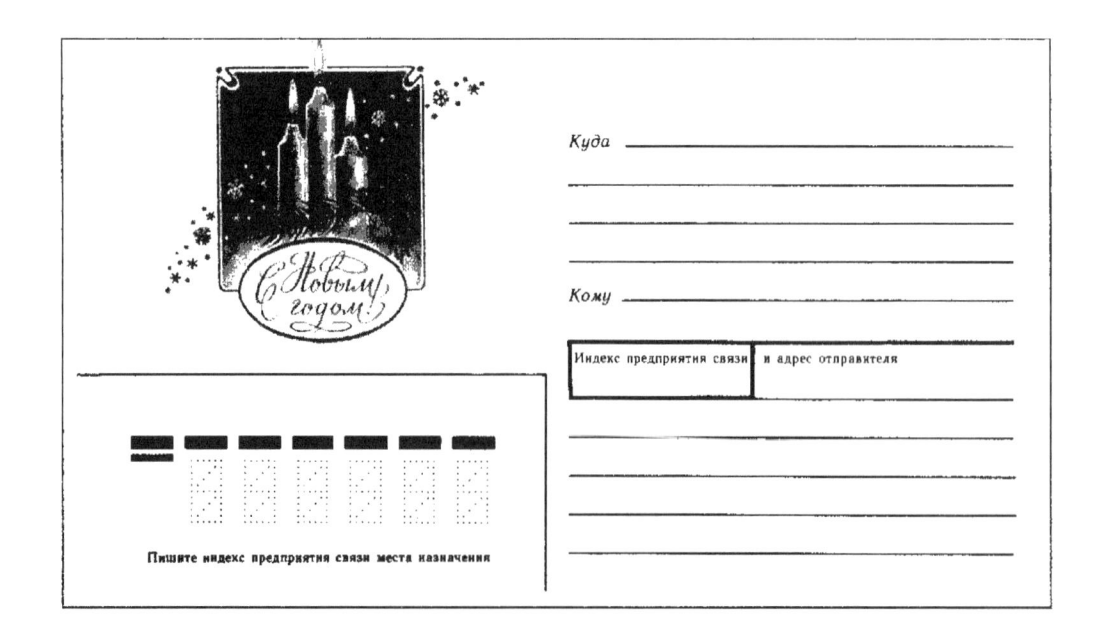

Name_____ Date_____ Class_____

Numerals: Case usage with 1–4

Б. Below is a picture of the living room in your apartment. Complete the following sentence by listing how many you and your roommates have of each of the following items: telephone, table, couch, armchair, television, lamp, shelf, rug. The first one has been done for you.

У нас в квартире...

1. <u>два телефо́на</u>_____,
2. _____,
3. _____,
4. _____,
5. _____,
6. _____,
7. _____,
8. _____.

Г. Solve these math problems.

1. У Ва́си одно́ письмо́, у Мари́ны два письма́. У Мари́ны и Ва́си ...

   _____.

2. У на́шего сосе́да Оле́га Петро́вича две соба́ки, и у сосе́да Макси́ма Васи́льевича то́же две. У нас в до́ме ...

   _____.

3. У Бори́са одна́ газе́та, и у его́ де́душки одна́. У них ...

   _____.

4. В на́шей кварти́ре две ко́мнаты, в ка́ждой ко́мнате два окна́. В на́шей кварти́ре ...

   _____.

5. У меня́ два стола́, я купи́л ещё оди́н. Сейча́с у меня́ ...

   _____.

Уро́к 6, Часть тре́тья   223

Ordinal numerals 5–30

Д. Russian students generally refer to their classroom as **аудито́рия** and use an ordinal number for the room number. In English it would be translated as *twenty-seventh room*. How would you tell somebody in Russian where your classes are located?

ОБРАЗЕ́Ц: room 27   два́дцать седьма́я аудито́рия

1. room 14 _____
2. room 5 _____
3. room 29 _____
4. room 17 _____
5. room 23 _____
6. room 10 _____
7. room 21 _____
8. room 7 _____
9. room 28 _____
10. room 22 _____

Е. You've just arrived in Moscow with your travel/study group. The group's rooms are scattered throughout the hotel. On which floor are individual students located?

Ed and Brian—23rd
Damon, Alan and Nate—21st
Robin and Leah—20th
Chris and Jim—18th
Katie and Sara—14th
Erin and Kelly—11th
Steve and Brendan—8th
Lee and Tim—7th
Angela and Sonya—2nd

ОБРАЗЕ́Ц: На како́м этаже́ Э́рин и Ке́лли?   На оди́ннадцатом.

1. На како́м этаже́ Ли и Тим? _____
2. На како́м этаже́ Кэ́ти и Са́ра? _____
3. На како́м этаже́ А́нджела и Со́ня? _____
4. На како́м этаже́ Крис и Джим? _____
5. На како́м этаже́ Эд и Бра́йан? _____
6. На како́м этаже́ Ро́бин и Ли́а? _____
7. На како́м этаже́ Де́ймон, А́лан и Нэйт? _____
8. На како́м этаже́ Стив и Бре́ндан? _____

Name_____ Date_____ Class_____

Months (Ме́сяцы) in Nominative and Genitive

Ж. Translate the months into Russian and mark where the stress falls. Then list the months in the Genitive case, again marking the stress. Remember that months are *not* capitalized in Russian.

	NOMINATIVE CASE	GENITIVE CASE
1. January		
2. February		
3. March		
4. April		
5. May		
6. June		
7. July		
8. August		
9. September		
10. October		
11. November		
12. December		

13. What stress pattern do you see if you compare the spring and summer months with the fall and winter months?

_____

_____

Calendar dates (day + date + month)

З. **Како́е сего́дня число́?** You have been asked what the date is. Use the cued dates to respond.

ОБРАЗЕЦ: May 22nd   <u>Сего́дня два́дцать второ́е ма́я.</u>

1. March 4th _____

2. October 18th _____

3. April 6th _____

4. May 28th _____

5. September 1st _____

6. June 23rd _____

7. December 16th _____

Additional meanings of «у» phrases

И. Answer the following questions, using a phrase with the preposition «у» along with another location phrase where necessary.

ОБРАЗЕЦ: Где у́чатся Ми́ла и Ро́ма? (*at our university*)
У нас в университе́те.

1. Где рабо́тает Серге́й? (*in our office*)

2. Где Мари́я Константи́новна? (*at Aunt Nina's*)

3. Где де́ти? (*at Petya's [place]*)

4. Где мо́жно купи́ть конве́рты и ма́рки? (*at our post office*)

5. Где Ка́тя? (*at grandmother's*)

6. Где мо́жно купи́ть америка́нские журна́лы? (*at our kiosk*)

7. Где вы игра́ете в ша́хматы? (*at our house*)

Перево́д

К. Translate the following dialogue into Russian.

"Has the mail already come?"
"Yes. There are two letters and a magazine for you."
"And who is the package for?"
"For me. From Grandma."

Name_____ Date_____ Class_____

Повторе́ние — мать уче́ния

Л. Following is a summary of the reading in Part 3. Fill in the blanks with words that maintain the context of the reading. You will have to change the form of some of the words. You will need to use one word twice. Do not use any of the other words more than once.

> Вот почтальо́н. Она́ отдаёт ба́бушке письмо́ и
> _____¹ пе́нсии, а Илье́ Ильичу́
> два _____² и бандеро́ль. На
> одно́м _____³ краси́вые
> _____.⁴ Илья́ Ильи́ч даёт их
> _____.⁵ Все получа́ют ра́зные
> газе́ты.
> Кругло́вы _____⁶ «Изве́стия».
> Си́лины получа́ют «Моско́вские но́вости», а Серге́й
> Петро́вич _____⁷ ещё и «Коммерса́нт».
> А вот письмо́ Во́ве. На конве́рте его́ фами́лия и
> _____⁸ — В. С.

Во́ва
два
инициа́лы
конве́рт
ма́рка
письмо́
получа́ть

Ситуа́ции

М. How would you . . .

1. say that in your town there is one post office and two libraries?

   _____

2. say that in your town there is only one stadium but three gyms?

   _____

3. say that this evening you will be at Nina's place?

   _____

4. say that you live on the seventh floor of the dorm?

   _____

5. say that you are already drinking your fifth cup (**ча́шка**) of coffee?

   _____

6. ask what today's date is?

   _____

7. say that today is Monday, April 17th?

   _____

Ва́ша о́чередь!

Н. Answer the questions that are asked of you.

1. У тебя́ до́ма оди́н компью́тер?

2. Я не по́мню, у тебя́ в гости́ной одно́ кре́сло и́ли два?

3. У вас в университе́те есть библиоте́ка? У вас одна́ библиоте́ка?

4. На како́м этаже́ ты живёшь?

5. Како́е сего́дня число́?

6. Како́й журна́л ты получа́ешь?

Сочине́ние

О. Write a short paragraph (five or six sentences) about your dorm room, apartment, or house. Ideas: Tell what you have and how many of each are in your living room, dining room, kitchen, bedroom, and so on. Use «у» phrases as you did in #1–3 of exercise **H** above.

РАБОТА В ЛАБОРАТОРИИ

ДИАЛОГИ

Диало́г 1 Ваш па́спорт? (Asking for your mail in a post office)

АА. Follow along as you listen to the dialogue.

А. Пожа́луйста, да́йте мою́ по́чту.
Б. Фами́лия?
А. Ольхо́вская.
Б. Ваш па́спорт?
А. Вот он, пожа́луйста.
Б. Вот ва́ша по́чта. Два письма́ и две газе́ты.

Name_____ Date_____ Class_____

- Now read and repeat aloud in the pause after each phrase.
- Now read the lines for speaker **Б** aloud.
- Now read the lines for speaker **А** aloud.

1. What does the woman have to show to receive her mail? _____

2. What does she receive? _____

Диалог 2   Почта уже была? (Asking about mail)

ББ. Follow along as you listen to the dialogue.

А. По́чта уже́ была́?
Б. Да, вот она́. Письмо́ па́пе, письмо́ мне и два письма́ тебе́.
А. А кому́ бандеро́ль?
Б. Бандеро́ль то́же тебе́. Она́ тяжёлая. Наве́рно, кни́ги.
А. Да, э́то а́нгло-ру́сский слова́рь (*dictionary*).

- Now read and repeat aloud in the pause after each phrase.
- Now read the lines for speaker **Б** aloud.
- Now read the lines for speaker **А** aloud.

How would the second line read if there had been three letters for the father, two for speaker **Б**, and one for speaker **А**?

_____

АУДИ́РОВАНИЕ

ВВ. You will hear descriptions of various places, including a house, a city, and a university. Record how many of each item is found in that place.

ОБРАЗЕ́Ц: У нас в го́роде две библиоте́ки, три спортза́ла и одна́ по́чта.
In this town there are . . .

_3_ gym(s)
_1_ post office(s)
_2_ library(ies)

1. At our university there are . . .

   _____ dorm(s)

   _____ library(ies)

   _____ gym(s)

2. In our house there are . . .

   _____ piano(s)

   _____ violins(s)

   _____ cello(s)

3. In my room there are . . .

   _____ lamp(s)

   _____ chair(s)

   _____ bed(s)

4. In our living room there are . . .

   _____ table(s)

   _____ lamp(s)

   _____ armchair(s)

5. In our town there are . . .

   _____ stadium(s)

   _____ post office(s)

   _____ park(s)

ГГ. You will hear a listing of students and the dorm rooms that they live in. Write down the number of the room next to the student's name.

ОБРАЗЕЦ: Нина живёт в двадцатой комнате.
Нина ___20___

1. Паша _____
2. Алёша _____
3. Марина _____
4. Настя _____
5. Лёня _____
6. Стёпа _____
7. Катя _____
8. Петя _____

ДД. Какое сегодня число? You will hear a series of dates. Write down the date as you would in English.

ОБРАЗЕЦ: Сегодня пятое сентября. _September 5th_

1. _____
2. _____
3. _____
4. _____
5. _____
6. _____
7. _____
8. _____

ГОВОРЕНИЕ

ЕЕ. How would you say that you have the following items?

ОБРАЗЕЦ: *You hear and see:* (*three newspapers*)
You say: У меня три газеты.

1. (*two magazines*)
2. (*four letters*)
3. (*one book*)
4. (*three envelopes*)
5. (*two stamps*)
6. (*one radio*)
7. (*three cassettes*)
8. (*one backpack*)

Name_____ Date_____ Class_____

ЖЖ. How would say *Today is* ... followed by the dates below?

ОБРАЗЕЦ: *You hear and see:* (*June 17th*)
You say: Сегодня семнадцатое июня.

1. (*January 31st*)
2. (*May 1st*)
3. (*December 6th*)
4. (*April 18th*)
5. (*March 27th*)
6. (*October 23rd*)
7. (*November 19th*)
8. (*February 29th*)

33. How would you say each of the following in Russian?

ОБРАЗЕЦ: *You hear and see:* (*at Sonya's house/place*)
You say: у Сони

1. (*at grandmother's house*)
2. (*at our university*)
3. (*in our town*)
4. (*in my room*)
5. (*at Aunt Anna's place*)
6. (*at our bank*)

Name_____ Date_____ Class_____

ЧАСТЬ ЧЕТВЁРТАЯ
Нам нра́вится э́та иде́я!

РАБО́ТА ДО́МА

ПИСЬМО́

Понима́ние те́кста

А. Review the reading on page 266 of the textbook. Each of the following statements about the reading is false. Rewrite them so that they are true.

1. В кварти́ре, где Све́та и Та́ня снима́ют ко́мнату, живу́т ещё Татья́на Дми́триевна и её муж.

   _____

   _____

2. В их ко́мнате нет ме́бели. _____

   _____

3. У Са́ши в ко́мнате стои́т кни́жный шкаф. _____

   _____

4. Са́ша мо́жет писа́ть то́лько на столе́. _____

   _____

5. Стол сто́ит до́рого, потому́ что он о́чень ста́рый. _____

   _____

6. Они́ все пьют ко́фе. _____

   _____

Missing, lacking in the past and future: <не́ было, не бу́дет + Genitive>

Б. Complaints! One person had something that another didn't. What are the complaints that you hear?

ОБРАЗЕ́Ц: У Джи́ма была́ гита́ра. А у Ви́ктора <u>не́ было гита́ры.</u>

1. У тебя́ был о́фис. А у меня́ _____

2. У молодо́го челове́ка бы́ли конве́рт и ма́рка. А у де́вушки _____

   _____

3. У меня́ был их а́дрес. А у моего́ дру́га _____

4. У мое́й подру́ги была́ валю́та. А у меня́ _____

5. У до́чери А́нны Васи́льевны была́ соба́ка. А у сы́на А́нны Васи́льевны

   _____

6. У нас был его́ но́мер телефо́на. А у них _____

   _____

В. Andrei was looking forward to his vacation in **Ялта** (a popular resort in **Украйна**), but his hotel turned out to be a complete disappointment. Read what his expectations were; then write what he actually encountered on his trip.

ОБРАЗЕЦ: В холодильнике будет минеральная вода.
→ В холодильнике не́ было минеральной воды́.

1. В комнате будет микроволновая печь.

2. В комнате будет холодильник.

3. В гостинице будет сауна.

4. В ванной будет хорошее мыло.

5. В баре будет холодное пиво.

6. В ресторане будет джаз-оркестр.

Г. Your host sister is having second thoughts about a camping trip that she has signed up for. She is concerned because there won't be many of the comforts of home that she is used to. What does she say?

ОБРАЗЕЦ: (toaster) Там не будет тостера.

1. (washing machine) _____
2. (vacuum cleaner) _____
3. (mixer) _____
4. (microwave oven) _____
5. (shower) _____

Name_____ Date_____ Class_____

Telling what you need

Д. **Что вам ну́жно?** Read each of the following situations and use the pictures below to decide what you need.

ОБРАЗЕЦ: Когда́ у вас у́тром заня́тия, вы всегда́ опа́здываете.

Мне ну́жен буди́льник.

1. Вы пи́шете письмо́. _____
2. Вы хоти́те знать, како́е сего́дня число́. _____
3. Вы хоти́те чита́ть но́чью. _____
4. Вы купи́ли но́вую маши́ну. _____
5. У вас кни́ги везде́ — на крова́ти, на полу́, на столе́.
   _____
6. Вы хоти́те слу́шать кассе́ты. _____
7. У ва́шего дру́га бу́дет новосе́лье. _____

What one must (not) do: <Dative + (не) на́до + Infinitive>

Е. Fill in the blanks with the appropriate <Dative pronoun + на́до> phrase according to context. The first one has been done for you.

У нас новосе́лье. Сего́дня ве́чером у нас го́сти. _____Нам на́до_____ гото́вить у́жин

(*dinner*). Но никто́ не хо́чет помо́чь мне. Моя́ сестра́ у́чится в консервато́рии и говори́т, что

_____[1] ка́ждый день игра́ть. Мой брат у́чится на истори́ческом

факульте́те и говори́т, что _____[2] писа́ть курсову́ю. Мой па́па о́чень не

лю́бит гото́вить. Он говори́т, что _____[3] рабо́тать. Моя́ ма́ма —

журнали́стка, и _____[4] писа́ть статью́. Ба́бушка и де́душка не мо́гут

помо́чь, потому́ что _____[5] гуля́ть. Хорошо́, что в на́шей семье́ есть я. Я

о́чень люблю́ гото́вить.

Уро́к 6, Часть четвёртая 235

Short-form adjectives

Ж. Fill in the blanks of the following sentences with the correct form of one of the short-form adjectives **до́лжен, похо́ж, рад,** or **уве́рен.**

ОБРАЗЕЦ: Моя́ сестра́ о́чень ___похо́жа___ на ма́му.

1. Та́ня, ты _____, что конце́рт бу́дет сего́дня ве́чером? По-мо́ему, он бу́дет за́втра ве́чером.

2. Де́душка Гре́га учи́лся в Бо́стоне, и его́ оте́ц там учи́лся. Грег _____, что он то́же бу́дет учи́ться в Бо́стоне.

3. Тим и Том — бра́тья. Они́ о́чень _____ друг на дру́га.

4. Де́ти о́чень _____, что мы идём в парк.

5. Ди́ма, жаль, что ты _____ идти́. Андре́й бу́дет игра́ть на гита́ре.

6. Как вы ду́маете, Ве́ра _____ на отца́ и́ли на мать?

З. Below are two letters written to the magazine **16** and its **Клуб одино́ких серде́ц** (*Lonely Hearts Club*). Skim through the letters to find the answers to the questions below. Write your answers in English.

1. What is the name of the young girl? How old is she?
   _____

2. Name at least two things that she likes to do.
   _____

3. What do you think the sentence **Я хоте́ла бы перепи́сываться с па́рнями 16–25 лет** means?
   _____

4. What is the name of the young man? How old is he?
   _____

5. What types of things does he like?
   _____

6. What word might give you a clue to his personality?
   _____

Name_____ Date_____ Class_____

Перево́д

И. Translate the following dialogue into Russian.

"Excuse me, are you selling these chairs?"
"Yes. They're not new, so they're not very expensive."
"I like them very much. And I need chairs. I want to buy them. How much are they?"

_____
_____
_____
_____

Повторе́ние — мать уче́ния

К. Following is a summary of the reading in Part 4. Fill in the blanks with words that maintain the context of the reading. You will have to change the form of some of the words. Do not use any of the words more than once.

Та́ня и Све́та _____¹ ко́мнату у Татья́ны Дми́триевны. В ко́мнате есть всё, что _____.² Им не _____³ ничего́ покупа́ть. Там не́ _____⁴ стола́, но Са́ша, их но́вый сосе́д, подари́л (*gave*) им стол. У _____⁵ в ко́мнате стои́т роя́ль, и нет _____⁶ для стола́. Писа́ть Са́ша мо́жет на роя́ле, а _____⁷ на столе́ он не мо́жет. Та́ня и Све́та о́чень _____,⁸ что стол _____⁹ не ну́жен.	быть игра́ть ме́сто на́до ну́жно он рад Са́ша снима́ть

Ситуа́ции

Л. How would you ...

1. say that you wanted to buy your sister a present but you didn't have any foreign currency?

   _____
   _____

2. say that the advertisement will not be in the city newspaper? It will be in the university newspaper.

   _____
   _____

3. say that you want to do your homework, but you need a pen?

   _____

4. say that your vacuum cleaner isn't working and you need to buy a new one?

5. say that you like this café because everything here is very tasty and the waiters are very polite?

6. ask your classmate if she's glad that her brother will be studying in Moscow?

7. ask your classmate if he looks like his mother or father?

Ваша очередь!

M. Answer the questions that are asked of you.

1. Ты снима́ешь но́вую кварти́ру? А новосе́лье уже́ бы́ло?

2. Что тебе́ на́до де́лать сего́дня?

3. Что ты бу́дешь гото́вить? Что тебе́ для э́того (*for that*) ну́жно?

4. На кого́ ты похо́ж (похо́жа)?

5. Что тебе́ на́до купи́ть?

6. В но́вой кварти́ре у тебя́ бу́дет стира́льная маши́на? А ми́ксер? А пылесо́с?

Сочине́ние

Н. Write a short paragraph (five or six sentences) about your life growing up. Ideas: What things did your family have? What did it not have? Maybe one of your siblings had something that you didn't or vice versa? Or one of your friends?

Name_____ Date_____ Class_____

Fun with grammar! Case review

O. Fill in the blanks of the following sentences with the appropriate case endings. Not all blanks, however, will have an ending. Then enter the words into the crossword puzzle below to help check your spelling. The letter-number combinations (e.g., **г**12) at the end of each sentence indicate the location of the word or words in the puzzle. The first letter and number are for the first word and so on. Note that **г** is for **горизонта́ль**, or horizontal; **в** is for **вертика́ль**, or vertical.

1. Мы купи́ли но́в_____ учи́тельниц_____ цветы́. (г14) (в6)
2. У ва́ш_____ дру́г_____ есть гита́р_____? (в7) (в3) (г19)
3. Т_____ (you) нра́вится э́тот фильм? (г18)
4. Ты хорошо́ зна́ешь Алексе́_____?(в16)
5. М_____ (me) на́до писа́ть курсов_____. (г21) (г5)
6. У нас до́ма два дива́н_____, одно́ кре́сл_____ и четы́ре ла́мп_____. (в4) (в15) (г20)
7. Мари́на сейча́с идёт на концерт_____. (г2)
8. Та́ня рабо́тает в ма́леньк_____ рестора́н_____ в це́нтре го́род_____. (г13) (г11) (в12)
9. Мо_____ бра́т_____ два́дцать три го́да. (в9) (в10)
10. Вот в_____ (you) бандеро́ль от ба́бушк_____. (в17) (г8)
11. Как_____ стать_____ ты чита́ешь? Интере́сная статья́? (г15) (в1)

РАБОТА В ЛАБОРАТОРИИ

ДИАЛОГИ

Диалог 1 Я могу́ дать вам... (Giving things to others)

АА. Follow along as you listen to the dialogue.

А. Вам нра́вится ва́ша но́вая кварти́ра?
Б. О́чень нра́вится.
А. Там есть ме́бель?
Б. Там всё есть, нет то́лько стола́.
А. У меня́ есть ли́шний стол. Он большо́й, о́чень хоро́ший. Я могу́ дать его́ вам.
Б. Спаси́бо.

- Now read and repeat aloud in the pause after each phrase.
- Now read the lines for speaker **Б** aloud.
- Now read the lines for speaker **А** aloud.

Rewrite the dialogue so that speaker **Б** has just moved into a new dorm rather than an apartment. And she needs a lamp rather than a table. (Note: The word **ли́шний** in line 5 will be **ли́шняя** when it modifies a feminine noun.)

А. _____
Б. _____
А. _____
Б. _____
А. _____
Б. _____

Диалог 2 Мне о́чень ну́жно кре́сло (Doing a favor for someone)

ББ. Follow along as you listen to the dialogue.

А. В мое́й но́вой кварти́ре есть стол, сту́лья, ла́мпы, кофе́йный сто́лик. Там о́чень краси́вый ковёр. Есть почти́ всё, что ну́жно, но, к сожале́нию, нет кре́сла, а мне о́чень ну́жно кре́сло.
Б. Я зна́ю, что мои́ сосе́ди продаю́т ме́бель. У них есть отли́чное кре́сло, но я не зна́ю, продаю́т они́ его́ и́ли нет. Е́сли хо́чешь, я могу́ спроси́ть (ask).
А. Спаси́бо!

- Now read and repeat aloud in the pause after each phrase.
- Now read the lines for speaker **Б** aloud.
- Now read the lines for speaker **А** aloud.

How would you say, "Unfortunately there's no couch, and I really need a couch."

Name_____ Date_____ Class_____

АУДИРОВАНИЕ

ВВ. When Lara went to collect her luggage upon arriving in Moscow, she found that her bag and the bags of two other passengers had come open and the contents were all mixed up. Listen as she tells an airport official what she had and what she didn't have. Write **да** next to the items that she had and **нет** by the items that she did not have. The first one has been done for you.

1. _____ backpack
2. _____ blouses
3. _____ boots
4. _____ jacket
5. _____ shampoo
6. _____ skirt
7. _____ soap
8. __да__ toothpaste
9. _____ toothbrush

ГГ. Who needs what? Match the name of the person on the left with the item needed on the right.

ОБРАЗЕЦ: Пе́те нужна́ валю́та.

Об. __г__ Petya
1. _____ our neighbor (female)
2. _____ you
3. _____ Vitya
4. _____ our neighbor (male)
5. _____ Maria Stepanovna
6. _____ we
7. _____ Professor Vasilev

а. a nice, big easy chair
б. a good music teacher
в. coffee
г. ~~foreign currency~~
д. an aspirin
е. envelopes and stamps
ж. address book
з. tickets to the soccer game

ДД. What would be the most appropriate English translation of the sentences that you hear?

ОБРАЗЕЦ: Я ра́да, что тебе́ му́зыка нра́вится.

    а. _____ I'm sure that you will like the music.
    б. _____ I am supposed to show you the music.
    в. __X__ I'm glad that you like the music.

1. а. _____ He's sure that Misha will be there this evening.
   б. _____ He has to go with Misha this evening.
   в. _____ He's glad that Misha will be there this evening.

2. а. _____ Nina and Lyonya look alike.
   б. _____ Nina is glad that Lyonya has to go.
   в. _____ Unfortunately Nina and Lyonya have to leave.

3. а. _____ Does your sister have to go?
   б. _____ Does your sister look like you?
   в. _____ Are you sure that's your sister?

4. а. _____ Lyuda needs a ride to the airport.

   б. _____ Lyuda has to work at the airport today.

   в. _____ Lyuda doesn't have to go to the airport.

5. а. _____ We're glad that you like our city.

   б. _____ We're sure that you will like our city.

   в. _____ We should show you the sights of our city.

6. а. _____ Do you think that our neighbors look French?

   б. _____ Are you sure that our neighbors understand French?

   в. _____ Are you glad to be able to speak French to our neighbors?

ГОВОРЕНИЕ

ЕЕ. How would you say that the following items weren't there?

    ОБРАЗЕЦ: *You hear and see:*   (*tasty cheese at the store*)
                      You say: Вку́сного сы́ра в магази́не не́ было.

1. (*address book in the purse*)
2. (*a washing machine at the neighbor's*)
3. (*mineral water at the café*)
4. (*an envelope on the table*)
5. (*my size at the store*)
6. (*the passport in the backpack*)

ЖЖ. How would you say that you need the following items?

    ОБРАЗЕЦ: *You hear and see:*   (*toothbrush*)
                      You say: Мне нужна́ зубна́я щётка.

1. (*table*)   4. (*lamp*)
2. (*easy chair*) 5. (*stamps*)
3. (*chairs*)   6. (*envelope*)

33. How would you say that the following people must do the following things?

    ОБРАЗЕЦ: *You hear and see:*   (*my brother; buy a bookcase*)
                      You say: Моему́ бра́ту на́до купи́ть кни́жный шкаф.

1. (*the boy; read a lot*)
2. (*Aleksei; write a term paper*)
3. (*grandmother and grandfather; walk every evening*)
4. (*Masha; listen to cassettes*)
5. (*Igor; buy Lena a present*)
6. (*we; go to the university every day*)

Name _____ Date _____ Class _____

ЖИЗНЬ ИДЁТ

УРОК 7

ЧАСТЬ ПЕРВАЯ
Когда́ бу́дет новосе́лье?

РАБО́ТА ДО́МА

ПИСЬМО́

Понима́ние те́кста

A. Review the reading on pages 282–283 of the textbook. Mark the following statements **В** for **ве́рно** (*true*) or **Н** for **неве́рно** (*false*). Correct the false statements so that they are true (you should have to change only one word).

1. _____ Све́та у́чит францу́зские слова́.

2. _____ Са́ша ду́мает, что у Све́ты плоха́я систе́ма.

3. _____ Све́та рабо́тает в понеде́льник, в сре́ду и в суббо́ту.

4. _____ Са́ша рабо́тает на ско́рой по́мощи.

5. _____ Све́та у́чится на второ́м ку́рсе.

6. _____ Днём и ве́чером у Све́ты заня́тия.

7. _____ Ле́том Та́ня рабо́тала три ме́сяца.

8. _____ Новосе́лье у Та́ни и Све́ты бу́дет в сре́ду.

9. _____ Са́ша хо́чет пригласи́ть сосе́дку, Ле́ну Си́лину.

10. _____ Та́ня хо́чет пригласи́ть Ви́ктора.

To study: учи́ть and занима́ться

Б. Fill in the blanks with correct form of **учи́ть** or **занима́ться**. The first one has been done for you.

Я учу́сь на факульте́те журнали́стики. Я _____учу́_____ францу́зский язы́к, но говорю́ по-францу́зски о́чень пло́хо. Мой брат Вади́м ду́мает, что я ма́ло _____.¹ Вади́м _____² неме́цкий язы́к. Он _____³ ка́ждый день и уже́ хорошо́ говори́т по-неме́цки. Моя́ сестра́ И́ра у́чится в университе́те на математи́ческом факульте́те. Ей на́до мно́го _____.⁴ У́тром у неё ле́кции в университе́те, а ве́чером она́ _____⁵ до́ма. Она́ _____⁶ англи́йский язы́к. Я понима́ю, заче́м она́ _____⁷ англи́йский язы́к: она́ матема́тик, и ей на́до чита́ть статьи́ по-англи́йски.

В. Fill in the blanks with the correct form of **учи́ть** or **занима́ться**.

ГЁНА. Како́й язы́к ты _____?¹

ВАЛЕ́РА. Испа́нский. А ты?

ГЁНА. Я _____² япо́нский.

ВАЛЕ́РА. Э́то тру́дный язы́к?

ГЁНА. Ужа́сно тру́дный, я о́чень мно́го _____.³

"On" a certain day of the week: в суббо́ту

Г. Following is a chart of your activities for the past week. Some activities may have occurred on more than one day. Answer the questions accordingly.

понеде́льник	собра́ние баскетбо́л рабо́та
вто́рник	уро́к му́зыки рабо́та
среда́	ле́кция о Толсто́м курсова́я
четве́рг	ле́кция о Толсто́м фильм «А́нна Каре́нина»
пя́тница	курсова́я рабо́та теа́тр
суббо́та	те́ннис конце́рт
воскресе́нье	новосе́лье у Да́ши

Name_____ Date_____ Class_____

ОБРАЗЕЦ: Когда́ был конце́рт? <u>Конце́рт был в суббо́ту.</u>

1. Когда́ (в како́й день) бы́ло собра́ние? _____
2. Когда́ бы́ло новосе́лье у Да́ши? _____
3. Когда́ ты игра́л (игра́ла) в баскетбо́л? _____
4. В каки́е дни ты рабо́тал (рабо́тала)? _____
5. Когда́ ты писа́л (писа́ла) курсову́ю? _____
6. В каки́е дни бы́ли ле́кции о Толсто́м? _____
7. Когда́ был фильм «А́нна Каре́нина»? _____
8. Когда́ ты ходи́л (ходи́ла) в теа́тр? _____
9. Когда́ ты игра́л (игра́ла) в те́ннис? _____

Д. Svetlana is trying to decide which evening to have her housewarming party. She has gathered the following information about her friends' plans. She is now discussing various possibilities with them. How would she respond to their suggestions?

У Светла́ны бу́дет новосе́лье, но она́ пока́ (*still*) не зна́ет, когда́ оно́ бу́дет. Она́ хо́чет пригласи́ть Андре́я, И́горя, Ва́лю и Со́ню. Светла́на рабо́тает в суббо́ту ве́чером. Андре́й рабо́тает в сре́ду ве́чером, а во вто́рник ве́чером у́чится. И́горь рабо́тает в воскресе́нье ве́чером. Со́ня рабо́тает в понеде́льник ве́чером, а у Ва́ли заня́тия в четве́рг ве́чером.

ОБРАЗЕЦ: АНДРЕ́Й. Я предлага́ю в понеде́льник.
СВЕТЛА́НА. <u>Нет, в понеде́льник нельзя́, потому́ что Со́ня рабо́тает.</u>

1. СО́НЯ. Я предлага́ю в четве́рг.

   СВЕТЛА́НА. _____

2. И́ГОРЬ. Я предлага́ю во вто́рник.

   СВЕТЛА́НА. _____

3. СО́НЯ. Я предлага́ю в суббо́ту.

   СВЕТЛА́НА. _____

4. ВА́ЛЯ. Я предлага́ю в сре́ду.

   СВЕТЛА́НА. _____

5. АНДРЕ́Й. Я предлага́ю в воскресе́нье.

   СВЕТЛА́НА. _____

6. Как вы ду́маете, в како́й день у Светла́ны бу́дет новосе́лье?

   СВЕТЛА́НА. _____

Уро́к 7, Часть пе́рвая 245

Introduction to aspect

E. If the following sentences were written in Russian, would the verbs require the imperfective aspect or the perfective aspect? Check the correct column on the right.

		IMPERFECTIVE	PERFECTIVE
ОБРАЗЕЦ:	I <u>fixed</u> dinner tonight.	_____	__X__
1.	I <u>used to walk</u> to school every day.	_____	_____
2.	I <u>finished</u> the book last night.	_____	_____
3.	She <u>studied</u> all weekend.	_____	_____
4.	She <u>was</u> still <u>doing</u> her homework …	_____	_____
5.	… when I <u>came</u> home.	_____	_____
6.	Every Sunday when I was a kid we <u>would visit</u> Grandma.	_____	_____
7.	I'll <u>call</u> you at three this afternoon.	_____	_____
8.	My dog <u>is</u> always <u>barking</u>.	_____	_____
9.	<u>Will</u> you <u>be</u> in Moscow …	_____	_____
10.	… when I <u>arrive</u>?	_____	_____

Ж. Following is a portion of the story of Little Red Riding Hood. If the sentences were translated into Russian, would the verbs require the imperfective or perfective aspect? Why? Do the verbs denote ongoing, repeated, or habitual action (imperfective)? Or do they denote the completion or result of an action (perfective)? Mark an **X** in the appropriate column for each of the underlined verbs. The first one has been done for you. Good luck!

> One day Little Red Riding Hood <u>decided</u>[1] to go visit her grandmother. Her mother <u>gave</u>[2] her a loaf of freshly baked bread for Grandmother, and Little Red Riding Hood <u>set out</u>[3] on the path through the woods. As she <u>walked</u>[4] along she <u>picked</u>[5] flowers for Grandmother, <u>listened</u>[6] to the birds, and <u>admired</u>[7] the beautiful trees. Suddenly a wolf <u>appeared</u>[8] on the trail and <u>said</u>[9] to her: "Little girl, where <u>are</u> you <u>going</u>[10]?" "I'<u>m going</u>[11] to visit my grandmother," <u>answered</u>[12] Little Red Riding Hood.

	IMPERFECTIVE (ONGOING, REPEATED, OR HABITUAL ACTION)	PERFECTIVE (COMPLETION OR RESULT OF ACTION)		IMPERFECTIVE (ONGOING, REPEATED, OR HABITUAL ACTION)	PERFECTIVE (COMPLETION OR RESULT OF ACTION)
1.	_____	__X__	7.	_____	_____
2.	_____	_____	8.	_____	_____
3.	_____	_____	9.	_____	_____
4.	_____	_____	10.	_____	_____
5.	_____	_____	11.	_____	_____
6.	_____	_____	12.	_____	_____

Name_____ Date_____ Class_____

The perfective aspect: One-time completion

3. How would you translate the following sentences into English? Note that all the sentences use the perfective aspect of the verb.

ОБРАЗЕЦ: Свéта закóнчила медицúнское учúлище.
<u>Sveta finished nursing school.</u>

1. Друзья́ пригласи́ли меня́ на новосе́лье.

2. Ви́ктор роди́лся в январе́.

3. Я уже́ вы́учила но́вые ру́сские слова́.

4. Вчера́ на́ши сосе́ди купи́ли но́вую маши́ну.

The imperfective aspect: Ongoing, repeated, or habitual/characteristic actions or states

И. Again, how would you translate the following sentences into English? Note that this time all the sentences use the imperfective aspect of the verb.

ОБРАЗЕЦ: Вчера́ ве́чером я учи́ла но́вые ру́сские слова́.
<u>Last night I studied (or: was studying) the new Russian words.</u>

1. Когда́ он был в Москве́, он говори́л то́лько по-ру́сски.

2. Мы чита́ли газе́ту ка́ждый день.

3. Ты вчера́ игра́л в волейбо́л?

4. Когда́ я учи́лся в университе́те, я мно́го занима́лся.

Aspect: Imperfective and perfective counterparts

К. Fill in the blanks with the correct aspect of the verb required by context. Use past tenses throughout.

1. Ва́ля. Что ты _____ де́лала _____ (де́лать / сде́лать) вчера́ ве́чером?

   А́ня. Я занима́лась, _____ (учи́ть / вы́учить) но́вые слова́.

   Ва́ля. Ты _____ (учи́ть / вы́учить) все но́вые слова́?

2. Сла́ва. Где была́ О́льга вчера́ ве́чером?

   Ка́тя. Она́ была́ до́ма, _____ (писа́ть / написа́ть) письмо́ ма́ме.

   И́горь. А я ви́дел её в па́рке, она́ _____ (чита́ть / прочита́ть) газе́ту.

3. Алёша. Пе́тя, что ты _____ (де́лать / сде́лать) вчера́?

   Пе́тя. Я _____ (писа́ть / написа́ть) курсову́ю. А ты уже́ _____ (писа́ть / написа́ть) курсову́ю?

   Алёша. Да, я уже́ почти́ всё _____ (писа́ть / написа́ть).

4. Же́ня. Что ты _____ (чита́ть / прочита́ть) вчера́ ве́чером?

   То́ля. Статью́ об америка́нской поли́тике. Очень интере́сная статья́. Ты не хо́чешь её прочита́ть?

   Же́ня. Хочу́. Ты её уже́ _____ (чита́ть / прочита́ть)?

   То́ля. Да, если хо́чешь, я могу́ её за́втра принести́ (*bring*).

Когда́? Parts of the day and seasons of the year

Л. Answer each of the following questions indicating a time of the day or a season of the year. For some answers you may be able to give more than one time of day or more than one season.

ОБРАЗЕЦ: Когда́ ты рабо́таешь? <u>Днём и ве́чером.</u>

1. Когда́ ты спишь? _____
2. Когда́ ты занима́ешься? _____
3. Когда́ у тебя́ ле́кции (*lectures*)? _____
4. Когда́ в Росси́и игра́ют в футбо́л? _____
5. А когда́ в Аме́рике игра́ют в америка́нский футбо́л?

   _____
6. Когда́ нам нужны́ свитера́? _____
7. Когда́ нам нужны́ сапоги́? _____
8. Когда́ нам нужны́ джи́нсы? _____

Name_____ Date_____ Class_____

M. Answer the following questions based on the calendar, which shows Ivan's appointments from last week. Do not write the exact time. Instead, write the day and appropriate adverb for "in the morning," and so on.

	ПН	ВТ	СР	ЧТ	ПТ	СБ	ВС
9.00	заня́тия			заня́тия			
10.00	заня́тия		футбо́л	заня́тия			ша́хматы
11.00	заня́тия		футбо́л	заня́тия	ша́хматы		ша́хматы
12.00		врач			ша́хматы		
1.00			чай у				
2.00			Воло́ди	те́ннис			
3.00				те́ннис		чай	новосе́лье
4.00						у Зи́ны	у Ма́ши
5.00							
6.00					рестора́н		
7.00			фильм				
8.00	концéрт		фильм			теа́тр	о́пера
9.00	концéрт					теа́тр	о́пера

ОБРАЗЕЦ: Когда́ Ива́н ходи́л в теа́тр?

   Он ходи́л в теа́тр в суббо́ту ве́чером.

1. Когда́ Ива́н ходи́л в рестора́н?

_____

2. Когда́ у Ива́на бы́ли заня́тия?

_____

3. Когда́ Ива́н игра́л в футбо́л?

_____

4. Когда́ Ива́н был на новосе́лье у Ма́ши?

_____

5. Когда́ Ива́н был у врача́?

_____

H. Look again at Ivan's schedule. What if it is now Tuesday morning of that week? Instead of using the day of the week, how would you answer the following questions, using **вчера́** (*yesterday*), **сего́дня,** or **за́втра** (*tomorrow*) and the part of the day?

ОБРАЗЕЦ: Когда́ Ива́н бу́дет игра́ть в футбо́л?

   Ива́н бу́дет игра́ть в футбо́л за́втра у́тром.

1. Когда́ у Ива́на бы́ли заня́тия?

_____

2. Когда́ Ива́н бу́дет у врача́?

_____

3. Когда́ Ива́н бу́дет у Воло́ди?

4. Когда́ Ива́н ходи́л на конце́рт?

What if today is Saturday morning of that same week?

5. Когда́ Ива́н ходи́л в рестора́н?

6. Когда́ Ива́н бу́дет на новосе́лье у Ма́ши?

7. Когда́ Ива́н идёт в теа́тр?

8. Когда́ Ива́н бу́дет игра́ть в ша́хматы?

Перево́д

O. Translate the following dialogue into Russian.

"Excuse me, is Petya home?"
"Yes. He's studying. Come in."
"Thanks. Hi, Petya! What are you doing?"
"Hi, Kolya. I'm studying biology. On Monday there'll be a test."

Name _____ Date _____ Class _____

Повторение — мать учения

П. Following is a summary of the reading in Part 1. Fill in the blanks with words that maintain the context of the reading. You will have to change the form of some of the words. Use each word only once.

Света _____¹ в медицинском институте. Кроме того, у неё есть диплом медсестры. Света работает _____² скорой помощи. Она работает в _____,³ в среду и в _____.⁴ Она работает и вечером _____,⁵ а утром и _____⁶ у неё занятия. Света много _____.⁷ Сейчас она _____⁸ английские слова, которые ей надо _____.⁹ Таня тоже много занимается. Она сейчас не работает, но _____¹⁰ она работала два месяца.	выучить днём заниматься летом на ночью понедельник пятница учить учиться

Ситуации

Р. How would you . . .

1. say that you will be studying Wednesday morning at the library?

   _____

2. say that you have to study Russian vocabulary (words)?

   _____

3. ask your classmate if he learned the new words yesterday?

   _____

4. say that you wrote (finished writing) your term paper on Saturday?

   _____

5. ask your host parents where they went in the summer?

   _____

6. say that you often go to Colorado in the winter?

   _____

Ва́ша о́чередь!

C. Answer the questions that are asked of you.

1. Ты рабо́таешь или то́лько у́чишься?
   _____

2. Когда́ у тебя́ заня́тия в университе́те?
   _____

3. Когда́ ты обы́чно занима́ешься?
   _____

4. Како́й язы́к (каки́е языки́) ты учи́л (учи́ла) в шко́ле?
   _____

5. Куда́ ты обы́чно е́здишь ле́том?
   _____

6. Куда́ ты обы́чно е́здишь зимо́й?
   _____

Сочине́ние

T. Write a short paragraph (five or six sentences) about your weekly schedule. Ideas: What do you do and when? Where? With whom? Stick to vocabulary that you know. If you're not sure how to say it, maybe you can say something else.

_____
_____
_____
_____
_____

РАБО́ТА В ЛАБОРАТО́РИИ

ДИАЛО́ГИ

Диало́г 1 Когда́ бу́дет...? (Scheduling a social event)

AA. Follow along as you listen to the dialogue.

А. Ни́на, когда́ у вас бу́дет новосе́лье?
Б. Я ещё не зна́ю. Наве́рно, в пя́тницу или в суббо́ту.
А. Пя́тница — э́то удо́бный день. И суббо́та то́же. Я хочу́ пригласи́ть моего́ дру́га Са́шу. Мо́жно?
Б. Коне́чно.

- Now read and repeat aloud in the pause after each phrase.
- Now read the lines for speaker Б aloud.
- Now read the lines for speaker А aloud.

How would you say in Russian, "I'd like to invite Professor Maksimov"?

_____

Name_____ Date_____ Class_____

Диало́г 2 Приходи́ к нам (*come over to our place*) в воскресе́нье
(Extending and accepting invitations)

ББ. Follow along as you listen to the dialogue.

А. Приходи́ к нам в воскресе́нье.
Б. Спаси́бо. А кого́ ещё вы приглаша́ете?
А. Мы хоти́м пригласи́ть Лю́ду, Ка́тю, Ма́шу, Серёжу и Оле́га.
Б. Отли́чная компа́ния! Мо́жно пригласи́ть ещё Джо́на, на́шего аспира́нта? Он в Москве́ неда́вно.
А. Прекра́сная иде́я! Пригласи́ его́, пожа́луйста!

- Now read and repeat aloud in the pause after each phrase.
- Now read the lines for speaker **Б** aloud.
- Now read the lines for speaker **А** aloud.

Rewrite the dialogue so that (1) the invitation is for Friday, (2) Olya, Anya, Boris, and Dima are being invited, and (3) the graduate student's name is Tina.

А. _____
Б. _____
А. _____
Б. _____
А. _____

АУДИ́РОВАНИЕ

ВВ. You will hear a series of sentences telling where Ivan went and on which days. Write the letter of the correct day next to the appropriate destination. The first one has been done for you.

ОБРАЗЕ́Ц: В теа́тр Ива́н ходи́л в сре́ду.

1. __в__ to the theater   а. Monday
2. _____ to the stadium   б. Tuesday
3. _____ to the library   в. ~~Wednesday~~
4. _____ to the electronics store г. Thursday
5. _____ to the post office   д. Friday
6. _____ to the law institute   е. Saturday
7. _____ to the grocery store   ж. Sunday

ГГ. For each of the sentences that you hear, decide whether the speaker is referring to an ongoing, habitual, or repeated action (imperfective aspect) or a one-time, completed action (perfective aspect) and check the appropriate column.

ОБРАЗЕ́Ц: Джон о́чень хорошо́ говори́т по-ру́сски.

	IMPERFECTIVE ONGOING, HABITUAL, OR REPEATED ACTION	PERFECTIVE ONE-TIME, COMPLETED ACTION
ОБРАЗЕ́Ц:	__X__	_____
1.	_____	_____
2.	_____	_____

	IMPERFECTIVE ONGOING, HABITUAL, OR REPEATED ACTION	PERFECTIVE ONE-TIME, COMPLETED ACTION
3.	_____	_____
4.	_____	_____
5.	_____	_____
6.	_____	_____

ДД. You will hear a series of sentences telling what time of the day or what time of the year people do or did certain things. Write the letter of the correct time next to the appropriate action.

ОБРАЗЕЦ: Вчера́ у́тром мы бы́ли в университе́те.

Об. __в__ We were at the university   а. tomorrow afternoon
1. _____ We're going to watch a movie   б. tonight
2. _____ I'm studying at the library   ~~в. yesterday morning~~
3. _____ I studied in Moscow   г. last night
4. _____ They were at their grandmother's in Novgorod   д. in the spring
5. _____ Tanya went to a restaurant   е. in the fall
6. _____ We watch a lot of football   ж. in the winter

ГОВОРЕНИЕ

ЕЕ. You will hear a series of questions asking you what activities are going to be on which days. Answer according to the cued weekday.

ОБРАЗЕЦ: *You hear:* Когда́ бу́дет новосе́лье?
          You see: (*Thursday*)
          You say: В четве́рг.

1. (*Sunday*)   3. (*Saturday*)   5. (*Wednesday*)
2. (*Tuesday*)   4. (*Monday*)   6. (*Friday*)

ЖЖ. How would you express the following ideas of *studying* or *learning* in Russian? Choose from the verbs **занима́ться** and **учи́ть / вы́учить**.

ОБРАЗЕЦ: *You hear and see:* (*I'm learning English.*)
          You say: Я учу́ англи́йский язы́к.

1. (*I'm studying at the library.*)   4. (*I've already memorized the words.*)
2. (*I'm studying the new words.*)   5. (*I'm learning Russian.*)
3. (*I study a lot.*)   6. (*I always study in the morning.*)

33. Expand the sentences that you hear, telling when the various activities will be done.

ОБРАЗЕЦ: *You hear:* Мы бу́дем игра́ть в те́ннис.
          You see: (*tomorrow morning*)
          You say: За́втра у́тром мы бу́дем игра́ть в те́ннис.

1. (*last night*)   4. (*in the summer*)
2. (*this morning*)   5. (*in the winter*)
3. (*tonight*)   6. (*in the fall*)

254   Уро́к 7, Часть пе́рвая

Name_____ Date_____ Class_____

ЧАСТЬ ВТОРАЯ
Я тебе́ позвоню́

РАБО́ТА ДО́МА

ПИСЬМО́

Понима́ние те́кста

А. Review the reading on pages 297–298 of the textbook. Then match the question on the left with the correct answer on the right.

1. _____ Како́й у Са́ши но́мер телефо́на?   а. Ле́ну
2. _____ Како́й у Ле́ны но́мер телефо́на?   б. 193-14-41
3. _____ Како́й но́мер телефо́на спра́вочной?   в. 155-94-79
4. _____ Како́й у Серге́я Петро́вича на рабо́те   г. Ната́лье Ива́новне
   но́мер телефо́на?   д. 155-94-89
5. _____ Кого́ Са́ша приглаша́ет на новосе́лье? е. Серге́ю Петро́вичу
6. _____ Кому́ звони́т Алексе́й Грачёв?   ж. 155-20-10
7. _____ Кому́ звони́т Серге́й Петро́вич?

Aspect: *To begin* (or *finish*) doing something

Б. Жизнь Ка́ти. Katya has led a very typical life for a Russian girl in regards to when she started to talk, walk, go to college, work, and so on. In the box below is a list of things that Katya did at some time during her life. Match each activity with the age when she would most typically have *started* the activity, using the verb **нача́ть**. One of them has been done for you.

> ходи́ть   говори́ть
> ~~ходи́ть в шко́лу~~
> чита́ть и писа́ть
> води́ть (*drive*) маши́ну
> рабо́тать

1. Когда́ Ка́те был год, _____
2. Когда́ Ка́те бы́ло два го́да, _____
3. Когда́ Ка́те бы́ло пять лет, <u>она́ начала́ ходи́ть в шко́лу.</u>

Уро́к 7, Часть втора́я   255

4. Когда́ Ка́те бы́ло шесть лет, _____

5. Когда́ Ка́те бы́ло восемна́дцать лет, _____

6. Когда́ Ка́те бы́ло два́дцать три го́да, _____

В. Stepan had a busy day yesterday. He finished several things he had been working on and started some others. From the pairs of phrases below, tell what he finished doing and what he started to do.

ОБРАЗЕЦ: писа́ть курсову́ю / писа́ть статью́

Степа́н ко́нчил писа́ть курсову́ю и на́чал писа́ть статью́.

1. чита́ть «До́ктора Жива́го» / чита́ть «А́нну Каре́нину»

_____

2. чини́ть маши́ну / чини́ть пылесо́с

_____

3. слу́шать кла́ссику / слу́шать рок-му́зыку

_____

4. смотре́ть «Гладиа́тора» / смотре́ть «Ва́ню с 42-ой у́лицы»

_____

Г. Choose one of the infinitives from the box below to complete each of the following sentences. Remember: When the verbs **начина́ть / нача́ть** and **конча́ть / ко́нчить** are followed by another verb, the second verb is always an imperfective infinitive.

```
де́лать      сде́лать
писа́ть      написа́ть
смотре́ть
             посмотре́ть
учи́ть       вы́учить
рабо́тать
             объясни́ть
объясня́ть
             зада́ть
задава́ть
    ~~игра́ть~~
```

ОБРАЗЕЦ: Когда́ Ва́ня и И́ра на́чали _____игра́ть_____ в ша́хматы?

1. Вчера́ ве́чером Оле́г на́чал _____ статью́ о поли́тике.

2. Ди́ма обы́чно начина́ет _____ телеви́зор в семь часо́в.

3. А́ня ко́нчила _____ дома́шнее зада́ние два часа́ наза́д.

4. Студе́нты ещё не на́чали _____ но́вые слова́.

5. Лю́да, когда́ ты обы́чно конча́ешь _____?

6. Преподава́тель ко́нчил _____ но́вую грамма́тику и на́чал

_____ студе́нтам вопро́сы.

Name_____ Date_____ Class_____

Time *when:* Когда́ ... ? В семь часо́в

Д. What is your roommate Anya up to? It is now noon. Use Anya's schedule below to tell when and where she has been and what she was doing there. Tell also where she will be at different times this afternoon and what she will be doing there. Write the numbers of the hours out as words. (Remember, however, that 1.00 will require no number.)

8.00	на стадио́не	игра́ть в те́ннис
10.00	у Га́ли	пить ко́фе
11.00	до́ма	учи́ть францу́зские слова́
1.00	до́ма	гото́вить обе́д
2.00	в университе́те	слу́шать ле́кцию (*lecture*)
4.00	в кинотеа́тре (*movie theater*)	смотре́ть фильм
6.00	у Воло́ди	занима́ться

ОБРАЗЕ́Ц: В во́семь часо́в А́ня была́ на стадио́не. Она́ игра́ла в те́ннис.

1. _____
2. _____
3. _____
4. _____
5. _____
6. _____

Expressing thanks

Е. Below is a picture of the room that the following people just helped you furnish. How would tell them thanks for the items they managed to find for you?

ОБРАЗЕ́Ц: Мари́на, спаси́бо за крова́ть.

1. Фе́дя, _____
2. Ни́на, _____

3. И́ра, _____

4. Све́та, _____

5. Ми́тя, _____

6. Бо́ря, _____

7. На́стя, _____

Aspect in the future: Imperfective

Ж. Tomorrow, Wednesday, is a holiday! What do you think your classmates are going to be doing? Choose an activity from the list below to match their interests and needs.

    занима́ться   смотре́ть пье́су А. П. Че́хова «Три сестры́»
    слу́шать му́зыку   ~~учи́ть испа́нский язы́к~~
    игра́ть в футбо́л   чита́ть «А́нну Каре́нину»
    гото́вить большо́й обе́д

    ОБРАЗЕ́Ц: Кристи́на хо́чет учи́ться в Испа́нии.

                      Она́ бу́дет учи́ть испа́нский язы́к.

1. Бра́йан лю́бит спорт. _____

2. Джон пригласи́л профе́ссора Вели́чкина и его́ жену́ на обе́д.

_____

3. У Кла́ры в пя́тницу контро́льная. _____

4. Билл лю́бит Толсто́го. _____

5. Са́ра и её друг Стив лю́бят теа́тр. _____

_____

6. Том — пиани́ст. _____

Aspect in the future: Perfective

З. Which of the following sentences refer to the present and which to the future?

		PRESENT	FUTURE
ОБРАЗЕ́Ц:	Что <u>ска́жут</u> на́ши роди́тели?	_____	X
1.	Куда́ ты <u>идёшь</u>?	_____	_____
2.	Кого́ ты <u>пригласи́шь</u> на новосе́лье?	_____	_____
3.	Семина́р <u>начнётся</u> в де́сять часо́в.	_____	_____
4.	Она́ <u>де́лает</u> дома́шнее зада́ние.	_____	_____
5.	Когда́ ты <u>прочита́ешь</u> э́ти статьи́?	_____	_____
6.	Вы <u>опозда́ете</u> на заня́тия.	_____	_____

Name _____ Date _____ Class _____

И. Olga has decided to plan her day carefully and write down what she'll do tomorrow and when. Finish her plan, following the example. Choose from among the perfective verbs below and use them with the items cued in parentheses.

посмотре́ть   купи́ть   вы́учить   позвони́ть
сде́лать   ~~написа́ть~~ прочита́ть

ОБРАЗЕЦ: (письмо́ подру́ге) У́тром <u>я напишу́ письмо́ подру́ге.</u>

1. (но́вые слова́) У́тром _____
2. (статья́ в газе́те) Днём _____
3. (сувени́ры сестре́) Днём _____
4. (дома́шнее зада́ние) Днём _____
5. (но́вый фильм) Ве́чером _____
6. (де́душка) Ве́чером _____

К. Following is a short children's poem that schoolchildren recite after having written a lot. The children exercise their fingers to give them a rest. You have learned all the words in the poem except the two underlined words, which are perfective future. How would you translate the poem into English?

Мы писа́ли, мы писа́ли,
На́ши па́льчики (*little fingers*) уста́ли (*got tired*),
Мы немно́го <u>отдохнём</u> (*perfective of* отдыха́ть),
И опя́ть писа́ть <u>начнём</u> (= начнём писа́ть).

_____
_____
_____
_____

Aspect and tense: Summary

Л. Can you identify the tense (present, past, or future) and the aspect (imperfective or perfective) of the verbs in the following Russian sentences?

		TENSE	ASPECT
ОБРАЗЕЦ:	Я <u>пишу́</u> письмо́ домо́й.	_present_	_imperfective_
1.	В э́том году́ Ва́ня <u>бу́дет учи́ться</u> в юриди́ческом институ́те.	_____	_____
2.	Вчера́ мы три часа́ <u>игра́ли</u> в ша́хматы.	_____	_____
3.	Сего́дня ве́чером я <u>вы́учу</u> но́вые слова́.	_____	_____
4.	Почему́ вы <u>опозда́ли</u> на ле́кцию?	_____	_____
5.	Что вы <u>бу́дете де́лать</u> послеза́втра?	_____	_____
6.	Кто у вас в семье́ <u>гото́вит</u> обе́д?	_____	_____
7.	Мы обяза́тельно <u>сде́лаем</u> дома́шнее зада́ние за́втра у́тром.	_____	_____
8.	Кого́ ты <u>пригласи́ла</u> на новосе́лье?	_____	_____
9.	Вы мно́го <u>занима́лись</u> вчера́?	_____	_____

Перево́д

М. Translate the following dialogue into Russian.

"Hi, Sasha. Whom are you calling?"
"I'm calling my friend. His telephone started working today."
"Do you already know his number?"
"Of course. And if his telephone isn't working yet, I'll call him tomorrow."

_____

_____

_____

_____

260 Уро́к 7, Часть втора́я

Name _____ Date _____ Class _____

Повторе́ние — мать уче́ния

H. Following is a summary of the reading in Part 2. Fill in the blanks with words that maintain the context of the reading. You will have to change the form of some of the words. You may use both the imperfective and perfective forms of one of the verbs.

У Си́линых (*at the Silins*) сего́дня _____¹ рабо́тать телефо́н. Им всё вре́мя _____². Са́ша _____³ Ле́не и _____⁴ её на новосе́лье. Пото́м позвони́л ста́рый _____⁵ Серге́я Петро́вича. Он сказа́л, что он в Москве́ в _____.⁶ И ещё звони́ли каки́е-то незнако́мые (*unknown*) лю́ди. Но́мер Си́линых _____⁷ на но́мер _____.⁸ Когда́ Серге́й Петро́вич позвони́л домо́й, Ната́лья Ива́новна попроси́ла (*asked*) его́ неме́дленно поменя́ть (*change*) но́мер.	звони́ть / позвони́ть знако́мый командиро́вка начина́ть / нача́ть похо́ж приглаша́ть / пригласи́ть спра́вочная

Ситуа́ции

O. How would you . . .

1. say that last night you finished writing your term paper and started reading a book?
   _____

2. ask your classmate what he was doing yesterday morning?
   _____

3. ask a Russian you met on the plane in which city she'll be living in America?
   _____

4. say that you're going to buy your brother a Russian book?
   _____

5. tell your parents thanks for the cassettes?
   _____

6. say that you all will start studying at seven o'clock?
   _____

Ваша о́чередь!

П. Answer the questions that are asked of you.

1. Ско́лько тебе́ бы́ло лет, когда́ ты ко́нчил (ко́нчила) шко́лу?
   _____

2. Когда́ ты обы́чно де́лаешь дома́шнее зада́ние?
   _____

3. Что ты де́лал (де́лала) вчера́ ве́чером?
   _____

4. Что ты ку́пишь ба́бушке на день рожде́ния?
   _____

5. Како́й сувени́р ты хо́чешь купи́ть дру́гу?
   _____

6. В Росси́и ты бу́дешь говори́ть по-ру́сски? По-англи́йски?
   _____

7. Кому́ ты звони́л (звони́ла) вчера́?
   _____

Сочине́ние

Р. Write a short paragraph (five or six sentences) about what you did yesterday. Pay attention to the verbal aspect—were the actions completed or were they in progress? Did you do them in the morning, afternoon, or evening?

_____
_____
_____
_____
_____
_____

Name_____ Date_____ Class_____

РАБОТА В ЛАБОРАТОРИИ

ДИАЛОГИ

Диалог 1 Ни́на до́ма? (Asking for someone on the phone)

АА. Follow along as you listen to the dialogue.

— А. Алло́, я слу́шаю.
— Б. До́брый день. Скажи́те, пожа́луйста, Ни́на до́ма?
— А. Её нет. Она́ в университе́те.
— Б. Вы не зна́ете, когда́ она́ бу́дет до́ма?
— А. Позвони́те, пожа́луйста, ве́чером.
— Б. Хорошо́, спаси́бо. До свида́ния.

- Now read and repeat aloud in the pause after each phrase.
- Now read the lines for speaker **Б** aloud.
- Now read the lines for speaker **А** aloud.

Rewrite the dialogue so that speaker **Б** is asking about Leonid (**Леони́д**) who is at work. Speaker **Б** should call again at eight o'clock.

А. _____

Б. _____

А. _____

Б. _____

А. _____

Б. _____

Диалог 2 Мне о́чень жаль... (Turning down an invitation)

ББ. Follow along as you listen to the dialogue.

— А. Ни́на, в воскресе́нье в университе́те конце́рт рок-му́зыки. Я тебя́ приглаша́ю.
— Б. Спаси́бо, но в воскресе́нье я не могу́.
— А. О́чень жаль. Конце́рт бу́дет о́чень хоро́ший.
— Б. Мне то́же о́чень жа́ль, но в воскресе́нье у нас бу́дут го́сти, и мне на́до быть до́ма.

- Now read and repeat aloud in the pause after each phrase.
- Now read the lines for speaker **Б** aloud.
- Now read the lines for speaker **А** aloud.

1. What is Nina invited to? _____

2. Why can't she go? _____

АУДИРОВАНИЕ

ВВ. Larisa's mother wants to know what her daughter was doing or where she was at specific times on the preceding day. You will hear what Larisa told her mother. Match the time of day with the appropriate activity or place. The first one has been done for you. There will not be an activity for each time given.

1. __e__ 9.00
2. _____ 10.00
3. _____ 11.00
4. _____ 12.00
5. _____ 1.00
6. _____ 2.00
7. _____ 3.00
8. _____ 4.00
9. _____ 5.00
10. _____ 6.00
11. _____ 7.00
12. _____ 8.00

а. was at a café
б. was fixing dinner
в. was studying her English vocabulary
г. was at the library
д. was at a club
~~е. was reading the newspaper~~
ж. went to the store
з. was calling a friend
и. was writing a letter to her friend in Boston

ГГ. You will hear a series of questions and statements. Write the letter of the question or statement next to the most appropriate response from the list below.

ОБРАЗЕЦ: Когда́ бу́дет новосе́лье?

1. _____ Ве́чером и но́чью.
2. _____ Мне о́чень жаль, но я не могу́.
3. _____ Нет, я ещё учу́сь.
4. _____ Де́душке.
5. __Об.__ В суббо́ту, в шесть часо́в.
6. _____ Нет, вы не туда́ попа́ли.

ДД. You will hear a series of sentences. Circle **P** if the sentence is in the present tense, **F** if it is in the future tense.

ОБРАЗЕЦ: *You hear:* Я учу́ но́вые слова́.

Об.	Ⓟ	F
1.	P	F
2.	P	F
3.	P	F
4.	P	F
5.	P	F
6.	P	F
7.	P	F

Name_____ Date_____ Class_____

ГОВОРЕНИЕ

ЕЕ. Why wasn't Patrick able to come by and help you yesterday? What does he give you as excuses?

    ОБРАЗЕЦ: *You hear and see:* (*10:00, reading the paper*)
                    You say: В де́сять часо́в я чита́л газе́ту.

1. (*11:00, working at the library*)
2. (*1:00, preparing dinner*)
3. (*2:00, studying at the library*)
4. (*3:00, explaining grammar to his brother*)
5. (*4:00, fixing the car*)
6. (*5:00, watching television*)
7. (*7:00, writing a term paper*)

ЖЖ. How would you thank somebody for the following gifts?

    ОБРАЗЕЦ: *You hear and see:* (*interesting book*)
                    You say: Спаси́бо за интере́сную кни́гу.

1. (*tasty chocolate*)
2. (*pretty flowers*)
3. (*invitation*)
4. (*photograph*)
5. (*wonderful present*)
6. (*postcard*)

33. How would you say the following in Russian?

    ОБРАЗЕЦ: *You hear and see:* (*I'm buying a car.*)
                    You say: Я покупа́ю маши́ну.
    or   *You hear and see:* (*I'll buy a car.*)
                    You say: Я куплю́ маши́ну.

1. (*I'm inviting Valya.*)
2. (*I'll invite Valya.*)
3. (*I'm calling my neighbor.*)
4. (*I'll call my neighbor.*)
5. (*I'm asking Nikolai.*)
6. (*I'll ask Nikolai.*)
7. (*I'm learning the new words.*)
8. (*I'll learn the new words.*)

Name_____ Date_____ Class_____

ЧАСТЬ ТРЕТЬЯ
Что принести?

РАБОТА ДОМА

ПИСЬМО

Понимание текста

А. Review the reading on pages 310–311 of the textbook. How would you complete each of the following sentences?

1. Таня и Света недавно говорили о _____
2. Они будут праздновать _____
3. Новоселье будет в субботу, в _____
4. Света и Таня уже купили _____
5. Джим умеет готовить _____
6. И в Америке и в России есть мужчины, которые _____
7. Джим, его друг Джеф и одна девушка, Николь, вместе _____
8. На новоселье Джим принесёт _____

Многие

Б. Disagree with the following statements using **многие.**

ОБРАЗЕЦ: Все женщины любят готовить.
А по-моему, многие женщины не любят готовить.

1. Студенты не любят учиться.

2. Американцы не говорят по-русски.

3. По-моему, американские студенты не любят классическую музыку.

4. Я слышала, что в Америке мужчины не умеют готовить.

5. Русские студенты не опаздывают на занятия.

Урок 7, Часть третья 267

Prepositional case of pronouns and это

Б. Fill in the blanks with the correct Prepositional case pronoun or form of **это** as required by context.

ОБРАЗЕЦ: У бабушки три собаки. Вы знаете об _____этом?_____

1. Иван Ильич очень строгий. Его студенты часто говорят об _____.
2. Я думаю, Валерий талантливый математик. Что ты думаешь о _____?
3. О _____ вы спрашиваете? Об экзамене?
4. Ты помнишь Петю Власенкова, который у нас работал? Я видел его на конференции, он спрашивал о _____.
5. Это моя старая гитара. Я на _____ учился играть.
6. Летом Ирина едет в Японию. Ты об _____ знаешь?
7. Это очень хороший фильм. В _____ играет мой любимый актёр.
8. Когда вы были в Сибири, мы часто говорили о _____.
9. Варя говорит, что готовить должны не женщины, а мужчины. Что вы думаете об _____?

What time is it? and A.M., P.M.

Г. Below are the times that Amanda usually does certain things. Answer the questions below about her activities. Write the numbers out and be sure to specify with **утра, дня, вечера,** or **ночи** whether the time is A.M. or P.M.

```
11.00 A.M.—drinks coffee
12.30 P.M.—plays chess
1.00 P.M.—calls her friend in Boston
2.20 P.M.—has class
3.40 P.M.—has lecture
5.00 P.M.—fixes dinner
```

```
8.00 P.M.—begins to watch TV
9.30 P.M.—begins to play guitar
11.00 P.M.—starts to study
2.30 A.M.—finishes studying
4.00 A.M.—sleeps
```

ОБРАЗЕЦ: Когда Аманда играет в шахматы?

В двенадцать тридцать дня.

1. Когда Аманда начинает играть на гитаре? _____
2. Когда она пьёт кофе? _____
3. Когда она начинает заниматься? _____
4. Когда у Аманды лекция? _____
5. Когда она заканчивает заниматься? _____
6. Когда она готовит обед? _____
7. Когда она начинает смотреть телевизор? _____
8. Когда Аманда звонит другу в Бостон? _____

Name_____ Date_____ Class_____

Verbs of "studying"

Д. Complete each sentence with the correct verb, as required by context.

ОБРАЗЕЦ: Я уже́ два го́да _____учу́сь_____ (учу́сь, изуча́ю, учу́) в медици́нском институ́те.

1. Мой брат _____ (у́чится, занима́ется, изуча́ет) ру́сскую исто́рию.

2. Вчера́ Ната́ша _____ (изуча́ла, вы́учила, гото́вилась) все но́вые слова́.

3. Она́ _____ (занима́ется, у́чится, изуча́ет) францу́зский язы́к в Моско́вском университе́те.

4. Вы должны́ _____ (учи́ться, изуча́ть, учи́ть) но́вые слова́ ка́ждый день.

5. Я не хочу́ _____ (изуча́ть, учи́ться, учи́ть)! Хочу́ рабо́тать.

6. Где ты предпочита́ешь (*prefer*) _____ (занима́ться, учи́ться, изуча́ть), до́ма и́ли в библиоте́ке?

7. Он сейча́с _____ (изуча́ет, гото́вится, занима́ется) к экза́мену.

8. В како́м университе́те ты хо́чешь _____ (занима́ться, учи́ться, изуча́ть)?

Е. In the following paragraph Nikolai is telling about his own college life and that of his brother Pyotr. Fill in the blanks with the correct verbs of studying: **учи́ться, занима́ться, изуча́ть, учи́ть / вы́учить,** or **гото́виться / подгото́виться.**

Мой брат Пётр _____¹ в Бо́стонском университе́те, как и я. Мы снима́ем вме́сте кварти́ру, но мы ре́дко ви́дим друг дру́га. Он _____² на хими́ческом факульте́те, а я _____³ на филологи́ческом факульте́те. Он _____⁴ хи́мию, а я _____⁵ францу́зский язы́к и литерату́ру. Он обы́чно _____⁶ до́ма, а я предпочита́ю (*prefer*) _____⁷ в библиоте́ке. Я хочу́ чита́ть и говори́ть не то́лько по-францу́зски, но и по-испа́нски, поэ́тому я _____⁸ ещё испа́нский язы́к. Ка́ждый ве́чер я _____⁹ но́вые слова́. Пётр сказа́л, что ему́ на́до бу́дет чита́ть статьи́ по-неме́цки, поэ́тому он _____¹⁰ неме́цкий язы́к. И коне́чно, мы хорошо́ говори́м по-ру́сски: ведь на́ши роди́тели из Росси́и. Сейча́с Пётр о́чень серьёзно _____¹¹ к экза́мену, и я то́же.

Ж. The following was taken from a website of a group of students studying together at Moscow State University. Read what the two young men have to say about themselves and answer the questions below in English.

403 группа

2000-2001 учебный год

Ларионов Илья Владимирович

Родился 28 мая 1980 года в городе Пущино. Учился там же, до 9 класса (включительно) в Пущинской средней школе 3. Учился плохо. В 1996 году поступил на химфак, состояние учёбы не изменилось, но первый семестр выдержал.

Потехин Иван

Я из Мурманска, живу в Москве, учусь хорошо.

1. In what month was Ilya born? _____

2. What was the name of the school where he studied until the ninth grade?
   _____

3. What kind of a student does he think he was in high school? Which sentence tells you? _____

4. In the last sentence he talks about entering the university. What do you think the term **химфак** means? It might help to see it as **хим/фак** and think of the various departments of the university.
   _____

5. Ivan says that he lives in Moscow. Where do you think he's from?
   _____

6. What sort of a student does he think he is? _____

Name _____ Date _____ Class _____

Перево́д

3. Translate the following dialogue into Russian.

"When will your friends celebrate their housewarming?"
"On Friday at eight P.M. They said I could invite a friend. I'm inviting you."
"Is that okay? I don't know them."
"Of course it's okay."

_____
_____
_____
_____
_____

Повторе́ние — мать уче́ния

И. Following is a summary of the reading in Part 3. Fill in the blanks with words that maintain the context of the reading. You will have to change the form of some of the words. Use each word only once.

Све́та и Та́ня бу́дут _____¹ новосе́лье и _____² Джи́ма. Новосе́лье бу́дет в суббо́ту, в семь часо́в _____.³ Сыр, _____⁴ и вино́ де́вушки уже́ купи́ли. Джим предлага́ет пригото́вить пи́ццу. Он уме́ет гото́вить не то́лько _____,⁵ но и о́вощи, и мя́со, и ры́бу. Его́ друзья́ говоря́т, что он _____⁶ совсе́м непло́хо. Джим говори́т, что в Аме́рике _____⁷ мужчи́ны хорошо́ гото́вят. Муж и жена́ ча́сто гото́вят обе́д _____.⁸

Та́ня зна́ет, что Джим _____⁹ игра́ть на гита́ре. Она́ про́сит Джи́ма _____¹⁰ гита́ру.

ве́чер
гото́вить
колбаса́
мно́гие
пи́цца
по о́череди
пра́здновать
приглаша́ть
принести́
учи́ться

Ситуа́ции

К. How would you . . .

1. say that you usually begin fixing dinner at six in the evening?

2. thank someone for a book and say that you like the photographs in it?

3. say that you already knew about that (what your classmates were talking about)?

4. say that your brother is studying physics and that he is a good student?

5. say that you usually start to study at eight or nine in the evening?

6. ask your sister if she studied her French vocabulary words last night?

7. say that you need to study for an exam in Russian literature?

Ва́ша о́чередь!

Л. Answer the questions that are asked of you.

1. Когда́ ты обы́чно занима́ешься?

2. Когда́ ты обы́чно начина́ешь занима́ться?

3. Ты ча́сто у́чишь ру́сские слова́? Почти́ ка́ждый ве́чер? Вообще́ (*at all*) не у́чишь?

4. Каки́е предме́ты (*subjects*) ты изуча́ешь?

5. Кто обы́чно гото́вит у тебя́ до́ма?

6. Скажи́, пожа́луйста, кото́рый час?

Сочине́ние

М. Write a short paragraph (five or six sentences) about your life as a student. Ideas: Where are you studying? What are you studying? Where do you usually study? What time do you have classes?

Name_____ Date_____ Class_____

РАБОТА В ЛАБОРАТОРИИ

ДИАЛОГИ

Диалог 1 Мо́жно попроси́ть . . . ? (On the phone: Asking to speak to someone who is absent)

АА. Follow along as you listen to the dialogue.

А. До́брый день. Мо́жно попроси́ть Ва́сю?
Б. До́брый день. Ва́си нет, он в университе́те.
А. А когда́ он бу́дет до́ма?
Б. Позвони́те ве́чером.

- Now read and repeat aloud in the pause after each phrase.
- Now read the lines for speaker **Б** aloud.
- Now read the lines for speaker **А** aloud.

How would you ask to speak to your friend Anna?

_____

Диалог 2 Приглаше́ние (Extending an invitation)

ББ. Follow along as you listen to the dialogue.

А. В воскресе́нье мои́ друзья́ бу́дут пра́здновать новосе́лье. Они́ пригласи́ли меня́, а я приглаша́ю тебя́.
Б. А э́то удо́бно? Ведь я их не зна́ю.
А. Коне́чно, удо́бно.
Б. Что принести́?
А. Мо́жно принести́ сыр и колбасу́. И́ли лимона́д (soda).

- Now read and repeat aloud in the pause after each phrase.
- Now read the lines for speaker **Б** aloud.
- Now read the lines for speaker **А** aloud.

How might you respond in Russian if someone invites you to a party at the home of people you don't know?

_____

АУДИРОВАНИЕ

ВВ. You will hear a series of questions and statements. For each one, circle the letter of the most appropriate response.

ОБРАЗЕЦ: Ди́ма, мы сего́дня у́тром говори́ли о тебе́.
 а. О ней?
 б. О нас?
 (в.) Обо мне?

1. а. Не зна́ю, но в них интере́сные фотогра́фии.
   б. Не зна́ю, но в ней интере́сные фотогра́фии.
   в. Не зна́ю, но в нём интере́сные фотогра́фии.

2. а. Нет, я ничего́ о нём не зна́ю.
   б. Нет, я ничего́ о ней не зна́ю.
   в. Нет, я ничего́ о тебе́ не зна́ю.

3. а. Да, в ней есть интере́сные статьи́.

   б. Да, в них есть интере́сные статьи́.

   в. Да, в нём есть интере́сные статьи́.

4. а. Да? Что он пи́шет о нас?

   б. Да? Что он пи́шет о тебе́?

   в. Да? Что он пи́шет обо мне?

5. а. Что ты хо́чешь знать о ней?

   б. Что ты хо́чешь знать о нём?

   в. Что ты хо́чешь знать о них?

6. а. О нас? Заче́м он э́то сде́лал?

   б. О вас? Заче́м он э́то сде́лал?

   в. О тебе́? Заче́м он э́то сде́лал?

ГГ. You have been asked to record appointments and business dinners for your company's president, who doesn't speak Russian. Write down in English the day and time of each. Be sure to include A.M. or P.M.

ОБРАЗЕЦ: В четве́рг в два часа́ дня.

Об. _____Thursday_____   _2:00 P.M._

1. _____   _____

2. _____   _____

3. _____   _____

4. _____   _____

5. _____   _____

6. _____   _____

7. _____   _____

ДД. You will hear a series of questions. Write the letter of the question next to the most appropriate response in the list below.

ОБРАЗЕЦ: Та́ня, где ты у́чишься?

1. _____ Италья́нский.

2. _____ Нет, на математи́ческом.

3. __Об.__ В Моско́вской консервато́рии.

4. _____ Нет, исто́рию Росси́и.

5. _____ В библиоте́ке.

6. _____ У меня́ за́втра экза́мен по биоло́гии.

7. _____ Нет, пло́хо.

Name_____ Date_____ Class_____

ГОВОРЕНИЕ

ЕЕ. You will be asked to tell about a certain thing or person. Respond that you don't know anything about it, him, her, or them.

ОБРАЗЕЦ: *You hear and see:* Расскажи́ нам о Ма́рке Тве́не!
You say: Я ничего́ о нём не зна́ю.

1. Расскажи́ нам о Джо́рдже Вашингто́не!
2. Расскажи́ нам о президе́нте Эйзенха́уэре и его́ жене́ Ме́йми!
3. Расскажи́ нам о Джу́лии Ро́бертс!
4. Расскажи́ нам о Бе́тси Росс!
5. Расскажи́ нам о Влади́мире Набо́кове и его́ жене́ Ве́ре Евсе́евне.
6. Расскажи́ нам о фи́льме Хичко́ка «Ми́стер и ми́ссис Смит»!

ЖЖ. How would you say each of the following times in Russian?

ОБРАЗЕЦ: *You hear and see:* 6:00 A.M.
You say: шесть часо́в утра́

1. 8:00 P.M.
2. 4:00 P.M.
3. 10:00 A.M.
4. 2:00 A.M.
5. 9:00 P.M.
6. 1:00 P.M.
7. 3:00 A.M.

33. How would you say each of the following in Russian?

ОБРАЗЕЦ: *You hear and see:* (*I'm studying Russian history.*)
You say: Я изуча́ю ру́сскую исто́рию.

1. (*I'm studying at a medical institute.*)
2. (*I always study at home.*)
3. (*I'm studying for an exam in geography.*)
4. (*I'm studing the new Russian words.*)
5. (*I'm studying math.*)
6. (*I will definitely learn the new words tonight.*)
7. (*I'm going to study at a university in California.*)

Name_____ Date_____ Class_____

ЧАСТЬ ЧЕТВЁРТАЯ
Было очень весело!

РАБОТА ДОМА

ПИСЬМО

Понимание текста

А. Sveta tells her mother about a lot of people in her letter. Review the reading on page 323 of the textbook and match each person on the left with one or more of the descriptions on the right.

1. Татьяна Дмитриевна _____
2. Саша Круглов _____
3. Илья Ильич Петровский _____
4. Лена Силина _____
5. Джим Ричардсон _____
6. Виктор _____

а. учится на факультете журналистики.
б. хорошо читает лекции (*lectures*).
в. бизнесмен.
г. подарил Свете и Тане стол.
д. работает в библиотеке.
е. приехал (*came*) в Москву на год.
ж. студент консерватории.
з. аспирант профессора Петровского.
и. живёт в том же (*the same*) подъезде, где живут Света и Таня.
к. хозяйка квартиры, где Света и Таня снимают комнату.

Past tense of verbs like мочь / смочь

Б. Complete the following sentences with the past-tense forms of the verb **мочь** or **помочь**.

ОБРАЗЕЦ: — Почему ты не сделал домашнее задание?
— Я не ____мог____ заниматься, у нас были гости.

1. — Почему ты не позвонил вчера?
   — Я не _____ позвонить, у нас телефон не работал.

2. — Ты сделала домашнее задание?
   — Да, мне _____ Вера. Она хорошо знает математику.

3. — Салат очень вкусный. Ты сама (*yourself*) его готовила?
   — Нет, мне _____ мама.

4. — Почему вы нам не писали?
   — Мы не _____ писать, у нас не было вашего адреса.

5. — Почему тебя не было на собрании?

— Я не _____ прийти.

6. — Кто тебе _____ починить компьютер?

— Олег. Он всё умеет.

Past tense of -ти verbs

В. The people and animals below found something appropriate for themselves. Match them with what they found. The first one has been done for you. Use each item only once.

1. Журналистка нашла __г__
2. Электрик нашёл _____
3. Бизнесмен нашёл _____
4. Кошки нашли _____
5. Водитель такси нашёл _____
6. Официант нашёл _____
7. Учительница нашла _____
8. Студенты нашли _____

а. телевизор, который не работает.
б. дом № 5.
в. сочинение Серёжи.
г. ~~ручку.~~
д. телефон брокера.
е. молоко.
ж. хорошую работу.
з. меню.

Г. It's Thursday evening, the dorm is empty, and you are recalling where everybody went.

ОБРАЗЕЦ: (Боб; stadium) Боб пошёл на стадион.

1. (Брандон; meeting) _____
2. (Лиса; institute) _____
3. (Ронда; ballet) _____
4. (Эрик и Билл; laboratory) _____
5. (Сара и Рон; restaurant) _____
6. (Тина; classes) _____

Д. Volodya had a party the night before and is trying to remember who came when and who brought what. Help him with his task. The items are pictured from left to right in the order they were brought. Write out all times as words.

Name_____ Date_____ Class_____

ОБРАЗЕЦ: 4:00 / Марина
В четыре часа пришла Марина и принесла сыр.

1. 5:00 / Наташа

2. 6:00 / Валера

3. 6:30 / Семён

4. 7:00 / Николай Петрович и Нина Алексеевна

5. 8:00 / Федя и Люда

6. 9:00 / Ира

7. 9:30 / Миша

Reported speech

E. Kirill and Oleg are having a party tomorrow night. Both called several friends and are now reporting back to each other. Below is the direct speech of their friends. What would Kirill and Oleg say? Remember that verb tense and aspect do not change in reported speech in Russian. Write the equivalent English subject and verb (for both sentences) to the right.

ОБРАЗЕЦ: Маша сказала: — Я принесу колбасу.   *I will bring*
Маша сказала, что она принесёт колбасу.   *she would bring*

1. Аня сказала: — Я умею готовить салат. _____

2. Толя сказал: — Я принесу гитару. _____

3. Лариса сказала: — Я приглашу подругу. _____

4. Петя сказал: — Я позвоню утром. _____

5. Коля сказал: — Я не могу, я завтра вечером работаю. _____

6. Наташа сказала: — Я опоздаю, у меня занятия в университете. _____

Whether (*or not*): **Inquiries using ли**

Ж. While talking with their friends, Kirill and Oleg naturally turned to other topics. Following are some of the questions that their friends asked. How would Kirill and Oleg report about their conversation with the other person? (Remember, in indirect speech, these yes/no questions will become *whether or not* statements requiring **ли**.)

ОБРАЗЕЦ: Маша спросила: — Ты работаешь в среду вечером?

Маша спросила, работаю ли я в среду вечером.

1. Аня спросила: — Петя знает Машу?

2. Толя спросил: — Вам нравится новая квартира?

3. Лариса спросила: — Аня хорошо говорит по-английски?

4. Петя спросил: — Ты читал «Евгения Онегина»?

5. Коля спросил: — Вы хотите петь песни?

6. Наташа спросила: — Толя хорошо играет на гитаре?

To wait for: <ждать + Genitive> vs. <ждать + Accusative>

З. How would you say or ask if somebody is waiting for the following people or things?

ОБРАЗЕЦ: Мы ждём <u>Катю</u>. (Катя)

1. Пётр уже два часа ждёт _____. (Николай)
2. Ты ждёшь _____? (письмо = *Are you waiting for a letter?*)
3. Мы час ждали _____. (автобус = *We waited an hour for the bus.*)
4. Почему вы ждёте _____ в машине? (Ирина)
5. Я уже три дня жду _____. (телеграмма = *I am waiting for the telegram.*)
6. Родители ждут _____. (сын)

280 Урок 7, Часть четвёртая

Name_____ Date_____ Class_____

Перево́д

И. Translate the following dialogue into Russian.

"Where did your brother go?"
"To a concert. He said Misha had invited him."
"Misha invited me to a concert last Saturday, but I couldn't go."
"Why not?"
"I was finishing a term paper."

_____
_____
_____
_____

Повторе́ние — мать уче́ния

К. Following is a summary of the reading in Part 4. Fill in the blanks with words that maintain the context of the reading. You will have to change the form of some of the words. Use each word only once.

Све́та пи́шет письмо́ ма́ме и _____,¹ каки́е у неё и у Та́ни сосе́ди и друзья́. Оди́н из них (one of them) — Илья́ Ильи́ч Петро́вский, профе́ссор ка́федры _____.² Они́ вме́сте жда́ли _____,³ и Илья́ Ильи́ч спроси́л Све́ту, лю́бит _____⁴ она́ литерату́ру. Она́ сказа́ла, что о́чень лю́бит. Тогда́ он спроси́л, _____⁵ ли она́, каку́ю литерату́рную герои́ню (heroine) зову́т Татья́на Дми́триевна. Све́та не _____⁶ вспо́мнить. Илья́ Ильи́ч _____⁷ ей. Он спроси́л, _____⁸ ли она́ зна́ет «Евге́ния Оне́гина».	ли мочь помо́чь хорошо́ авто́бус по́мнить расска́зывать исто́рия

Ситуа́ции

Л. How would you ...

1. tell a neighbor that you couldn't call because you couldn't find her telephone number?

2. say that your brother helped you fix your car?

3. say that yesterday your parents came and brought you a new television?

4. ask your classmate if she found the pictures of Nadya?

5. say that Dima said he would bring cheese and sausage to the housewarming party?

6. say that Vera asked if you were inviting your friend?

7. say that Lena wants to know if you play tennis well?

8. say that you've been waiting for a letter from your sister for two months already?

Ва́ша о́чередь!

М. Answer the questions that are asked of you.

1. Почему́ ты не позвони́л (позвони́ла) мне вчера́?

2. Кто тебе́ помо́г сде́лать дома́шнее зада́ние?

3. Когда́ ты пришёл/прие́хал (пришла́/прие́хала) в университе́т?

4. Когда́ ты слу́шаешь но́вости?

5. Что сказа́л Андре́й? Куда́ он пойдёт?

6. Кого́ ты ждал (ждала́) вчера́ в па́рке?

Name_____ Date_____ Class_____

Сочинéние

H. Write a short paragraph (five or six sentences) about some place that you went today. Ideas: Where did you go? What did you bring (with you)? Did anybody say anything to you or ask you something?

_____
_____
_____
_____
_____
_____

Fun with grammar! Case review

O. Fill in the blanks of the following sentences with the appropriate case endings. Not all blanks, however, will have an ending. Then enter the words into the crossword puzzle below to help check your spelling. The letter-number combinations (e.g., **г12**) at the end of each sentence indicate the location of the word or words in the puzzle. The first letter and number are for the first word and so on. Note that **г** is for **горизонтáль,** or horizontal; **в** is for **вертикáль,** or vertical.

1. В суббóт_____ мы ходи́ли на концéрт, а в воскресéнь_____ — на новосéлье. (г10) (г22)

2. От когó э́то письмó? От вáш_____ подрýг_____? (в12) (в4)

Урóк 7, Часть четвёртая

3. Мама купила мне красив_____ юбк_____. _____ (it) мне очень нравится. (г11) (в7) (г6)

4. Ты любишь играть в футбол_____? (в9)

5. Я рекомендую вам эт_____ журнал_____. В _____ (it) есть очень интересные статьи. (в18) (в8) (в2)

6. В нашем кинотеатре (*movie theater*) идут старые итальянск_____ фильм_____. Надо сказать об этом тво_____ отц_____. (в3) (г9) (г19) (в16)

7. Куда вы обычно ездите зим_____? (г15)

8. Профессора Иванова сегодня не будет. Разве ты об эт_____ не знала? (г5)

9. В сумке я нашла две ручк_____ и карандаш_____. (г17) (г13)

10. Дн_____ я работаю, а вечер_____ я занимаюсь. (г1) (в14)

11. Мы учимся на историческ_____ факультет_____. (г21) (в20)

РАБОТА В ЛАБОРАТОРИИ

ДИАЛОГИ

Диалог 1 Вы давно тут живёте? (Discussing living arrangements)

АА. Follow along as you listen to the dialogue.

А. Таня, познакомьтесь, это Миша и его друг Коля. Они снимают комнату у нашей соседки.
Б. Миша, вы давно тут живёте?
В. Нет, не очень. Мы сняли комнату месяц назад.
Б. Вам тут нравится?
В. Да, нам нравятся и комната и хозяйка. И автобусная остановка близко.

- Now read and repeat aloud in the pause after each phrase.
- Now read the lines for speaker **Б** aloud.
- Now read the lines for speaker **А** aloud.

How would you say, "We rented an apartment two months ago"?

_____

Диалог 2 Ты уже снял квартиру? (Discussing living arrangements)

ББ. Follow along as you listen to the dialogue.

А. Ты уже снял квартиру?
Б. Да. В очень хорошем районе.
А. Ты там живёшь один?
Б. Нет, конечно! Мы снимаем большую квартиру. Мне такая большая квартира не нужна. Кроме того, это дорого.
А. Кто это «мы»?
Б. Мы — это я и мои школьные друзья Вадик Ростовцев и Петя Гузенко. Мы всё делаем по очереди: покупаем продукты, готовим, убираем (*clean*) квартиру. В воскресенье моя очередь (*turn*) готовить обед. Ребята (*The guys*) говорят, что я готовлю неплохо. Приходи к нам (*to our place*) в воскресенье обедать (*to have dinner*)!

Name _____ Date _____ Class _____

- Now read and repeat aloud in the pause after each phrase.
- Now read the lines for speaker **Б** aloud.
- Now read the lines for speaker **А** aloud.

How would you say, "On Saturday it's my turn to clean the apartment"?

_____

АУДИРОВАНИЕ

ВВ. A three-way matching! Listen carefully to the following sentences and decide who (first column) helped whom (second column) do what (third column). Write the letters from the second and third columns next to the name in the first column.

ОБРАЗЕЦ: Нина помогла Борису починить пылесос.

	КТО? (*WHO?*)	КОМУ? (*WHOM?*)	ЧТО? (*WHAT?*)
Об. __г__ __дд__ Nina	а. student	аа. learn the Japanese vocabulary
1. ____ ____ Andrei	б. Katya	бб. write a letter in English
2. ____ ____ Rebecca	в. Lyuda	вв. do homework
3. ____ ____ Volodya	~~г. Boris~~	гг. find a nice apartment
4. ____ ____ neighbor	д. Marina	~~дд. fix the vacuum cleaner~~
5. ____ ____ Natasha	е. Anatolii	ее. make a salad
6. ____ ____ Professor Ivanov	ж. father	жж. fix the computer

ГГ. Another three-way matching! There was a party last night. Listen carefully to who arrived when and what they brought. Write the letter of the appropriate time and item next to the person's name. Times may be used more than once.

ОБРАЗЕЦ: В шесть часов пришёл Виталий и принёс кассеты.

Об. __б__ __дд__ Vitalii   а. 5:00   аа. guitar
1. ____ ____ Vika   б. 6:00   бб. salad
2. ____ ____ Liza   в. 7:00   вв. pizza
3. ____ ____ Viktor   г. 8:00   гг. cheese
4. ____ ____ Yulya   ~~дд. cassettes~~
5. ____ ____ Oleg   ее. wine
6. ____ ____ Tanya   жж. mineral water
7. ____ ____ Maksim   зз. sausage

ДД. Below is the indirect speech of a brief conversation that you will hear between Gena and Ira. Number the sentences in the order that they are spoken. The first one has been numbered for you.

а. _____ Ира спросила, можно ли пригласить Линду, их аспирантку.

б. _____ Гена сказал, что это прекрасная идея.

в. __1__ Гена сказал, что у него в воскресенье будет новоселье.

урок 7, Часть четвёртая   285

г. _____ Ге́на сказа́л, что он собира́ется пригласи́ть Ни́ну.

д. _____ Ге́на сказа́л, что он приглаша́ет И́ру.

е. _____ И́ра сказа́ла, что Ли́нда в Москве́ неда́вно.

ж. _____ Ге́на сказа́л, что он ещё хо́чет пригласи́ть Та́ню, Ва́сю и Ю́ру.

з. _____ И́ра спроси́ла, собира́ется ли он пригласи́ть Ни́ну.

ГОВОРЕНИЕ

ЕЕ. How would you say that the following people found the following items?

ОБРАЗЕЦ: *You hear and see:* (Natalya Stepanovna; watch)
You say: Ната́лья Степа́новна нашла́ часы́.

1. (the neighbors; our cat)
2. (Professor Nikonov; a taxi)
3. (the American students; an old map of Moscow)
4. (the waiter; Vera Ivanovna's purse)
5. (we; an old address book of Father's)
6. (the girl; a vacuum cleaner that works)

ЖЖ. You will hear a series of questions asking where certain people are. Say that they went to the cued location.

ОБРАЗЕЦ: *You hear:* Где Ива́н?
You see: (post office)
You say: Он пошёл на по́чту.

1. (meeting)
2. (museum)
3. (stadium)
4. (restaurant)
5. (home)
6. (university)

33. You will hear a series of statements and questions. Using the name cued below, tell what the person said or asked. Remember, if it is a yes or no question, you will have to paraphrase it with the word **ли**.

ОБРАЗЕЦ: *You hear:* — Я снима́ю кварти́ру недалеко́ от университе́та.
You see: Леони́д: — Я снима́ю кварти́ру недалеко́ от университе́та.
You say: Леони́д сказа́л, что он снима́ет кварти́ру недалеко́ от университе́та.

You hear: — Ты живёшь в общежи́тии?
You see: Тама́ра: — Ты живёшь в общежи́тии?
You say: Тама́ра спроси́ла, живу́ ли я в общежи́тии.

1. Па́вел: — Ты о́чень интере́сно расска́зываешь.
2. Ната́ша: — Мы вме́сте пра́здновали новосе́лье.
3. Кристи́на: — Ты ви́дела Ди́му на собра́нии?
4. Фёдор: — Вы пригласи́ли ва́шу сосе́дку?
5. Ани́та: — Зи́на помогла́ мне написа́ть курсову́ю.
6. Вале́рий: — Ты ви́дела фильм «До свида́ния, ма́льчики»?

CPSIA information can be obtained
at www.ICGtesting.com
Printed in the USA
BVHW07s0902100818
523777BV00006BA/19/P